Never Stop Dancing

A Memoir

ISBN: 978-0-578-52445-0
Library of Congress Control Number: 2019907369

Book design by Lance Buckley and John Robinette and Robert Jacoby

Image credits: John Robinette

Printed in the United States of America

Never
Stop
Dancing

A Memoir

JOHN ROBINETTE
and ROBERT JACOBY

Also by Robert Jacoby

Novels

Dusk and Ember
There Are Reasons Noah Packed No Clothes

Nonfiction

Escaping from Reality Without Really Trying

Though lovers be lost love shall not;
And death shall have no dominion.
　　　　　—Dylan Thomas

Dance, when you're broken open. Dance, if you've torn the bandage off. Dance in
the middle of the fighting. Dance in your blood. Dance when you're perfectly free.
　　　　　—Rumi

Dedications

John
To Adam and Bryan

Robert
To Gina

Introduction

It was late July 2010, and I was racing against a closing window of time. I told John I needed to talk to him in person; I could not do this over the phone or by email. Driving down to John's house to see him that first time to tell him about my idea for this book project—based on his miserable situation—I thought he might have one of two reactions: he'd see the value in it and really want to do it, or he'd punch me in the head. I thought my proposal might be complicated by the fact that in the almost ten years I had known John I had never met Amy. Now I was on my way to ask my friend to do something not for me, not for him or his children, but for something greater.

John and I met in 2002 while working on a large website project for Johns Hopkins University—John was a contractor leading a Web development team; I was the content lead for the project's online presence. We started talking, as colleagues do, about what was happening in our lives. I was going through a divorce after sixteen years of marriage and three children (one boy, thirteen, and two girls, ten and eight); John was becoming a parent for the first time. Our friendship developed immediately and deeply, with office and lunchtime discussions quickly going down the paths of shared interests in politics, philosophy, history, current events, and, undergirding all, the purpose of life and how best to live. Our conversations explored and centered on the meanings of things.

After four years we left our jobs but kept in touch. Our discussions meant too much to me—to him, too, I like to think—to just let them go. So we would meet every couple months or so for lunches and dinners and talk for two or three or more hours, picking right up where we had left off, as if we'd seen each other just the day before.

There are few people in my life with whom I've ever had the sort of friendship I enjoy with John. But "friendship" and "friend" aren't the most accurate descriptors. Ours is a kinship of the mind and soul and heart and spirit.

In April 2010, John lost his forty-two-year-old wife, Amy Polk, in a horrifying pedestrian traffic accident. She was killed instantly while crossing an intersection in Washington, DC. By that time I had a new life partner, Gina, and a new home for my three children. Gina and I visited John less than a week later; it was the first time I'd been to his house in Takoma Park, Maryland. I'd never met John's two young boys, Adam and Bryan, until that day.

John was shattered, and I was shattered seeing him. I remember sitting on the floor in his living room near the fireplace, with friends and neighbors, listening to John recount some recent experience with Amy. And I listened, because John needed to be heard.

By this time in my life, my own experiences of grief and tragedy had piled up. I'd suffered through bouts of depression since childhood and survived several suicide attempts. Both my parents were dead—my father, slowly, from lung disease, and my mother, instantly, from a fatal home accident. I'd gotten married too young, too foolishly, and lost myself in that relationship, giving up my dreams of writing when I declined acceptance from two different creative writing programs in favor of my young family's needs. Buried one unborn child. And through it all mourned the loss of my peak creative years.

I am curious about death and its attendant experiences, and I want to know the fears and fascinations and realities around it. As I've gotten to know certain people in my life I've earned their genuine trust, asked probing questions, and listened as they've shared their stories: a friend from China who had served two years in a reeducation camp; a friend from Argentina who had lost friends and family to kidnappings during that country's "Dirty War"; three coworkers I'd known over the years who had lost siblings to murder; an in-law whose sibling died as a teen; men who fought in wars and watched men die or lost limbs of their own. My father was a veteran of World War II and had fought in the Pacific Theater for two-and-a-half years, and what little he told me has always haunted me. Death and its subtler forms have affected me deeply many times over the years.

I share these stories to illustrate that we are survivors. Hearing others' stories made me realize, too, that most of us, if we live long enough, carry stories of heartache and loss that remain untold.

By July 2010 I had written two books. The first, a novel, about my struggles with depression, was *There Are Reasons Noah Packed No Clothes*, which chronicled a young man's search to find the will to live. That work provided me space to explore the same questions John was struggling with after Amy's death: Why are we here? What does it mean to live? What does it mean to love? And what of death? What should we make of loss and death? These are essential questions that ultimately each one of us attends alone. The other book was *Escaping from Reality Without Really Trying*, a nonfiction work based on forty hours of interviews with a sixty-one-year-old merchant seaman. I had conducted more than a hundred interviews in my professional career as a journalist, but never like that in such a concentrated effort and time. For that project I sat with the man over ten consecutive days, talking with him for up to six hours each day, listening to his wild, captivating, and hilarious stories, recorder on. Asking questions. Steering our conversation. Listening.

The inspiration for *Never Stop Dancing* came to me in the swimming pool at my athletic club. The imagery of water and rebirth is obvious, now. Then, I was floating on my back in the water, buoyed by Gina's hands under my shoulders, letting my mind wander over my life, my purpose, my fate. I was in a graduate program at the University of Maryland; something I knew I should be doing for my career. But was it enough? Was it right? I was starting to feel the press of time, and I wondered if I would be able to accomplish the goals I had set for myself, among them, writing five books over the next twenty years. My thoughts drifted to John and his recent loss of Amy, and I wondered what his life was like now, him a widowed father with two young boys, what he was doing, how he was coping. I knew people were helping him as they could, with food and laundry and child care. These were all physical needs. And I wondered what anyone could do—if *anything* could be really done—to help him in his grief, where he was living now. What can I do about it? I thought. How could I possibly help?

Something clicked in my head.

Immediately my thought was to interview John about Amy's death not in one interview session but over time, over *many* days, spanning the first full year after her death. I thought back to that terrible day when Gina and

I visited John in the raw first week after Amy's death and what he had shared in the midst of his grief. Dread mixed with excitement from the first time this idea occurred to me. My hunch was that this would be an important project. I didn't think anyone had ever done such a thing, let alone thought of doing it. Who would? On the surface, the idea itself felt wrong. Intrusive and disturbing. Even grotesque. But I wanted to hear more of his language of grief, and how he might possibly describe it. I wanted to know how someone could experience such a loss, put words to it, and come back from it. I wanted to know his experience of losing someone so close, so beloved. At the heart of it, I wanted to know the breadth and depth of love, and love lost. But I also wanted to know what it would be like for him living through it, as it seems that the older I get the more I realize that much of life is about survival. In a way, too, I thought John's grief might inform others' grief—how they manage it, how they talk about it, and how they process it—and, ultimately, how they move on. Perhaps, too, then, I was hoping to re-find some lost part of me. And I knew that these insights and stories John was experiencing might be forever lost if no one captured them. As I got out of the pool I knew I had to call John right away to tell him I needed to see him as soon as possible. I wanted to make the proposal before I changed my own mind about it.

I drove to his house the next day. It was Friday evening, July 30, 2010. His boys were over at a friend's house. We were in his living room, alone. Too nervous and excited and hopeful, I stood to explain; I can still see John leaning forward on his living room couch, listening intently. Listening as I laid it out. When I stopped talking John sat for just a moment, and I could see him thinking, and then he looked up at me, wiped his eyes, and said, "Yes, let's do it."

I think we were both shaking.

My first thought was, this is good, he's not going to punch me in the head. In my nervousness I shifted gears. I explained quickly some thoughts on how it would proceed. It was a safe conversation about dates and schedules, so as not to lose momentum, so he wouldn't change his mind, so *I* wouldn't change *my* mind. And throughout, even though John had agreed, I felt like I was trying to convince both of us there in that room in his home where Amy had lived that this was a good thing to do, that we needed to do this. We settled on a date for the first interview.

Then we shifted focus. We talked a little bit about his boys, how they were handling the death of their mother, the family's new life and schedule. It was small talk, and we both knew it. When we said our goodbyes we hugged a bit tighter than usual, and our goodbye looks to one another on his front porch felt heavier than normal. Of course. Nothing we'd discussed that night, nothing about this situation, was normal. And yet, I think we both knew it was very much normal, for us, for what we were about to do. What we were about to do was talk—simply talk—as two good friends. It's what John and I have always done.

I kept telling myself this as I left his house that evening. We were just going to talk. As we normally do. It's what we've always done. I was relieved. And unsettled. Because now I had to make it happen.

———

John and I met on eight different occasions throughout the following summer, fall, winter, and spring. I always drove down to John's house, about an hour south.

We recorded our first interview sessions in John's living room. His boys might interrupt us as they ran in and out, or asked their dad for help with something. I remember one session in the fall—we sat on his back porch, listening to the birds call to one another in the trees. It's very clear on the recording.

During the interview sessions we talked as friends have talked, I imagine, for thousands of years. Only now there was a recorder between us, and not much else. It felt like we were opening up the brutal places of human existence and emotion, holding things up for discovery and examination. When it got to be too much for John—when I felt like he was reaching the end of a point or a thought, or just trailing off, or when his voice would falter or tears would begin to flow—I'd turn off the recorder. There were times when we needed to weep, or hug, or be silent together. And sometimes it got to be too much for me, too, listening to John, watching him live and relive what he was going through. I had never met Amy, so I was simultaneously learning about her and losing her through John. His loss, his memories of Amy, this person he was making real for me—I was mourning her loss, with him, as I was also meeting her for the first time. It was a terribly odd and terribly painful experience for me.

The text developed for this book is the transcribed material from our conversations. John and I then worked, together and separately, to expand and deepen the narrative. We've kept true to the process, dividing the book into four seasons corresponding to our interview sessions. My story is intertwined with John's throughout, just as our lives were during the year after Amy's death. This book, then, is the product of who we were, and who we are—our conversations that year and each of us looking back.

Why did I do this? you might ask. I've asked myself that many times as I've read over this text and worked on it and wept and had to walk away from it. At the beginning, I wanted to help John, by exploring his grief as it was happening; help myself, by taking part in something special; and help others, by recording a history of a man's journey out of death and toward life. Through this experience I've learned there is nothing simple in our discussions and experiences of life and death, love and loss, and grief, and what these words mean to each of us, individually and together, and how those words change meaning through our experiences, over time. And how life moves on and moves us on. Through the conversations that make up *Never Stop Dancing* I was reminded that I am not alone in this; this is life. But in this life of pain and sorrow there is great joy and beauty, too. And there are gifts to be found in grief. I wanted to know what could be salvaged, what might be learned, and after, what new life might be found and enjoyed.

What John lived through may be common to humanity, but the experience he and I shared in and from this book is unique, perhaps, especially, for men.

My hope is that as you come along with me to engage in a conversation with someone who has endured the profoundest of losses, you'll incorporate John's story—and my story of being John's friend—into your own story, and discover and rediscover love and its wondrous, mysterious reach. And ultimately, like John, like me, find ways to unearth the treasures among the ruins.

Preface

When my wife Amy died, so suddenly and so tragically, I needed answers. I immediately started looking for books to help me understand, to cope. I found a book called *Swallowed by a Snake*, by Thomas Golden. Golden writes mostly about grief and recovery for men and how men deal with loss differently than women. The author describes the concept of a "grief container," a designated place for one's grieving. A vessel, if you will, to hold and protect the aggrieved. He describes different rituals or acts that become containers for the mourner.

This is a grief container for me.

—

I've called a friend who had a tree taken down. He's got these huge pieces of wood, just stacked in his front yard. So I think I'll rent a truck. Go over there and haul them over here. And the rest of the year—I don't know, every Saturday morning—chop wood for an hour or two. Then I can just give free chopped wood to the neighbors.

Summer

The wound is the place where the Light enters you.
— Rumi

I scheduled my first interview session with John for Saturday, August 7, 2010. The day was very hot and very bright. Close to ninety degrees and Maryland humid.

Interviewing people was exciting and fun for me; I always enjoyed learning new things about my subjects, how they lived, who they were. People open up in an interview session like they normally would not do. And I knew how to prepare, what tools to bring, how to "read" the subject during the session.

As I was preparing to talk with John I had to keep telling myself to do everything as usual. I checked the audio recorder. One, two, three. Testing, testing. One, two, three. Unpacked and repacked the batteries. Did it again. Checked the extra set. Did it again. Paper pad and pens. Checked twice. Pacing in my home office between tasks. I put everything into my writing bag and took it out to my car for the nearly hour-long drive south to John's house in Takoma Park, on the northeast border of DC.

I asked myself that first Saturday morning on the drive down if this was the right thing to do. If there wasn't something perverse about interviewing someone who had just suffered the most devastating of losses. There was still time to not do this, I told myself. To call John and call it off. But, as I thought that choice through, I knew that I had to do this. I had to do it.

I prepared by reading the blog John started soon after Amy was killed. He'd written about the immediate aftermath—May, June, July—and that's where I wanted him to start. I thought about questions to ask him. Usually I prepare a list, even if only as a framework for the interview. Back in my home office when I had written down the first question, I'd stopped. I looked at it. *How did you find out Amy was killed?* I wrote a second question. *How did you tell your boys, Adam and Bryan?* I stopped and looked at that one, too. This is horrible, I thought. I can't believe I'm going to do this, ask these questions, interview my friend. It seemed ghoulish and gross. I tore the sheet out of the notepad and threw it away. I resolved to simply talk with John, talk like we'd always done, as friends.

As I drove down that Saturday morning I wondered how Amy's death had changed him. How it was going to change him.

I wondered how it would change me.

I found out soon enough.

John's house is on an old street where the homes have no driveways, just street parking. I parked down a bit from his house and walked up. Our greeting at the door was a bit unusual for us both; we knew we were about to embark on something unprecedented, and neither one of us knew how it would turn out.

John asked me what he should do, where we should talk.

I tried my best as the interviewer to "act normal" and "be in charge." I told him I thought it would be best if we both were in a comfortable setting. I pointed and said, "How about right here, in the living room?" There was a sofa and two chairs.

He nodded his agreement, and I began to set up there so that he could be on the sofa and I would be in a chair across, and in between on a kitchen chair my audio recorder, pad, and pens. I unpacked my gear. I was checking the recorder, making sure it worked, fiddling with my pen and pad. I was nervous.

John sat down across from me.

I could sense John wanted to ask me how this would begin. I didn't really know where to begin, how to begin. I'd thrown out my first question and my follow-up questions. I had nothing written down to ask. But I didn't want to tell John that. I came back to what I wanted to do. I wanted us to talk, like we would normally do. I wanted to look with John into the wound to see what we could see. I wanted him to start, and I wanted to know how it happened. It's funny, now, thinking back on it. I clearly remember: John had to prompt me to start; he asked me the first question.

He said, "Where should I begin?"

I felt myself grow small, as if I were standing on the rim of a high cliff looking over an undiscovered valley. I heard myself whisper, "Start at the beginning."

—

It was the morning of April 29, 2010. I spooned up behind Amy, sliding my left arm under her pillow while letting my right arm gently trace along the curve of her hip up to her waist, then to her stomach. She curled her legs up so mine could fold in right behind hers and in the same motion with her right arm took my hand and pulled it up between her breasts. Her brown hair tickled my nose as I nuzzled my face up beside her. We had perfected this choreography years ago and now performed it without a thought. Our two bodies folded together just perfectly. I knew there wasn't time for it, and she would say no, but I asked anyway.

"Do you want to make love?"

Amy sighed, then said, "I knew you were going to ask that. But we have to get going."

And she was right, but we hadn't made love in nearly a week. Each day was sliding into the next. Our lives had become like so many others' our age: juggling kids and their school and sports activities, our jobs, volunteer work. We loved the life we were creating, but that life had changed so much since we'd met. Now, even things that seemed simple before, like making love, required at least some amount of forethought and planning.

The previous week I'd had Friday off, and with her part-time work schedule, Amy stayed home on Fridays and used it for the thousand and one things she did to keep our house going. The University of Maryland, where I worked, was on a schedule of budget cuts, which included mandatory furlough days. So on that previous Thursday, a week earlier, I proposed to her, "Sweetie, I have to take a furlough day tomorrow. What do you have going on? Maybe we can, you know, make a date?"

"Make a date" was code for us. It might include a candlelit meal at home, or a walk along the hiker-biker trail near us, but what it really meant was lovemaking. I would never have imagined that the act of planning sex with my wife would be nearly as exciting as executing that plan. But there it was.

"Oh, yeah, right. Friday," she started. "Don't forget Friday is kindergarten registration. I'm volunteering for the PTA table, and then there's one other thing I need to do for the birth center, but after that, one o'clock, two o'clock, I'm free."

Besides her campaign to start a nonprofit midwifery birth center in our town—Takoma Park—after two others had closed, Amy was a passionate and tireless volunteer. She was involved with the PTA, church, school events, our neighborhood association, you name it. She was the listserv moderator for more than one email group and was active in a national women's engineering professional society. She was a former member of Mensa (to meet guys, she told me), and when we met (I was decidedly *not* in Mensa) she was active in a group called GEMS (Girls Excelling in Math and Science) and lectured on career choices for teenage girls. One night each week she practiced with a local Middle Eastern dance troupe and occasionally performed as a belly dancer. (I'll be honest, I was never quite sure how this forty-two-year-old woman, born of Scottish and German stock with the remnants of Presbyterian blood running through her, decided to take up belly dancing—or "Middle Eastern folk dancing," as she would correct me—but it was a hobby I unwaveringly supported.) With all of that going on, for me to be able to get a couple of hours with her on her "day off" was great.

So it was about two o'clock when she returned home from her various activities. We had maybe three-and-a-half hours to ourselves before picking up the boys. Bryan, four, attended preschool at a nearby church and Adam, seven, took the bus from his elementary school to the same preschool, which offered an after-school care program. Pickup time was six p.m. sharp or we'd start to accumulate late fees. Not wanting to waste one precious moment, I poured each of us a glass of white wine, and we sat on the couch. I turned to Amy and rested my elbow on the back of the couch and my head on my hand. I sipped my wine as she recounted her morning. Then we shifted to talking about a trip to upstate New York we had planned for the summer. It was a marriage retreat that we were really looking forward to. We talked about the kids. A yard project I wanted to do. She talked some of her dream of building a birth center in our town and some progress she had recently made. She had been lobbying our state delegate to get a law changed to make the licensing of midwives easier. We just talked about what couples a month away from a ninth wedding anniversary talk about. We were sitting together on the couch, sharing our thoughts about our life together, the wonderful and the mundane.

There's no other way to really describe it. We were happy. Happy with our lives. Happy with our family. Happy with each other. She moved closer to me. I set my wineglass down, and we held each other.

Then Amy said, "You know, I get home, you've cleaned the house, and now we've been talking for an hour. This is the best foreplay *ever*." We both laughed and then started kissing.

We went upstairs and made love, and it was beautiful. Making love with Amy was always beautiful, but something was changing.

In the decade since we'd met we had moved from mad, passionate lovers to newlyweds, to parents. Now we were just beginning a shift from the frantic exhaustion of being young and naïve parents to something else. We were developing more fully as individuals, as partners, and in that process we were rediscovering each other as lovers. We were finding new ways to enjoy ourselves, our bodies, with each other.

This was the memory, of our last lovemaking, that swirled in my mind that Thursday morning, April 29, as I lay there in bed with the warmth of her body against mine. I was reliving that last time we'd made love and anticipating the next. I just needed to get through the next day and a half until we could make love again.

We dragged ourselves out of bed. Got the coffee going, breakfast, the kids out of bed, dressed, fed, and so on. For our normal morning routine I'd walk our second-grader, Adam, a half-block to the school bus stop, then I'd head off to work. Amy would drive Bryan to his preschool, park in a lot near the Metro, and commute to work in downtown DC. So it was our normal, sort-of-controlled chaotic morning.

"Normal time tonight?" I asked.

"Yup, normal time."

"Normal time" meant no late meetings or other activities afterwards. Normal was increasingly rare, and a normal night home was something to look forward to.

She complimented me on my tie, I think, and then I said goodbye. At least I think I said goodbye—I don't remember, which really bothers me—as I ran out the door with Adam.

It was a beautiful day, late April in the mid-Atlantic. At the bus stop I chatted with the other parents—idle chatter as we waited, and then the bus came and the neighborhood kids filed onto the bus, and off they went. Then I drove to work, and Amy took Bryan to preschool, and off she went to work. Or, that's what I assumed had happened, since that is how our mornings went.

I got to work and went about my day. Cleared out emails. A meeting here and there. The day was late-spring warm, maybe eighty degrees, but not oppressive. Sunny. Clear. Not too humid yet. A nice day to have meetings across campus. My first of two afternoon meetings had ended, and I was walking back to the building where my office was for the second meeting. I checked the agenda on my phone as I entered the building and headed up to a conference room where the meeting was going to be.

I came up the stairs into the hallway and saw somebody out of the corner of my eye. He pointed toward me and said, "That's John."

I looked down the hallway toward the voice and saw two men, backlit. I couldn't quite make out who they were. One started toward me. It was a police officer.

I was still thinking about the agenda for the meeting I had to get to. That a police officer wanted to see me wasn't necessarily unusual. Having spent about twenty years doing IT work in and around the DC area, much of it for the federal government, I'd had a couple dozen or more interviews for security and background checks. Former employees applied for other jobs; neighbors listed me on their background check forms. It didn't register with me that a uniformed DC cop was not the right person to be conducting such a background check, but that's what I told myself, to make sense of it. He introduced himself and then asked me, "Are you John Robinette?"

"Yeah." I was still thinking about the meeting, not quite paying attention.

"And your wife's Amy Polk?"

I tilted my head to the side and squinted my eyes and then heard myself slowly respond, partly answering, mostly questioning, "Yeah?"

This was not how someone conducting a background check should introduce himself. He should have shown me his credentials. He should have given me a name, someone who had worked for me five years earlier.

An electric shock started at the base of my spine and shot up into the back of my head. My mind started to race, trying to create a reasonable explanation for his presence in my life and his peculiar questions. His words echoed in my skull.

And your wife's Amy Polk?

He guided me into the nearest empty office. My heart started to race. He slowed down. This police officer slowed down, and the world around me slowed down. He reached up and guided me with his arm. I could hear my pulse slamming against my eardrum like a car racing down the highway with a stone stuck in a tire tread: ba-dum, ba-dum, ba-dum, ba-dum.

And your wife's Amy Polk?

Now we were standing in the empty office. I was near the door, and the police officer slowly turned to me.

His face.

I was seeing his face now, really seeing it, for the first time. I had looked him in the face but hadn't noticed until now. It was the face of pain. Deep,

deep pain. His brow twitched, and he blinked once, twice. His lips, the corners turned down a bit too much, slowly opened.

"Your wife was in an accident."

Accident?

In that moment it made no sense. My mind was racing. She didn't even have to drive two miles to drop off Bryan and then get to the Metro station, and never does the speed limit go over thirty. She's a very capable driver. Bryan? Is Bryan okay? The officer didn't say anything about him, so this is clearly some mistake, I thought. Typical police incompetence. Or wait, maybe someone bumped into her from behind at the one stoplight between the day care and the Metro stop. That's it. That's what happened. And maybe it was just hard enough for the airbag to deploy and they took her to the hospital just to make sure she's okay.

"Is she okay?"

"She didn't make it."

Didn't make it? What does *that* mean? "What?"

"She was in an automobile accident."

This couldn't be. How could she have possibly been in an automobile accident in our little town that was so severe that a police officer would have to use "She didn't make it"? It's not possible! Where did this happen? Did she decide to not ride Metro for some reason? Why was she driving somewhere else? What was she doing?

I said to him, "What was she doing driving a car? *Where?* It's not possible! She rides Metro to her office in downtown Washington."

"No," he said. "She was hit."

"*What?*"

"It was a pedestrian accident."

Oh, dear God.

Horrible.

Shock.

"*No!*" I screamed. "You have it all wrong! Are you sure? *Amy Polk? Amy Ellen Polk?*"

No. This can't be. How can this be? This is all wrong. There's some horrible, terrible mistake here. I knew it couldn't be true, and as I was trying to make sense of it all, it started. I started to cry. But it was a cry I had never cried before. An unfamiliar cry. Low, deep, primal—howling moans. I felt nausea rise up from my toes and settle in as a tightness halfway between my throat and chest.

What do I do? I didn't know what to do. What do I do? Who do I call? I have to call people. My boys. I have to get my boys. Synapses started firing. One, then another, then another went off, trying to create something resembling a coherent thought. Amy is supposed to pick up the boys. They're going to be waiting for her.

Now two colleagues entered the office.

I heard their words in an auditory slow motion just over a muffled pulse in my eardrums. "John, how can we help?"

My mind was reeling, racing. It felt like there was another voice talking to me, trying to guide me. *Amy is supposed to pick up the boys. I have to get my boys.*

The police officer said he was sorry. His voice sounded as if it was in slow motion and muffled. He handed me his card and said something about a police investigator being in touch.

"John." It was one of my colleagues talking. "Is there someone we can call?"

A fog started to roll in.

Amy is supposed to pick up the boys, said the voice. *I have to get my boys.*

I was staring at these people and feeling my world closing in around me, an invisible membrane beginning to surround me. Through the membrane the others' voices were becoming more muffled and were slowly being drowned out by a low, pulsating, rumbling sound from some dark and previously hidden part of the universe that resonated directly in my eardrums. The tightness between my throat and chest was growing into a ball of nausea pulsating with the rumbling in my ears.

I dry heaved and tasted vomit.

"John, is there someone here we can get?" Their fading voices barely registered.

Amy is supposed to pick up the boys. I have to get my boys.

"Amy is supposed to pick up the boys. I have to get my boys." Somehow the words let themselves out of my throat and passed my tongue and slid out through my lips. Did they hear me?

I need to call people so I can get my boys.

"I need to call people so I can get my boys." More words slid out.

My hands shaking, I reached into my pocket for my phone. Every utterance, every trivial body movement required a will of concentration and strength I'd never had to summon. I fumbled with my phone. I'd been at this job just six months and had gotten a new cell phone at work. Most of my phone numbers were still in my old phone; I hadn't taken the time to transfer my address book completely. I stared blankly at the screen; it waited quietly for me to command it to do something.

What do I do now?

"What do I do now?" This would become a question I'd ask myself frequently. And right at that moment I had to ask it with every heartbeat.

What do I do now?

I stared at my phone.

Unlock the phone.

I needed to unlock my phone. What's my passcode? My thumb shakily keyed it in.

What do I do now?

Activate the phone app.

My thumb touched the phone app.

What do I do now?

Press the button to get to the phone's number pad.

I pressed the button to get to the phone's number pad.

What do I do now?

Nothing.

I felt—

Adrift. The membrane closed in tighter. The room started to list ever so slightly to the left. Through the membrane the colors of the room washed out and faded to various grays. I felt the ball of nausea again, and I prepared to throw up as my diaphragm clenched. Maybe if I could just vomit it all out it would subside and go away. But I only dry heaved again, and it didn't go away.

My thumb started to instinctively tap out the phone number for my parents in New Jersey. The phone number I grew up with. The first phone number committed to memory. So that is what I would do. That's what I would do first.

I used both hands in a vain attempt to steady the phone against my ear as it started to ring. What do I say? I've never had to tell someone my wife is dead before. How do I say it?

My mom answered the phone.

"Hello?" It was the same sing-songy "hello" I'd heard from her my whole life. She holds the final 'o' and goes up a note, then comes back down on the final beat. It was a happy, I'm-so-glad-someone-is-calling kind of hello, with three syllables.

"Mom?"

"Oh hi, Johnny."

"Mom?"

"What is it?"

"Amy."

"Yes?"

"Mom—Amy."

"What's wrong, dear?"

"Amy's—Amy's dead."

"Oh, dear God! Oh, John. Oh, dear God."

The low moaning sobbing returned. Tears and snot were running down my face. I tried to wipe them away, my hands getting sticky and wet. I heard my mom in the background say to my father, "Joe, come here right now, something terrible has happened."

I heard the handset in New Jersey fumble from my mom to my dad.

"John. What is it?"

I told him.

He asked what happened.

I told him what the police officer told me.

He asked where I was.

I told him at work.

He said he'd call right back.

I said okay.

I pulled the phone from my ear and my thumb pressed the button to end the call.

Convulsing. Moaning. Now what? What do I do now?

I had to figure out what to do next. I still didn't know what to do. My colleagues were desperate to help, asking me all sorts of questions. "Who here on campus can we call?" "Who can come here and help?" "What do you need?" I was standing there, shaking, tears and snot and saliva running down my face. With the back of my hand I tried to wipe my face so I could see better. I just stared at them. I saw their mouths slowly moving and making sounds. I heard their muffled words. Nothing made sense. Nothing at all.

Get home. Get the boys!

By now I was completely surrounded by the membrane. My chest tightened and the low rumble grew louder.

Get home. Get the boys!

What's that? Get the boys? I was in no condition to get behind the wheel of a car. My whole body was shaking. I could barely see through my tears. I could barely hold a cell phone. Operate a car?

John! Get home. Get the boys. Now!

My mouth blurted out, "I gotta get home. I gotta get my boys."

Then my dad called back. Very businesslike he asked, "Have you called Bonnie yet?" Bonnie is Amy's mom.

"No."

"You need to do that next."

"Okay."

"And here is what I think you should say ..." He started giving me instructions on what to say to her. Giving me my lines, which is so much my dad—a writer and director falling back on what he knew how to do. I love my dad, but nothing he said registered at all. I simply could not follow any instruction more complex than one simple item.

"Dad?" I cut him off. "Dad, I can't—I can't even follow your instructions right now. I just have to call her and do it however it happens."

"Okay," he said. Then he told me he and my brother Mike were coming right down from New Jersey.

"Okay."

I hung up.

And then I called Bonnie.

—

No one—*no one*—should ever have to tell a mom that her daughter's dead. No one. But I couldn't let anyone else tell her. It had to be me. I turned away from the others in the room. I looked at the phone I was holding in both hands. Shaking. I hesitated for a moment and then I took a deep breath. I pressed buttons. Right then, there was a lag time in her reality. I realized as I was dialing that Amy's mother was still living a happy retired life, thirty minutes from us in Springfield, Virginia, married to her second husband, Donald, with a son and a forty-two-year-old daughter. A daughter who was beautiful and successful and full of life. For Bonnie, at that moment, as I lifted the phone to my ear, Amy was very much alive. A wife and a mother active in so many wonderful causes, trying, with what she had, to make the world a better place, working out what it meant to have two young boys, to be married, and to hold a career. The phone started ringing and I imagined Bonnie walking to answer it with her natural belief in this living, vibrant Amy. Then she answered the phone.

"Hello?"

"Hello, Bonnie?"

"Yes. John. Hello?" Maybe she sensed something off. Maybe. Her voice was about the same as it always was—straight and to the point.

"Bonnie? I have terrible news."

"Oh, yes?"

"Amy ..."

"What about Amy?"

"Amy's dead."

The deep, low moaning sobs came again. I felt a hand on my arm. I was now sitting in a chair. She asked what happened, and I told her. She asked about the boys. I told her they were still at their aftercare. She asked me where I was. I told her I was at work. She asked how I was going to get the boys. I told her I was not sure, maybe someone here could help, which I had not thought of at all. I heard her calling out to Donald. Muffled sounds. Then she came back on and told me to figure out a way to get the boys home and that she was coming right over. I hung up sobbing.

The church. I needed to call our church. I asked someone to look up the number. Our minister was on sabbatical. Our church administrator answered, and I told her what had happened. I could tell she was horrified, but she also had a plan. She called other people: the assistant minister, lay leaders, and our head minister, who was in Cape Cod. I had to figure out how to get the kids. It was 3:30 now. I had to get them by six. I was sitting at the desk and sobbing and trying to figure out my next phone calls. I asked coworkers to look up numbers. Who could help me get home? Then I thought of a coworker who lived in our neighborhood. And I thought of another coworker I had gotten to know pretty well. I asked for someone to get them.

I was fumbling now with the handset of the desk phone—one of those console-type phones with two lines and extra buttons to press. I could barely see. My hands were shaking. Nothing was working. I couldn't even press the button on the desk phone to get the line. I leaned over the phone and threw the handset down. Even that I couldn't do right—the handset jumped right back at me with such startling force that it caught me in the corner of my eye, hard. Split the skin right on my eyebrow. Started bleeding, swelling up.

I heard someone say, "Put ice on it, put ice on it!"

"No," I said. "I want a scar. I want a big scar." The pain, something about now experiencing pain—I wanted to feel physical pain. I needed that pain. And the crying came back as a wave, bigger than the last.

I was in a daze. I was floating, being pulled forward, back to my office. Then I was trying to collect my things. My laptop, papers. I didn't know what I needed.

What did I need?

What do you need from the office when your wife dies?

Pictures.

On my desk was a framed photo of Amy, my bride, on our wedding day, with an almost imperceptible smile. On a bookshelf behind my chair was a picture of the boys with Amy she had taken at Sears. And the picture of us from the previous summer on a trip to Florida—the classic cheesy tourist photo from Gatorland with a snake around me and a small, harmless, well-fed gator across our laps. I gathered them up. I stood and turned to leave. The membrane closed in. The low rumbling increased. Time slowed down even more.

I looked around my office, and everyone and everything began moving in a surreal slow motion. I wasn't imagining it—the world really was this way. I heard my heart racing through the pulsing in my eardrums; my breaths came fast and shallow. I desperately needed to blow my nose, but all I had was a shirtsleeve. And everything around me just kept slowing down—and then it stopped. I felt for a moment I could just walk right out of the room and no one would notice, and to them, when the world restarted, I would have simply disappeared. My next steps would be into a whole new branch of time, off into a dark parallel existence I had never imagined. I stood there. In that moment there was simply nothing. No time. No sound, except the rumbling, pulsing in my eardrums. I was alone with the world around me as I entered into a reality where death lived. I was stepping from an old reality that no longer existed—one where I am married and where Amy lives—into another one where Amy is dead.

I looked around. Everything was off-kilter. Perhaps someone had slipped me some mild hallucinogenic. All the color in everything around me washed out, leaving behind just pallid two-dimensional remnants. The blue wall and green rug and brown wood desk were all now varying shades of gray. My colleagues had been replaced by two-dimensional cartoonish cut-outs. The wall behind them was tilted—not much, maybe just ten degrees from center. And then I noticed that all the walls were this way. The whole room, I realized for the first time, had been built at an angle. I looked at the cardboard cutout coworkers, and they just stared back in their frozen silent desperation.

Then a sound pierced through the silence.

"John, give me your keys. I'm going to drive your car home." One figure was gesturing to another figure. "And Laura will drive you home."

A hand took me by the arm and led me toward the door, and then we were outside. The gray sun blinded me, and I couldn't see for a moment. I squinted and blinked, then noticed that it wasn't just my office—everything was tilted the same ten degrees. As I stepped forward it felt like the whole earth was listing to one side. I looked for something to hold on to because I was sure I was going to slowly slide toward the edge of the Earth and drop off into oblivion. Then the lump in my chest returned. My whole torso contracted and dry-heaved, but nothing came out. The nausea and dizziness continued. I wondered if I had a really high fever. I could feel myself moving, walking, I think, but it was as if some of me had been left behind. And I remember thinking that it will catch up with me, eventually.

Then I was in the car and riding home. It was a short ride. Maybe fifteen minutes. Suddenly I was walking up my front steps. I fumbled with my keys. I started to cry again. I got inside. I stood there, not sure of my next movement. In the prior world, where Amy lived, I would have subconsciously set my backpack down, kicked off my shoes, gone to the bathroom, and so on. I would not have had to consciously think about those actions. But as everything around me was being reset to this new world where Amy was dead, I had to stop, concentrate, and deliberately investigate my body's state.

Do I need to pee?

Yes. Go to the bathroom, lift the lid, open your fly, pee.

Am I thirsty?

No, I don't think so. Wait, yes, yes I am. Go to the kitchen, get a glass from the cupboard, move toward the sink, turn on the tap, fill up the glass with water, turn off the tap, lift the glass to your mouth.

As I stood there waiting for the signals from my body to tell my brain what it needed, these spasms, these grief spasms, short-circuited the signals and welled up from down low, deep inside the bottom of my chest. It felt like I had to cough something out. I imagined black tar balls—tumorous growths inside me, expanding—not part of my physical body, but inside me somewhere. Bloody, black, waxy tar masses were growing inside me, and I had to expel them, force them out. And as soon as one would go, another one would start to grow deep inside. They'd come every minute or two, spasmodically, and I would have to moan them out. I had this image of the way a snake swallows a rat or a pig, and then disgorges the hair and the bones and the skin, in a mass. It contorts its whole body and dislocates its jaw to expel this mass. In my mind's eye I saw my jaw opening up to the width of my torso and peeling back, exposing bone and muscle and tissue to allow this bloody, black mass to come out. Like some freakish Hieronymus Bosch painting of doomed souls being ripped apart by Satan's helpers.

Our assistant minister and a friend from church went to pick up the boys. We had talked it through at some point after I got home. They weren't going to say anything to the boys. They were just going to pick them up and say your daddy and mommy couldn't get you, so we're going to get you today. Of course, we had to tell the afterschool care so that they would know it was okay for these two people who weren't on the emergency pickup list to come get them.

Then Bonnie arrived.

We just held each other and cried. Convulsive, spasmodic sobbing. More tears. Now our clothes were wet from our sobbing as we clutched on to each other for—what? Strength? Comfort? We didn't know what to do but hold each other and cry. Sometimes it was uncontrolled sobs. Sometimes full-throated moans. Then at some point we realized we needed to compose ourselves—the boys would be home soon.

We sat on the couch.

But what would we say when they arrived? What was there to say?

We would just have to say it when they got there. And when they did, Adam and Bryan came bounding up the front porch stairs, like they do, with their backpacks. Like they do.

Adam sensed something was off. Something had to be off, of course. It was a little early to have been picked up; people from church had come to get them; and there were other people at the house—Amy's mom, and these strangers from my work, too.

I told my boys to come over to the couch.

I knew I was about to destroy their worlds.

"I have terrible news," I said. "Mommy was killed in a car crash."

We all just sat there and cried. And my boys started to cry a cry I had never heard before. If you're a parent, you know your child's cry, whether it's a cry of pain or fear or anger. Whether it's a real cry, or a fake cry. I had heard all of those, and I knew those cries. I had never heard this cry before from them.

Adam said, "It's not fair. It feels like a dream. The most horrible, worst dream ever."

He was right, and he and his brother were being ripped from their old reality and forced into this new reality.

Then from somewhere Adam asked, "Are we gonna get a new mommy?"

Oh my God! Jesus Christ—how do I answer that question?

I said, "I don't know. We'll figure that out later."

I imagine that moment will be seared into their memories forever: *The day Mommy died, and the time when Daddy told us Mommy was killed.*

I hate that.

I hate that thought.

———

John said he needed to take a break.

I did, too.

This was like no other conversation we had ever had.

I turned off the recorder and watched him start to cry and at the same time felt my own tears welling up. Seeing my friend in so much pain was overwhelming.

I sat there thinking, My God, what have I started? What am I doing here? Why am I doing this? I didn't know if I could do this, if I wanted to keep doing this. I sat there looking at a man—one of my closest friends—shattered, and knew there were no words to fix any of this. What could I ever say to assuage this pain? I told him the only thing I had. I told him how sorry I was for his loss and that this happened to him and his boys. I could feel myself starting to shake; it took everything I had to control myself and not burst into tears. John excused himself and went into the kitchen.

All of the questions I hadn't been able to write down two hours earlier were swirling around in my head now. Who was Amy? What was she like? What about their relationship and marriage? And, how did he and his boys cope in the days and weeks after her death? I didn't want to pepper John with too many questions in his current state. I knew I needed to go slowly and let him tell his story, help him get his story out. But there had to be some structure, too, some sense of meaning and timing. That's the job of the interviewer, I kept telling myself. I had a job to do here.

John called out from the kitchen that he needed to check on his boys, who were in the basement watching TV. Typical Saturday morning stuff. I called out, "Okay, take your time." I stopped my tears, blew my nose, gathered my thoughts. What did I want him to talk about next? It felt like we needed to back up just a bit. Maybe talk about pleasant memories.

He came upstairs and into the kitchen. "Do you need something? Water? Coffee?"

"Sure," I said. "Water. I could use some water." I followed him through the dining room and into the small kitchen. He lived in a part of Takoma Park, Maryland, where the homes had been built in the 1930s and 1940s. They were small and cozy. The trees were thick and established up and down the street and all around the houses. You could look outside the windows in any room and see green.

John asked, "How did it go?"

"This?" I said. "This right here?" I stopped myself from bursting out loud with an absurd laugh. As I looked at John in disbelief, he caught my incredulousness, shook his head, and took a deep breath. I could tell he hadn't realized how ridiculous his question was. I was still shaken from his words. It was all so painful. Too painful? But John had moved to a different place. In that moment that realization was unspoken but understood between us. We had to give each other permission to look at this for what it was to each of us and step out of the intensity of the grief from time to time. Maybe even laugh. He needed my permission, and I needed his.

If we couldn't grant each other that, we wouldn't make it. I finally broke the silence.

"I think what you went through that day is horrible, John. And I can't believe this is the first time I'm visiting your house. Well, not the first time. The first time was that first week, after—" I had to look away to the trees outside or I thought I would burst into tears again. It was a little over three months since the April day she had been killed. I told John, "I'm sorry I never met Amy or your kids. Before all this." I needed to focus on what we were trying to do. "Let's talk about that. Let's talk about something good." We got ourselves back into the living room, and I asked him to tell me about Amy and his children, Adam and Bryan.

—

The Sunday before Amy was killed, I'd gone to the gym and come back; we had dinner, and it was getting on about 7:30, 7:45, a school night. Our routine was to leave the TV off and just hang out and do family stuff. Some Sunday evenings we would have what amounted to a family meeting. Maybe discuss how things were going, talk about an issue that had come up or make sure everyone was clear on the rules for something, like keeping rooms clean, screen time, or wrestling in the house. Just a way for Amy and me to feel like we could assert some control over our lives. On this particular Sunday, after our meeting time, I put some music on, jazz, I think, and we were all milling around the living room.

Bryan said, "Daddy, put on some rock music we can dance to. Play the 'We're Not Gonna Take It' song."

I was kind of tired and hoping to get the kids to bed on time for a change, and in the back of my mind I knew if I honored Bryan's request I could say goodbye to an on-time bedtime. But that didn't seem like a good enough excuse to say no.

For my fortieth birthday the year before I had treated myself with a wireless audio system in the house. Any music I can stream from the Internet or play on my computer I can play through the house. I convinced Amy this was a good idea because I could get rid of the stereo, stacks of CDs, and speaker wires. I picked up the controller and searched for Twisted Sister, selected the song, and turned up the volume just a bit. The boys got into it, started jumping up and down in the living room. Adam was playing air guitar.

"Dad, play the Shrek song."

I queued up "Rock Star" by Smash Mouth.

Then we just started going through songs: "Chumbawamba" by Tub-thumping, Michael Jackson, Madonna, other songs the kids liked. Then Amy started dancing with the boys. She took little Bryan by the hands, and they started jumping and dancing in circles, and Bryan's blond hair was bouncing right along with him. Adam looked like rubber with his lanky arms and legs going in all directions. I was still sitting on the couch, thinking of the next song to select and starting to think, oh man, it's getting on toward eight o'clock; we should really start wrapping this up; I've got stuff I need to prep for work tomorrow.

Amy started dancing toward me, kind of tilting her head, and she reached her arms toward me, and said, "Is something wrong? Why aren't you dancing?"

"Nothing's wrong," I half-lied. She smiled and raised one eyebrow skeptically at my response, and I shook out of my head the list of things we had to do the rest of that Sunday night—baths, dishes, laundry, lunches for the next day, email for tomorrow. I queued up more songs and got up, and we were all dancing, right there in the living room, jumping up and down, raving like we were at a nightclub, spinning around. Adam would drop down on his knees and play his air guitar and toss his head up and down. At one point Bryan took his shirt off and swung it around his head and kept on dancing with his skinny naked torso. Then Adam took his shirt off, too, so now there were two skinny kids with no shirts on. Amy had a blouse on over a halter top, so she took off her blouse and tossed it on the floor. I got caught up in the moment and took my shirt off, too.

Before our wedding Amy and I had taken ballroom and swing dance lessons. I took Amy and swung her under my arm and twirled her around. I grabbed Adam to get him to try, but he was too busy with his air guitar. Bryan wanted to try, but we settled for him standing on my feet and grabbing my legs as I danced around.

It was getting dark outside. And I wondered if people could see us inside, half-dressed, playing fake guitars and singing into invisible microphones. See us jumping up and down like maniacs. I wondered if they could hear our music from outside.

It was great.

That's my last memory of us as a family. Four days later she was dead.

—

That first night after Amy died I couldn't eat, I couldn't drink, I couldn't sleep. I was barely functioning. My heart was still beating and my lungs were still breathing. But I physically could not eat. People had to remind me to drink.

One of those people was my dear friend, Jim, who had been the best man at our wedding. He had known Amy about as long as I'd known Amy, so it was hard for him, too. My dad and my brother Mike showed up sometime after dinner, I don't exactly remember. It's mostly a blur now, what they did or what I did or what they said or I said. I know they were trying to console me. Help me through each moment. I know it must have been hell for my dad, seeing his son in utter anguish. At one point we were in the basement on the couch in front of the TV. He tried to console me by sharing a story about a play he recently saw. It was about a woman, I think, who had lost her husband or sons, or both, in the war, but at the end of the play it all worked out, somehow, and she was able to get on with her life. It pains me to tell this story because I don't want to criticize my dad. He was trying to help me see that "this too shall pass." But it just made me angry. I was in the shock of sudden grief and my brain couldn't consider any future, let alone make sense of some play. My brother just sat there. I'm not sure what he was thinking. But even at that moment, just hours after Amy's death, I started to sense the chaos that now surrounded me, and the way the chaos was engulfing those closest to me, too. I needed them for support. To remind me to eat, and pee, and breathe, and yet they were suffering, too.

At some point in the evening I could feel one of those black, waxy, tar masses—a very large one—coming on. I was afraid for how I would disgorge it—how it would possibly pass—and that it was going to be very painful. I was concerned for my boys, that they would see it, see me. It wasn't that I wanted to hide my grief from them—I hadn't, really—but there was something different about this one; I could sense it.

I went to my brother and Jim. I said, "Get Dad's keys. You gotta drive me somewhere. I have to be out of this house."

My brother drove Jim and me down to the end of the street, where there are only a few houses on the one side and the road dead ends at a park. As the minivan came to a stop I practically fell out onto my hands and knees. I could see my shadow from the streetlight on the black asphalt, and it just came out. I screamed and moaned and hit the pavement with my fists. It was as if all the demons and all the dark forces and all their manifestations were channeling through me. I clenched every muscle in my body and shouted as loudly as I could and as hard as I could and as long as I could.

I felt a convulsion, a clenching of my bowels and a low groan rising to moaning, and I arched my back as I wailed at the universe. Then gasping for breath. Rapid gasping. Then another convulsion. Dizziness. Another convulsion, clenching, wailing. Gasping for breath. Then again. And again one more time. How many more? One more. Get it out. I had to get it out now. It was the only way to push that black mass out.

It was exhausting.

I don't know how long it lasted. A minute, maybe two minutes? Whatever the time, I had been in a complete full-body spasm. A complete contortion of my intestines and gut to force out the pain. It was draining—physically, emotionally, and psychically. I screamed myself so hard and so loud that I was hoarse. It was like howling at the moon. But in the moment, through that pain, came some new awareness. I felt connected in a horrible and human way to a deep, primitive source of all the pain and grief of humanity. I had only heard of it before this, and now I was connected to it. Our short time on this Earth was now undeniably and exquisitely real to me, and I felt it. I started imagining the pain Amy must have felt when she was hit. I hoped her death was sudden, but I wanted to know that pain. Somehow I felt I needed to know what that pain was like for her. And then this horrible image in my mind's eye played out of her final moments alive. This would be my curse for living: to never know what really happened to her on that street that morning, and to only be able to create horrible fantasies in vain attempts to understand it.

How could someone go through this and not essentially become bare to the universe and just scream it out? And as the last of the howls started to subside, I thought about something that we've all seen—images or videos on the news after some terrible thing has happened in the Middle East, or amid some other war zone. It could be a suicide bombing, or a child has been killed, or any of the various crimes or atrocities we commit against one another. You'd see the women and men in the streets, rending their garments, pulling at their hair, beating themselves on the head. And I suddenly realized I was doing that. That's what I was doing there on the side of that street. I was instinctively grabbing at my hair and at my head, pulling at my shirt, and howling. I didn't plan to do it. My body just did it.

And there on the dark street, looking around at the few houses, lit from the inside, I thought, why are we *all* not in the street? We should *all* be out in the street, howling, screaming at the sky, and tearing at our clothes, because that's what felt right. That's what felt right to do, right there and then. But we weren't doing it. We don't grieve that way. Now, looking back, I'm kind of sad about that, because I think that would've been helpful for all of us, to express what we were really feeling. My dad, Mike, Jim, other family and friends. I thought, they need to rend their clothes and pull their hair, too.

—

Later that night the obvious question came up from the boys: Where's Mommy?

Well, that's a hard question to answer when you haven't really thought it through all the way. I had been raised Catholic and schooled in the classic Catholic concepts of heaven and hell. I didn't really understand how it worked, but that's what I believed. Over time, and as I had moved away from the Church, I had come to a different understanding. I couldn't get my mind around a loving God who would create original sin and hold a grudge against the unbaptized. And later the notion of hell for nonbelievers made no sense, either. Eventually, as I came to believe in a more universal salvation, the need for a hell for fallen souls disappeared. Nor did I feel there was any need to threaten with hell to prevent sinful behavior. And then even the notion of heaven began to fade. I didn't feel the need for that existential punishment-and-reward system in order to be a good human being; being compassionate should be its own reward. So I probably could have said to the boys, "Sorry. There is no afterlife. There is no God. Mommy lives on in our memories and the good deeds she did while she was alive." But I chickened out.

And who doesn't like the idea of a heaven where we can be reunited with our loved ones? But I couldn't just say, "She's in heaven." So I explained how Mommy was in the spirit world. It seemed convenient, and it avoided the whole heaven-and-hell conversation. It allowed me to punt for a later day.

Sleep would not come easily that first night. As completely and physically wrung out as we were, somehow the utter despair and loneliness warded off sleep. What happened? How could this be? Why us? What do we do now? All these questions kept popping up with no possible answers. After folks left and my dad and brother went to bed, I just stayed in the basement with my boys, watching TV. I laid out blankets and pillows and sleeping bags, and we bunked on the floor. Bryan had his favorite stuffed animal, a baby Winnie-the-Pooh he called "Baby." I could barely even stand to go into our bedroom, my bedroom, and the boys didn't want to sleep alone. Nor did I. We held each other and snuffled and cried and eventually the boys fell into fitful sleep. Bryan was squeezing Baby. I tossed and turned and wrestled with new demons. At about four in the morning one of the boys wet the bed. In some ways it helped me focus on a task. I now had something to clean up, and I knew how to do it.

—

Bryan came bounding up the basement stairs and into the kitchen and showed himself in the doorway, shy and smiling, like any four-year-old boy, and that stopped us both. John looked at me and I knew what he had to do. I turned off the recorder.

Seeing them together, John helping Bryan get a glass of orange juice in the kitchen, I felt like an intruder. Yet somewhere in my head I told myself we were off to a good start—a good grim start.

I started packing up my things. I went into the kitchen just as John was scooting Bryan back downstairs into the basement.

I told John we could call it a day.

He looked a little surprised and a little curious. "How did it go?"

I took a deep breath. Earlier, his question upset me. Now, I could focus to think about what we were doing. "I think it went great," I said. "I think we have something to work with." Both of these statements were true, but as I was saying the words they seemed hollow. "We can stop here," I told him. "I'm packed up." I felt that if I kept on talking I would start crying all over again.

John walked me to the front door, and we talked and planned of meeting over the following two weekends. On his front porch we shook hands, but that did not seem to be enough, at all. We hugged and held onto each other.

"Thank you," I said.

When we pulled away John looked at me like I'd never seen him look at me before. His expression was a mix of love and kindness and sorrow and grief. He said, "Thank you, too," and I realized he meant for everything—me being there, us talking.

It was a beautiful Saturday. Sun shining. Bright blue sky. I walked down the street to my parked car, put my writing bag in, got in behind the wheel, and burst into tears. I cried, I think, for a solid minute. Over everything. John, Amy, his boys, us, the world we live in. It was overwhelming. After that minute I was able to calm myself down just enough to drive. I drove home in a state of shock.

It seemed to me there was someone in my head, walking around, poking at things on the shelves of my memories. I drove home thinking about how our friendship had started and how we had become such immediate and close friends. By outward appearances you wouldn't think we would get along at all. John is a progressive Democrat, active with environmental causes; I've been a registered Independent all my life. John is a Unitarian Universalist (I had to look that up when he first told me); I'm a Christian. John is outgoing and gregarious, your typical first-born. I'm an average middle child; the peacemaker. The labels of our differences are varied and many, but I think it was just these great differences that attracted us to each other, to test our worldviews, and to test ourselves and what we believed to be true.

When we first met at the Johns Hopkins University Center for Communication Programs, I was the editor of Internet Technologies (what today you'd call a Web content manager) and John was the project manager on a contract team hired to revamp our website. From the start we had to work closely. I had a nice office overlooking Baltimore's Inner Harbor. My office was comfortable. I'd brought in hanging plants and books for the shelves, personal knickknacks, a desk lamp, and a lava lamp. At a local pawnshop I had picked up a boom box with detachable speakers; music was always an incredibly important part of my life. Still is.

On John's first day on the project, the song "Edge of the Ocean" by Ivy was playing on my boom box. That caught his attention. I think after introductions we must have gone through part of my CD collection—Radiohead, Moby, Built to Spill—talking likes and dislikes in music.

Soon after that we had our first lunch. We engaged immediately on current events and politics and our worldviews, topics most people try to avoid. John and I hit each other head-on, though; I think we both relished the opportunity to hear a different viewpoint, to explore details of why a worldview is formed one way or another.

In the car driving home after our first interview session, I thought about all the intervening years since then, all the times we'd shared together, just the two of us, sitting and talking for hours, enjoying each other's company and conversations. Every time I left I would wonder if other men enjoyed this type of camaraderie. My life experience told me no. Once John had asked me if I wanted to "invite the ladies" (his wife, my girlfriend) to our next meeting. I always declined; I needed this space too much for our friendship. I told him, "This time is our time, John. It's for you and me. I'd like to keep it that way."

I thought about the last time John and I had met for dinner. It was December, before Christmas. We were having our typical conversation—exploring current events and politics and then earnestly debating the challenging "Why?" of things in those areas—when it struck me that we did not really touch on the challenging "Why?" of things in our personal lives. I told John that I'd never told anyone (other than Gina, and she lived through it with me) the details of the relief of my divorce, seven years earlier, and the awful years that followed. I told John how I had suffered in silence, and how my three children had suffered, too. In that moment I wanted John to know my grief, and about me through my grief, in a way I'd never shared before with a friend.

As I was telling my story there in the restaurant, I broke down crying. It was such a relief to let things go. John told me how sorry he was for me and my children, for what we had all gone through. As I wept he rested his hand on mine, and that touch lifted me.

In modern America men aren't supposed to do what we were doing: crying, comforting each other with a handhold.

I felt relieved. Cleansed.

It had been a confession. More.

It was my own interview session with John at that restaurant that night.

Driving home thinking about why I was doing this project with John, I must have smiled to myself, thinking, John listened to me that night; now, I would listen to him. I think part of me wanted to escape the pain of my own life by focusing on someone else's life, too. Solace can be found in learning you're not alone in life's struggles, in grief, no matter what you're grieving. So in some way, I thought, perhaps this project could be some type of therapy for me. Not as a grief container, as John had told me it would be for him, but as a grief release.

I thought of losing Gina like John had lost Amy—suddenly, violently. What would I do if I were in John's place? Right away my imagination stopped; I could not bear those thoughts.

Home, I talked with Gina about the interview, and I cried with her, too. I told her that listening to John had raised so many conflicting emotions in me, outside of the project itself. I think that when I cried I was mourning all over again the loss of my creative years during my marriage, the eventual loss of my marriage, the estrangement from my children, and my children's difficult years. Talking with John, I told Gina, made me acutely aware of the pain I had gone through during my own life, but also the blessed love I was able to share with her. I didn't know where this project would go, I told her, but now that I had started it I needed to keep going. Her support was unwavering.

All that week my thoughts ended up with John and his boys, how they were managing their new lives. And Amy. I knew we needed to talk about Amy.

Six days later I met with John for our second interview session. It was Friday, August 13, 2010. It was just after dinner with a couple hours of summer sun left in the day. His boys were over at friends' homes, so we wouldn't be interrupted. I set up our space in his living room, the same as in our first session. I pulled over a chair from the dining table and put on the seat my recorder and pad and pen and sat across from him in a living room chair to take notes.

When he walked in he seemed at ease with our arrangement—this sitting down to talk—and eager to engage. I was wondering if he felt as though he was in a psychiatrist's office, sharing himself in ways he normally wouldn't. I didn't ask—I didn't want to steer us off our interview session—but it felt that way to me. John asked me what I wanted him to talk about.

I said, "Let's pick up where we left off. Tell me about the first few days after. After Amy died."

—

We weren't even a week into this new life and I had to start thinking about how I was going to get the kids back to school. And beyond that, how was I going to get on with the other basics of life? I mean, how much time could I take off work? I got a few days of bereavement leave and had some vacation time stored up. But should I use it? If the kids were going to start back to school, what would I do? Just sit around the house?

I needed help, and the elementary school counselor came over. The principal came over. It was amazing, the amount of support that came from all sorts of different places—neighbors, family, church, school, my work, Amy's birth center community. Hundreds of people came through this house that first week—hundreds. In talking to the school counselor and the preschool folks, we decided it was important for the boys to try as best as possible to get back to a routine of some sort. We decided the next Thursday, the first week in May, they should start back to school. That way they would start Thursday, then they would have Friday, and then the weekend. We could ease them back into it.

Beyond school for the boys, I couldn't even really see what else needed to be done on a day-to-day basis. I had to refigure everything out.

My family was still coming and going. We started a routine with that. I'm blessed with a large family. I'm the oldest of five, with a sister and three brothers. I said to them, "Look, let's take advantage of this. It's better if I have one of you here each of several days rather than all four of you and your families here at the same time. So go back and figure out a schedule, and let's parcel it out. Ration yourselves."

I knew they had their own lives to deal with, too, and work and family stuff. The idea was for them to spread it out so that they would have the energy to support me. Because having too many people in this little house is difficult over time. It's fun for a party, but it's a small house.

So a week passed, and I arrived at the first Thursday after Amy had been killed. This was the day the boys would be getting back to their "normal" routine. I had to drive Bryan, but I started imagining Adam on the bus, and if I were in his shoes, would I want to ride the bus? I thought to just tell him I would drive him, too. But then another voice warned me, *Don't start a new habit. He'll want you to drive him to school for the rest of his life.* Such a simple thing—how to get to school—but I was wrestling with it, wanting to make the best decision I could. Finally, I gave up trying to figure it out and simply asked Adam, "Do you want to take the bus or have me drive you?"

"I'll take the bus."

"Okay."

And I let out a subtle sigh of relief—riding the bus is what he'd normally do, and I was craving anything resembling normalcy for all of us. But as we were getting ready that first morning, he started to cry. He decided he didn't want to take the bus after all.

I stood there. Juxtaposed with my desire for normalcy for my boys was my craving to do everything humanly possible to protect them from the pain of the world. What would I now do to shield him from even the slightest pain? I knew the answer. I would do anything. It was as if everything could now be prefaced with the words "now that Mom is dead" in order to guide our next decision. Even the most mundane thing.

Now that Mom is dead, should Adam ride the bus or should I drive him?

Now that Mom is dead, do we have mac and cheese or spaghetti with tomato sauce?

I wanted—*craved*—to get back to normal, but at the same time this horrible reality stuck its nose into everything I did or thought.

I stood there struggling like that and finally said to Adam, "Look, if you don't want to take the bus, that's fine. If you want me to drive you in, I'll drive you in. Just let me know."

"Yes, drive me in."

"Okay. That's what we'll do."

Except there was one small hitch. Our little elementary school was going through a huge renovation project, so Adam and all his schoolmates were riding the bus each day to the holding school, which was halfway across the county. It was a long bus ride for him. Before the construction he'd had maybe a five-minute bus ride. Now it was closer to thirty minutes, or longer on a bad day. For me, that day, it meant a drive around the top of the beltway, in morning rush hour, up to Grosvenor. It's one of the worst commutes around here.

I was nervous. This was not my first time back behind the wheel, but it was the first time in DC rush hour on the beltway. And because Amy had been killed by—I mean, just the thought of what could happen in a car now had me on high alert. I buckled Adam and Bryan into their car seats. I got behind the wheel and took a deep breath, turned the key, and started the engine.

It had been a week, and the color of the world had mostly returned. The low rumble was still there, but it wasn't drowning out all the other sounds anymore. The ten-degree list had almost corrected itself. But there was a lingering feeling of disorientation, dizziness. There should be a warning sticker somewhere, you know, people "on grief" shouldn't operate heavy machinery, right? I had to concentrate and think before every move. I'd been driving a car for more than twenty years, and much of it had become subconscious, automatic. And this particular drive I've easily done a thousand times in my ten years commuting in the Maryland suburbs near DC. It's one of those drives I normally wouldn't have thought about; I'd just subconsciously drive.

Not that day. Every act required white-knuckle concentration and thought. When should I signal a turn? When should I start applying the brake? How hard should I accelerate onto the beltway? I thought of a couple times in my life when I'd had a bit too much to drink and should not have driven but did and felt I had to really stay focused. This was like that.

But with determined concentration I got us to the holding school, parked, and we all walked into the office because we were a little late. I signed Adam in and watched him as he walked out of the office to his classroom. Just like that. It seemed so strange because it all happened so normally.

I walked out carrying Bryan in my arms. I was numb. I was just trying to stay focused on the task: safely get the kids to school, safely get the kids to school, safely get the kids to school. If I didn't focus my brain on that, I would remember that Amy was dead and I would lose it. And I couldn't lose it driving sixty miles per hour on the DC beltway in rush-hour traffic. As I crossed the parking lot to my car I became vaguely aware that a woman's voice was calling out, "John. John. John!"

You know when someone calls your name, but you're not sure it's *your* name they're calling? In that moment I was simply trying to focus on the immediate task of getting back in that car. I was doing everything I could to block out everything else. I hesitated, and then it registered: Oh, wait, I think she's calling out to *me*.

I turned around, and this woman I didn't really know came running up to me.

"You don't know me," she said, "but I knew Amy, and this is so horrible." She hugged me, and she was crying.

I was standing there holding little Bryan, and this woman is crying—not a little cry but big, open sobbing. And there we were, the three of us, in an elementary school parking lot. I was trying to focus on getting back in my car, but how would I do that *now*? She told me that she and Amy had worked together in the PTA, I think, and she maybe asked me how we were doing.

Then this fight started in my body. I could feel the grief welling up again, building pressure, and I needed to let it go. I just needed to let go and start crying right then in this awkward hug with Bryan and this woman I didn't know. And another part of me was saying, *Goddammit! Get the hell out of here! Now! You are going to be getting back in that car and driving your four-year-old son on a road with lots of cars driving fast because they are all late for work!* And then I became very self-conscious. How do I react to this? How *should* I react to this? I hadn't really been out in public yet. I remember thinking, is this something that now happens? Up to that moment I'd been very open—chest-ripped-open—with my grief. But now I found myself in a very different place. I was in a parking lot at my older son's elementary school with my younger son, asking myself if this is the time and place for me to just break down and collapse on the pavement, before attempting to drive a car halfway around the county in rush hour to get Bryan to preschool.

No. I had to bottle it up and keep it bottled up.

She was telling me through her tears how sorry she was and how horrible it was, just the most horrible, most terrible thing ever, and she was thinking of me and my boys, and on and on.

I said, "Yes, I appreciate that, thank you. And how did you know Amy?"

She explained again.

We shared some more, but I don't remember it. She finished what she needed to say, and then I got Bryan in the car.

I was shaken by that encounter. I had to compose myself, all over again. And I was thinking: This. Fucking. Sucks. I *really* didn't want this. I got in the car and started the engine. Took a deep breath and let it out. Then I looked at Bryan in the rearview mirror. It had taken so much energy and concentration to get through that encounter that I had hardly paid attention to Bryan. I looked at him and he was just sitting there, looking straight ahead from under his blond mop of hair that I'd forgotten to comb. This little boy, just sitting quietly, waiting to go. I wanted to say something to him, but what could I say?

Then it sunk in a little more. There was this whole community of people, beyond our family and close friends, who knew and loved Amy, and they were grieving her loss, too. It was obvious, of course. But how their grieving would affect us was not obvious.

All our close friends and immediate family had come by those first few days. And there had been a regular stream of neighbors and good friends who had come over to offer their condolences and grieve with me. As tiring as it was, I welcomed it, and it was necessary. But now I was becoming aware of the large group of people who knew Amy, whom I may *not* have known very well, or may *not* have had the opportunity to run into regularly. Now, as I was getting back into the routines of life, and doing the things that Amy would have been doing, like taking our boys to school and preschool, and birthday parties, play dates, and the like, I was going to start bumping into them. I'd go to the grocery store, or I'd be in town to run some errands.

"Oh, you're John. You don't know me, but Amy and I did this thing together." The person would start to cry, and they'd want to hug, and I'd be trying to buy milk or mac and cheese, or just get somewhere.

This might sound really shitty, but I didn't want that, at all. After a while it started to feel like I had to be consoling *others* in *their* grieving. After a while I started to prep myself for what I needed to do next. Okay, I could tell myself, I need to get my shit together for the next thirty minutes so I can go to the store to get food. So if I bumped into somebody out of phase with me, I'd experience this destructive interference of the waves. I know this sounds ridiculous, but it's the best way I can explain it. So if I were to bump into somebody I would be prepared. I had to gird myself for these encounters. Honestly, it would have been better if they could have waited until I was ready for "grief time." But that isn't how it works.

I realized that our culture doesn't have structured, ritualized grief mechanisms. It's ad hoc and chaotic, and so these interactions are not just likely to occur, they're *bound* to occur. Because of this, I think we unwittingly put an extra burden on those who are grieving.

So I started to think about this from the other perspective, that *other* grieving person's perspective. Let's say I'm at the grocery store, and I see somebody I kind of know, and they just had this horrible thing happen to them. If we see each other and I *don't* acknowledge it, right there, it becomes a *thing*. It's as if I *have to* acknowledge it. I *have* to go up to that person, I *have* to express my sorrow, I *have* to offer help. I have to. Because if I don't—if you don't do it that first time—the moment is lost forever.

I think it's a very strange thing in our culture. Everybody wants to help, but no one really knows what to do. And the person who's grieving often doesn't even know what to ask for.

So my exchanges became some variation on:

"What can I do for you?"

"Oh. Well. I don't know. We could always use food."

In short order I had freezers full of bread and oven roast chickens and baked casseroles. I had plenty of food. Food overflowing. Then I mentioned to someone something about how Amy did all the laundry. Before I knew it five families had volunteered to take turns with our laundry. And the compulsions to help me those weeks extended beyond the obvious ways of helping, too. During one of those first days when my house was full with visitors, a friend said to me, "I know you don't know what you need right now, but there are a lot of people who just want to help in any way they can." I was sitting on the floor and I looked up at the windows, which were dirty with dust and pollen, water spots and cobwebs. I half-joked, "I've been meaning to clean the windows for months." My friend walked away and about thirty minutes later he came back and said, "I know you were kind of joking about the windows, but next Saturday three people will be here to clean your windows." I was dumbfounded.

But it was also simple things. Probably without even realizing it, friends and neighbors offered little encouragements that helped a lot, too. It may have been a day or two after Amy died when a neighbor asked, "Is Adam playing baseball this year?"

I said, "No, he's not signed up." I hadn't really thought about it, and Adam hadn't asked.

He said, "You should sign him up. It's after the deadline, but I'm sure we could work something out. It's not like there are too many kids."

Amy and I had wanted to get the boys involved in sports, but we hadn't pushed them too hard. If they wanted to do it, we'd sign them up, and if they didn't, we weren't going to force the issue. One year Adam wanted to play flag football. Another year it was lacrosse. He tried each and had some fun, but neither really stuck. I had grown up with baseball, and then the Washington Nationals moved to DC in 2005, and Adam was starting to get into baseball and appreciating the sport. The month before Amy died I had taken the boys down to spring training in Florida. We met my dad and mom and one of my brothers and his wife for part of it. We drove all over the middle part of Florida for a week. It was a lot of fun. Each day the boys were getting to understand the game a bit more. A couple years ago we got a Wiffle ball and bat and we'd play in the street. My boys would get some of the neighborhood boys together, they'd choose teams, and one of the other dads or I would pitch.

From the way my neighbor asked about Adam playing baseball I sort of suspected he was thinking, or hoping, it might be something that would help Adam. So I asked Adam if he wanted to play. He said yes, and the league got him on a team.

Their first practice was a week and a day after Amy died. Beginning of May. Clear, blue skies. The oppressive heat and humidity of summer hadn't set in yet. And the juxtaposition of *she's gone* against the backdrop of this pure American sport mythologized beyond any sport in our country—it was a lot to take in. There was a moment as I was watching Adam out on the field when I thought, here's my boy, playing little league, like I did, and like my dad did, and his dad did, and … no mom. And as the season unfolded for us it continued to be both beautiful and heartbreaking, but it became clear to me it was a gift from a neighbor to our family and one that I still cherish.

Another friend and her family came over a couple weeks after Amy died and brought us dinner. I was describing how so many people had extended themselves, offered help, even the most mundane things like planting flowers in our front yard. She said, "John, you have to understand how hard this is on *us*. Because the one thing we want to do, we *can't* do. We can't bring back Amy."

That's when it clicked for me. Everybody wanted to bring back Amy, and no one could do it. But they feel compelled to *do something*. Our culture demands it. Our bodies demand it. Our sense of what's right demands it.

Thinking back on those first few weeks—and after having read *Swallowed by a Snake*—I'm wondering about how other traditions and cultures have set structures and rituals around grief and loss. What would it mean for everyone to have specific periods of time to grieve? Day one, immediate family arrives. Day two, other people arrive. Now it's quiet time. Here it's noisy time. Here's when we dance. Here's when we chant. Here's when we take the body. Here's when we burn the body. Here's when we scatter the ashes. Here's when we beat the drums. Whatever it is, it's prescribed. There's a time for everything. That's what Ecclesiastes says, right? There is a time for all things. Everything has a season. But somehow we got rid of that. Lost it. Why?

—

I drove back around the beltway to Takoma Park and parked in front of the Presbyterian Church that houses the Takoma Park Child Development Center, Bryan's preschool. We went in, and I walked down the hall with Bryan to his room. We got to the door and looked in, and there were all the other four-year-olds. By now it was about 9:30, and they were working on art projects. The teacher saw us and came over, and all the kids turned and looked our way. Bryan and I stood there.

"Go on, Bryan," I said.

He started to sob and moved out from the doorway to the hall so the others wouldn't see him cry. I dropped to one knee, set his backpack down, and hugged him.

"Daddy, I don't want to go," he stammered through his sobs.

"Sweetie," I said, "let's give it a try. All these people are really happy to see you." Which I knew was true. The staff and teachers were all first-rate. As hard as all this was, I knew Bryan would be safe here.

"Daddy," he said, still sobbing, "can you stay?"

I sighed. Part of me so badly wanted to say, "Yes. I'm going to stay here all day with you, every day, forever. I'm never going to leave you."

But I knew that if I didn't say goodbye that day, we'd go through it the next day, and if I didn't do it the next day, we'd do it Monday. It was like that first day of school, when you drop them off and they don't want you to leave and you don't want to leave, but if you don't do it, it just prolongs the pain.

I leaned into the room and motioned to one of the teachers, and she came out into the hall. She and I set up a little plan. I went back to Bryan and sat him down and said, "Okay, Bryan, I'm going to hand you off to your teacher, and she has my phone number. Let's double-check on my phone that she can call me." And the teacher showed Bryan her phone and how she'd be able to call me any time. She dialed, and my phone rang, and I answered to show Bryan how easy it would be to get me. "So, Bryan, if you want to call during the day, any time, here's how to reach me."

This was another moment, one of many that would come, when if I had let myself think of what was going on, *really* going on, I wouldn't have been able to function. What I mean is this: It had been exactly one week earlier when Amy did this exact same thing. She had brought Bryan in, probably carrying his backpack, walked him to this room, and handed him the backpack so he could hang it on his hook. Then she probably bent down and hugged him and said, "Goodbye, see you later," and that was it. But last week there had been no later. To Bryan, Mom dropped him off, like I was doing now, and then disappeared and never returned. And now, here we were, and I was saying goodbye to him in the very same place. And I realized that there are no guarantees anymore. No promises. If he'd asked me to promise that I'd pick him up at 5:30, what could I say? I couldn't make that promise anymore.

All this flashed through my mind as I paused there, on my knees, and said goodbye to Bryan. But I had to put it all aside for that moment. I had to pack away all my grief and wobbliness and fears and uncertainties for a moment—*this* moment—to deal with the present task. In some ways it helped me get very focused. The grief, that is. It forced me to focus on one single thing in one single moment in time.

It was exhausting.

—

John stopped, and I took that as a signal.

Break? I asked him with my eyes.

He nodded.

I turned off the recorder.

"Do you want to stop?" I asked. I almost wanted him to tell me yes. I felt wrung out, listening to him relate that terrible first week after Amy's death. I looked around. Early evening light played in through the living room windows, and outside on the quiet street the trees were beginning to cast their long shadows. I would be driving home in darkness tonight. I looked back at John.

He shook his head no. "Let's talk about something else."

"Okay," I said. I thought quickly, about Amy. "Let's talk about Amy. You've never told me how you two met."

—

Amy and I met on a blind date.

Except she wasn't my date.

Several months before I met Amy, in the summer of 1998, my girlfriend and I had broken up. It was a tough breakup for me. We'd been a couple nearly three years and had moved in together that third year, and for a while I thought she and I would be together forever. But eventually, we realized it was not to be, for a variety of reasons, not the least of which was I wanted to have children and she did not. That fall I dated a few women. A few false starts, nothing particularly serious, and I grew a bit frustrated with the dating scene. I was in my early thirties and just wasn't sure I even wanted to be dating. Being single with no relationship constraints had its benefits. I was renting a great two-bedroom apartment in downtown Arlington, Virginia. I could walk to my Metro stop, and there were plenty of bars and restaurants nearby. Life was good. I was enjoying my freedom. Then one day a friend of mine, Alev, called me up, and asked me what I had planned for that Saturday.

"Oh, nothing. I was just going to stay in, maybe watch a movie." I was kind of looking forward to a relaxing weekend.

"Some friends and I are going to a party at Studebakers. It's a surprise birthday party for a friend's ex-girlfriend."

"What?"

She did her best to explain the several degrees of separation between her and this friend whose girlfriend had broken up with him, but he had already gone to the trouble of scheduling this big party, and so on.

I'm not sure when I stopped paying attention. I was silent. Was this really my best offer on a Saturday? Studebakers was this B-list bar with a DJ and dance floor out in Tyson's Corner. I had no desire to drive out to the suburbs for that experience.

"Friend's ex-girlfriend? I don't know, I think I'll just stay in."

But she had buried the lede!

"Well, my friend Marcia is coming. Maybe we could meet for dinner first. And they're running a special at Studebakers—twenty-five-cent rail drinks if we get there before nine o'clock. I'll drive."

Wait, what was that? Marcia? Well, that was the name of a woman I didn't know yet. I was being set up! Okay, fine, I didn't care. Plus, there was cheap alcohol and a designated driver. "Okay, I'm in!"

We discussed time and logistics and hung up. Alev lived close by, so it was an easy walk to her apartment building. I put on my classic post-grunge, upscale, casual going-out clothes: blue jeans with black T-shirt and unbuttoned, un-tucked casual Oxford shirt. Brown leather shoes and belt completed the look. It was January and dark by the time I got to Alev's place, about 6:30. I knocked on her door. It opened, and there was Marcia.

You know those times when you first see someone and your pulse quickens, you nervously swallow, and think, "Wow, could she be the one"?

This was not that time.

Immediately I regretted agreeing to this, and I could only envision having to endure dinner, then a drive to the suburbs, drinks, and half-hearted dancing in a lame dance club. What was I doing?

Marcia and I introduced ourselves and politely shook hands, and then we all headed out to a nearby Mexican restaurant. I can't remember what I ordered, besides margaritas. We exchanged light conversation. She was a middle school or elementary school teacher. I don't remember. She probably asked what I did, and I tried to not bore her about the IT industry. IT was hot in the late 1990s, and everyone had an opinion or had some question about computers then, and I often dreaded getting into that conversation by admitting to what I did. It seemed like half the people I met at parties were having some problem with a printer.

I'm sure Marcia picked up on my vibe or came to her own equal conclusion that this was going nowhere and that we'd just have to make the most of the night.

At some point Alev said, "We need to wrap up so we can get to Studebakers before nine."

Oh. Yeah. I was studying my second margarita so intently I had nearly forgotten the cheap booze that was waiting. So we paid our check and headed off to the 'burbs.

Studebakers was attached to a hotel just off the beltway on Route 7 in Tyson's Corner. We parked in the hotel parking garage, walked around to the hotel entrance, and then into the nightclub—a nondescript dark space with a bar on one side, some flashy lights, and loud techno music thumping. Including the three of us, and the two bartenders, there were maybe a dozen people total.

Ugh.

This sucks, I thought. I had never really been into the whole nightclub scene, and it occurred to me that the only people who went to nightclubs before nine o'clock were losers or those lured by the cheap drinks. At that moment I was still clinging to my self-identification with the latter.

We walked to the bar, got our cheap drinks, and joined the small clutch of people standing in a circle. Alev introduced me to another person. "John, this is Steve. He's the one throwing the party."

We shook hands and I recalled that the original motive for the gathering was a surprise party for a friend's ex-girlfriend.

"Nice to meet you," he said. "Glad you could make it. So my girlfriend—well, my ex-girlfriend—should be showing up sometime around 9:30, and we can surprise her then." He was explaining the whole setup, and I tried to look interested while also trying to pull my hand out of the too-long handshake.

I stepped back into the circle and just stood there and sipped my drink. I couldn't quite see who was next to me. It was pretty dark, but I could tell the person to my right was a petite woman with dark hair. When a few seconds started to turn into uncomfortable silence, I turned to her and, hoping to reaffirm my status as "not a loser," asked, "So are you here for the twenty-five-cent drinks, too?"

She turned to me, smiled, and said without hesitation, "Speaking of quarters, have you seen the new state quarters?"

It was January 1999, and the first of the state quarters, Delaware, had recently been released. It was novel and in the news and I *had* seen one.

"Yes!" I said perhaps a bit too excitedly, but I sensed she was relieved she wouldn't have to stand there alone any longer, either. So I continued, "And have you seen the new twenty-dollar bill?"

"Yeah!" she replied. "And what's up with Andrew Jackson's big head?"

We laughed, and that started us off. There was something in that first exchange. Her wit. Her confidence. Something. We turned to each other and kept talking. Why are you here? Friend of a friend. Same. My name? John. Yours? Amy. Where do you live? What do you do? All the normal first questions. I asked her about an interesting Native American–looking medallion on a leather strap she wore around her neck she had gotten on a recent trip to visit friends in Alaska. We talked about travel and how we each loved it. We talked about where we had gone to school and what we studied. She was a computer science undergrad, so we had that in common. And we kept talking. Politics, Bill Clinton, Monica Lewinsky, and so on. We got another drink. Before I knew it people were starting to fill the nightclub and were dancing. The DJ queued up Madonna's "Ray of Light," and Amy grabbed my hand and pulled me onto the dance floor.

"I love Madonna!" she screamed over the music.

And man, oh man, could she dance. I did my best to keep up. I had always thought I was a decent dancer, but she was good. Really good. And sexy. She was mixing in belly dance hip moves, and I could make out her figure for the first time. With the dance floor lights I finally saw her green eyes and perfect red lips. I can't exactly say I fell in love with her at that moment, but I knew I was falling for her right there on the dance floor. The song ended and another came on, and we kept dancing for a couple more songs. Eventually we stopped, I bought her a drink, and we kept talking. Then at one point in our conversation there was a pause and I said, "Amy, I'd like your phone number, because I am going to call you tomorrow and ask you out on a date."

She tilted her head, raised an eyebrow, and gave me a subtle, mischievous grin, a grin I'd grow to love. She reached into her handbag and pulled out a business card and wrote her number on it.

"I'd like that," she said as she handed me the card. We kept on talking and occasionally danced. Before I knew it, it had gotten late, and my designated driver and former blind date had to leave. Amy and I shook hands and said goodbye.

That's how we met.

—

John paused on the edge of tears.

"Let's take a break," I said.

John nodded and grabbed a tissue and went into the kitchen.

Listening to the story of how Amy and John met reminded me of the hope we all feel for new love. I sat there, watching this man I cared about going through this grief for the woman he loved so much. I thought of the dreams he and Amy must have had, like we all have, when creating new love. My attention flipped to Adam and Bryan, the product of that love, playing at a friend's house. I was looking out the window when John came back into the living room with a glass of water and broke my mental wandering by asking, "Can I get you anything?"

"What? No," I said. "I'm good."

He settled back onto the couch. "How are you doing?"

Typical John. Here we were talking about how he'd lost Amy, and he's asking me how I'm doing. "I'm okay," I said.

"What do you want to talk about now?"

I wanted to get back to where we'd started the session. "Let's get back to that first week, John. Back to those first days right after she died. Tell me what happened, what you were going through. How did you cope?"

—

In the days right after Amy's death, I began to sit on the floor. I just needed to be low, low to the ground. If I could have melted into the earth I would have gladly done so. If I could have prostrated myself, sunk into the earth and just stayed there, I would have gladly done that. Instinctively. I never came into the living room and thought, "Hmm, should I sit on the couch or the floor?" Something just led me to sit on the floor.

Sometimes I would sit cross-legged. Sometimes I would kneel on the floor and lean forward, the way Muslims pray. If I were sitting on the floor when others stopped by, they would sit on the floor with me. I'd sit, sometimes saying nothing, sometimes crying, sometimes talking, and people would visit.

I'd sometimes sit quietly, but eventually those tumorous balls of grief would come back up. I'd feel each one coming—it felt like I was about to throw up—and it would come up, and I'd start to cry and moan, and from my kneeling position, I'd throw myself forward and lay my head down on the floor.

Some people would pat me on the back and say, "Yeah, that's it," or "You're doing well," or "You're going to be fine." They meant well, I know, and they were doing what they could do to help, but the things they were saying didn't sound right to me. After all, I was not doing well, and I was not thinking at all about being fine. I wanted to grieve. I hated the pain, but I needed the pain. I wanted it to end, but I didn't want it to end. I was aware of a direct connection between my love for Amy and my pain, and how the pain reflected the love we'd shared. If my pain were to end, would that signal the end of our love?

I didn't really know what would have been better for people to say. Maybe "I miss Amy, too," or "I'm so sorry this happened." There really is no good thing to say to someone who has just experienced this type of loss, I suppose. I've since tried to think of what I might have said to someone in the same position, but sometimes there are no words. It was simply presence and touch that I found most supportive and meaningful many times.

One particular time members of my church came over. I was kneeling on the floor, and the balls of grief were expanding in my chest. I leaned forward, put my arms forward, and rested my head on the floor. I couldn't see what was happening around me, but I was aware of hands on me, just resting on me, holding me. No one said anything; no one needed to say anything. There were maybe ten people, all around me, laying their hands on me. That was the right thing to do for me then. I moaned and cried, and they all were on the floor with me, laying hands on me.

As sorrowful a moment as that was, there was something beautiful about it. I could feel my sorrow and my pain and my grief vibrating out of me and through them. There was a connected energy I could feel through their touch. I began crying even harder—loud wailing and moaning with my forehead down on the floor and my arms in front of me. And they just continued to hold me; their hands held my back, my arms, my legs. I could feel the bone-ache of my grief pulsate from deep inside and radiate out to their hands. And then I felt their love and compassion passing back through their hands and into my body. It lasted for a minute, maybe two. The sobbing subsided. I lifted my head slowly, and as I pushed myself back to a kneeling position those around me let go, one by one. I was exhausted. I was in pain. My diaphragm and ribs hurt. My chest and throat burned. My head throbbed. But I felt a calmness, for the first time. It was that laying on of hands. Healers, they were. We sat in silence for another minute or so. No one spoke. We just sat there. Then when it was time I thanked them. It was a very powerful experience.

I would want that for others.

—

At some point in those early days it occurred to me that the Jews have been doing this for quite a while. I had a Jewish coworker whose father died, and he shared with me some of the tradition of sitting shiva and the guidelines for the bereaved and for those visiting the bereaved. As I understood it, the person in mourning sits on the floor, and there are established times for certain things to happen. The grieving person is on his own sometimes, and then there are certain times for people to visit. Before Amy died I didn't really understand what was behind the practice of sitting shiva; never considered it. But there on the floor of my living room, I was starting to get it. It just felt right to sit on the floor. I didn't track the days, but the experience of sitting or kneeling on the floor, by myself, or with others, went on for a week or so.

And with it a routine of sorts started to emerge. One thing that the boys and I did happened spontaneously. It grew from this compulsion I felt to gather Amy's things and collect them in one place, at the fireplace. A shrine emerged, made of pictures and veils from her dancing, and books she liked to read, and her glasses and jewelry and mementos and stuffed panda bears and things other people brought over. I told the boys, "If there's something you think Mommy would like or something that reminds you of Mommy, get it, place it here." Part of it started because I had to have things of hers near me, right away, like a headband, or a hair scrunchie. There was that necklace with a medallion from Alaska she had worn the day we met. I had to find it. I started wearing it.

It was very difficult for me to go into our bedroom. That space we shared reminded me of the magnitude of my loss of the woman I had committed to be with—the woman with whom I'd created the two children in our house. Going into our bedroom brought that into sharp focus, and reminded me of what was gone, and that I could never take her in my arms and spoon up behind her, ever again. But I couldn't avoid going in there. I needed some things—all my clothes were there, of course—and after a couple days of sleeping on the floor with the boys, I decided to move, and the three of us slept together in our big bed for a couple weeks until the boys decided they wanted to be back in their rooms. So part of creating the shrine around the fireplace was to be close to her while I sat in the living room. Somehow, retrieving a few artifacts from our bedroom and moving them somewhere else in the house had the effect of shifting the power the bedroom itself had over me. With that shift, the bedroom was not the only sacred place in the house, so I could more easily enter it.

There was also something important about having a central focal point for Amy. The fireplace with all its mementos became the space where I would sit and grieve those first couple of weeks. Especially in the morning. Mornings were difficult. Particularly so. I'd wake up. There would be this fraction of a moment as sleep was sliding away when there was nothing. Just nothing. Then as fast as that moment had come it was replaced with the realization that Amy was still dead. It was another day I was alive and Amy was still dead. I'd force myself up and I'd hurry to the living room before the sobbing would start so I could be in the right place. I had to sit in the right place on the floor. I'd hold it in until I could get there. Hurry to the bathroom, grab a drink of water, then quickly go to the living room, sit on the floor, and just start to moan and cry—ten minutes, half an hour, I don't even remember. It was different each day. Some people meditate, or exercise, first thing in the morning. I'd sit on the floor and cry. Then I'd get up from the floor, wake up the boys, make breakfast, and get them off to school.

So there I was, beginning to create some new patterns. Wake up. Grieve. Pull myself together long enough to get the kids going.

And while we were creating new patterns in our day-to-day personal lives, there was also other work to attend to. Almost from the first day people would ask me when the service was.

And that was easier said than done. Because of how Amy had died and the ongoing investigation, we had no idea when we were going to get her body back. How do we schedule a memorial service? Can I have a memorial service without Amy's body? Isn't there usually a coffin with the body, or at least an urn?

It was as if these two parallel worlds—our grief, and the cold logistics of getting Amy back—fed off of each other somehow, and no one really seemed to know what to do. We were all making it up as we went, as if Amy was the first human being ever to have died.

I was lucky, in a way, that a friend from our church is also a lawyer. He had seen how the "system" works—or doesn't work, sometimes, I should say—so he was there for me to be an intermediary and to basically look over the shoulders of those involved. Closing out the official business of the identification with the medical examiner took almost three weeks. So it was that much time before we could recover her body, go to a funeral home, make the arrangements to have her body cremated, get the remains, and so forth. But I could not wait that long to have a memorial service. And at first we really didn't even know how long that would take. We needed to have a memorial service soon, and we needed to do *something*. I needed to honor her.

But how?

The weekend after Amy died, our minister returned from her sabbatical and came over, and we worked it through. And thank God for my minister, for guiding me through this. I'm not even sure I knew how to eat, yet I had to start making decisions about things. When should we have the service? Did I want music? Who should be invited? And so on. That's when we realized we'd need two services. One, as soon as possible, for family only, and a second, larger public service for the hundreds of people who would want to honor Amy. We scheduled the family service for the Tuesday after her death. Five days after she'd been killed.

For the public service, we started looking at the calendar, trying to guess when the authorities would be done, when we would be ready, and we landed on a date in June. It was partially because our minister had interrupted her sabbatical and would have to return again, partially because my dad already had some travel lined up. But mostly it was because of the information we got from the medical examiner's office about when they'd be able to release Amy. They said it could be two to four weeks more, or *longer*.

When I heard that I thought, what does *that* mean? "Two to four weeks, or longer?" Longer? What does "longer" mean? Five weeks?

Because five weeks is "longer." Or is it *six* weeks? Six weeks is also longer, and so is a *thousand* weeks. They might as well have just said in five weeks or maybe *forever*.

Faced with that, once we looked out past three weeks or so, as crazy as it sounds, it just became a matter of convenience, and lining up people's schedules. I wanted to have something that felt right, and I couldn't have a service that felt right without all my family there for the public service, so we decided we would have it whenever we could make it work. That's how we came up with June 18.

But it still felt wrong. It was almost two months in the future, but it might as well have been forever.

—

So there we were. Lacking any formal guidelines or rules, we decided to do what made sense for us.

For the family service, on Tuesday, May 4, I'd also invited a couple of close friends. I wanted someone there who could take the boys out of the service if they wanted to step out. A woman from our church, a musician, agreed to sing. There were probably twenty people there altogether. It's hard to say what the most difficult thing was about that day, but speaking aloud of my loss is the first thing that comes to mind.

It was never something I'd deliberated—whether or not I should get up in front of my family and speak from my heart about the life Amy and I had shared, and about who she was to me. I knew I would do it. There was no doubt in my mind I would give the eulogy. I can't say whether it was from a sense of responsibility to Amy, or respect and honor for her, or some combination. But there was no doubt in my mind. There was really no choice.

But I didn't know exactly what I was going to say. I had difficulty with the words. In those first few days I could not—and still can't—grasp the senselessness of her death, the incomprehensibility of death, in general. Who really understands it? Buddha, maybe? Jesus? Maybe they got it, I don't know. But for most of us, or for me, at least, at some point, language fails. I think anything having to do with the time and moment of death, and what—if anything—comes after, is at worst speculative and at best a matter of faith. Death is ninety percent of the reason why religion exists, isn't it?

Because of this event we all have coming up. And our unfortunately large brains have the ability to comprehend our own existence, and comprehend *not* existing, in some way. It's scary, and it's something we don't understand, so we tend to shy away from it. Most of us don't have a lot of practical experience with death. At least I didn't. So for the first few days after Amy died I was grappling with the enormity of her death, my loss, our loss—and what I would say.

Death was in our family now, and it created so many questions. There were the almost mundane, day-to-day questions. What does it mean to live without a wife? Without a mom? How do we function now as a family? That was the mechanical part of it. But then there was the existential part of it. What does it mean to be alive? To be human, for such an infinitesimally small speck of time in the history of it all? Why is it that we have evolved to be aware of our own mortality? Can that possibly be helpful? Has anyone come up with a satisfactory answer to any of this? I didn't really think so, and yet, I was confronted with a desperate need for those answers.

So that Tuesday morning of the family service I started to develop some notion of what I might say about Amy, but not the exact words. I had some notes. The yin and yang, the two poles of grief and love, were very much part of my understanding, existentially, even in the first few days. I think I can honestly say that we had a special relationship. It helped me to hear other people testify to this. People were saying to me, "You two were perfect together." And as hard as that was to hear sometimes, it affirmed this sense I had in my own mind about who we were, which was really important for me. And still is. But the level and depth of the grief ...

Searching for answers, I was drawn to Rumi very quickly. He was a thirteenth-century Persian mystic who wrote a lot of beautiful poetry, and he wrote about how our profound grief is informed by the profound love for what we've lost. Rumi's language and imagery provided a sense of a true understanding I could almost grasp. Here was a man who had experienced the most ecstatic of love and the most desperate despair. One of his poems says something about grief being the garden of compassion that can open you to life's search for love. Something like that. At first, it made me mad. Grief is the garden? Why can't love be the garden? Why is it grief? But then it started to make sense. Even with my frustration with his words, in some peculiar way Rumi's writing helped with the awesome pain I felt. The more I read, the more I began to understand how love and grief coexist, and how each *requires* the other. I came to realize that the pain I felt so deeply was *because* of the love I felt so deeply. It has to be so, as this is a certainty of our love. How *else* would I feel? *Because* we had this amazing love, I *experience* this amazing grief.

It's not that I enjoyed feeling that way, that day, or the way I feel three months after her death. But it validated something that's extremely important for me as part of my own memory, and for my boys.

And I want my boys to understand, however they can, the nature of our love and the life force from it that created them. I think that's really important for them to understand. Over time, of course. I can't sit down with Bryan, a five-year-old now, and explain that to him. But, hopefully, someday, he will come to understand it in his own way and draw meaning or purpose from that.

The service that Tuesday was scheduled for two o'clock in the afternoon. That morning I went for a run. I ran hard. I ran down to the end of our street, and then into Sligo Creek Park, where there's a hiker/biker trail, for about four miles, along the stream in the dappled sunlight. As I was running, it came to me, and I knew what I would say. I think it was about eleven o'clock that morning. I got home, sat in front of the computer, and the words appeared on the screen as my fingers typed.

—

John motioned for me to turn off the recorder. After I did he asked if I wanted him to get the eulogy he'd read at the family service. "Should we have that in the book?"

"Yes," I said, "we should."

"Do you want me to get it now?"

I nodded. "Do you have it?"

"It's printed out near my computer. I could go get it right now. Or after. If you want to copy it in. Do you want me to read it in? Now? Into the transcripts? Should I go get it now?"

I nodded. If John was to read it now, I thought—that would be a sacred experience. One very meaningful for him, one I would want recorded.

He got up and went to get it. I waited. And I thought of Amy's reach in life, now in death, of the hundreds of people who had come through this house, this living room, to visit John that first week after Amy was killed.

John came back into the living room and sat down on the couch with the pages. He read.

—

Dear Amy,

Thirsty I wandered the desert in search of cool waters. I came to a small rivulet and drank from it, but the water was sour and made me sick. I then came to a shallow pool with reeds and drank from it. But the water was salty. It made me sick. I continued onward and came to a small oasis with a pool. I stopped and drank from it, but its source had dried and the pool became stagnant. I continued onward, digging here and there in the earth, divining for water, occasionally catching the morning dew for a small sip to wet my dry lips. I continued on.

I arrived at a sandy cliff. As I edged forward to look below it gave way and I fell. The weightless fall both terrified and exhilarated. I plunged headlong into a deep, rolling river fed by mountain streams. I gasped for breath. Finding my balance, I gulped in the cool, sweet waters. The water washed over and cleansed me. I was alive. The current swept forward and carried me into the most beautiful valley any man has ever seen.

I breathed in the fragrance of the loamy soil and perfume of the surrounding forest wood. The dappled sun passing through the embracing tree canopy warmed me. Sounds of the water dancing around large stones upon the bedrock and lapping the sandy banks weaved into beautiful hymns. This was sacred land. I rested upon the shore and built a fire. So abundant was this sacred land that new life sprang forth, and we all drank of the cool, sweet waters, played in the forest, and danced by the fire on the sturdy bank of the water.

For eternity we dreamed we would drink and play and dance. And then suddenly the land shifted and shook. The trees groaned with anguish and were uprooted. The bedrock moaned in despair and her sturdy bed gave way, plunging us back into the river. And now three of us hold on dearly and gasp for air and wonder to what unknown place the current takes us.

Oh, my Amy, I miss you so. Your beautiful eyes and sparkling smile. A mere glimpse and reflection of the passion and fire within. The passion and fire, which now burn strong among the multitude that stood witness to your life and received your many gifts. I feel them all around me, your

passion and fire. There are no words I have found to describe their profound nature.

That I love you fully and with all my heart and all my soul, I hope you
know. I believe you do. That others love you, too. So many. So, so many is
a reality I only now begin to comprehend. But that so many loved you is
manifest of your abundant love to us all. For me, besides the precious gift
of time, howsoever brief you shared it with me, was a gift of profound love.
And through that profound love you showed me how to be loved, the most
precious gift imaginable.

And I also know—and I do know you know—how much your two
beautiful boys love you. Please know they also feel your love, a love they
carry inside them for eternity. Thank you for those gifts.

And there's one more thing I kept meaning to tell you, but just never
did. Do you know how every morning after I got dressed for work you'd
tell me, "You look nice" or, "I like that tie"? Every morning. Every morning. I just want you to know I noticed it. I really did. It made me feel good
as I ran out the door. I kept meaning to tell you thank you, but never did.
I'm sorry I never got around to it. Thank you.

And now we are in a different place and a different time, Amy, you
and me and the boys. The dream you and I spoke of on our second date of
traveling around the country in a Winnebago and dropping in from time
to time on our grandkids must now change to something different. That is:
I have no idea yet. Somehow, I know you will help me discover it, for you
are with me and in me, now and forever.

My dearest Amy, I love you.

—

John stopped reading, and I watched the pages in his hand slowly drop
down. He began to weep.

I turned off the recorder and sat there mute, watching my friend convulse in tears, and seeing him in so much pain, I started to cry, too—for
his pain; for what he had gone through and was going through; for his two
young sons, Adam and Bryan, and their loss; and for our loss, our collective
loss at another human life gone. I wept for Amy.

But along with the overwhelming sadness I felt there was a sense of
release, of permission to grieve. John and I were mixing that boundary,

again, between interviewee and interviewer. We were friends now, and so I could weep for him, for his loss, for us here in this terrible situation, recounting that loss.

I'd never met Amy, but after listening to John read his eulogy for her, there in his living room—the eulogy he'd read to that small intimate group just after Amy's death—I felt that I had come to know about her. And this was proper, I thought. After all, who are we but reflections of what others say we are? I wanted to learn more about Amy, and John, and their relationship.

It took a few minutes for us to regain our composure and continue.

—

The family service in which I gave that eulogy was simple. It was at our church, the Unitarian Universalist Church of Silver Spring. Reverend Liz, our minister, and Revered Ellen, our minister of religious education, officiated, and Michael Holmes, our music director, provided beautiful music along with others who performed. We had all our family there, both sides. Bonnie and her husband, Donald, Amy's stepdad, were there. Amy's dad, Jim, and his wife, Cara, their daughter, Abigail. Amy's brother and his wife and his son. My parents and siblings came. I'd invited my good friend Jim and his wife. And our friends from church, Erik and Alison, to act mostly as shepherds for the boys.

Amy's mom had made little purple ribbons to wear in her honor. Purple had been Amy's favorite color. We had pictures of her, and veils from her folk dancing. The music was important, too. There was a traditional English folk ballad, "10,000 Miles." Amy and I had just seen the movie *Into the Wild*, and there's a song on the soundtrack called "The Wolf," in which Eddie Vedder just screams out a visceral yearning, crying, pain. No lyrics, just wailing. I was listening to it a lot in the days after she died. There was something about the melody and Vedder's wolflike yet very human howl. I imagined myself lying on my living room floor, or down the street with Jim and my brother the night Amy died, and hearing those howls off in the distance. Our music director from church adapted that song and played it on a large Native American woodwind. It was chilling and mournful. We also played "Gymnopédie," by Satie, a quiet and somber piece, which I fell in love with when I heard it played by a classical street guitarist in a park in Madrid when Amy and I were there in 2002.

It was a simple service. Reverend Liz, who had married us, opened with some words, followed by Reverend Ellen. They kept it short. In their respective ways they acknowledged the grievous loss. The capriciousness and finitude of life. The comfort we sought and the healing power of community. And then we had a time for sharing when anyone could say what they wanted. Amy's dad came over to the boys and got down on a knee and told them how they needed to look out for each other. He told the story of how when he had been a little boy his father, a merchant marine during World War II, had died. I had forgotten this family story and that Amy's father had grown up without a dad. After those who wanted to speak did so, I read aloud my letter to Amy.

—

In the days that followed, friends and family still came and went—not at the same level or intensity, but we had a pretty full household much of the time. Sometimes I think of myself as an introvert, but I'm really a borderline extrovert. I've talked to other people who've been through this, and they remarked, "I can't believe you had all those people over. I would want to just crawl under the sheets." But I don't do well alone. Not alone and depressed. That is a bad place for me, so having people around, as exhausting as it was, helped. It gave me someone to talk to. Someone to cry with. There were times when I would be wrung out. Not having slept well, end of the day, sheer exhaustion, and someone would come to the door and I'd say to myself, "Fuck. I don't have time for somebody to just stop by."

But I'd tell them, "Hey, come on in," and then I'd spend two or three hours talking to them. And it would make me feel good. The company of other people was very important.

Over time, though, I felt a very real tension growing. I knew that I needed solitary time, to be quiet with myself, with my own emotions. But I also feared being quiet with myself and my emotions and what that might mean, and I knew having a constant flow of people helped me to avoid going there—to avoid sitting with my own naked fears of being alone, not having a partner. Wondering if I would ever find someone again. When someone was with me it quieted those fears. When no one was around, the only way I could quiet them was with Scotch. But that is another story I'll get to. So there were those moments when I was moaning, "Ugh, I've got to pull down the blinds, close the door, and turn off the lights, so that people don't keep stopping by." But then people would stop by, and once I convinced myself I was okay, I'd let them in.

In the days after the family service, the large, public service was looming for me. From the first moment after her death I'd been telling myself: I've just got to get through this minute. Then: I've got to call Bonnie. Then: I've got to get through this hour. Then: I've got to get through telling the boys that Amy's dead. I've got to get through this one night. I've got to get through driving my car for the first time. I've got to get through getting the boys off to school. And now, looming ahead was the second service, the service for the community of people around us, and it was becoming a big one. Another huge marker, a milestone, to get through to the other side.

I have this obsession now with time, the passage of time. I think part of it is driven externally, culturally, like the Jewish mourning period, and how their process unfolds over the first year. Beyond the seven days of sitting shiva, there are markers throughout the year, and there are stages for mourning. And at one year you unveil the headstone, and then you're done.

However, part of it is that I have created in my mind what I imagine is expected of someone mourning. I feel compelled to mark off things to show progress to myself, but also as a way to say, I got through that, so I must be doing okay. And then I can say, I got through this other thing, so I must be making progress. And out of convenience, I guess, I oftentimes make up these markers or assign meaning to things, just so I can have the feeling of getting past it.

But the public memorial service was more than just a marker. It was another milestone to pass, of course, but there was something else, and I felt compelled to make sure it could *be* something. I felt that this service was *the* moment to honor Amy, publicly, and, as her husband, and loving her the way I did, I couldn't squander the opportunity. It needed to be perfect. It needed to be perfect, because that's how I imagined our relationship, and the way she was. I didn't want to lose that moment, that opportunity, to fully honor who she had been as a human being, or as my wife. I felt like this would be the time to do that.

So the words I spoke, the music we chose—many of those decisions were very important, and intentional. I went over what we had done at the family service, but thought it too intimate for this larger event. That meant finding more music and creating a second eulogy.

The memorial was set for June 18, seven weeks after Amy had died. I had no idea what would come after the service, but I just knew, somehow, that getting beyond it would be important for the boys and me. And the long wait gave it even more significance, more heaviness, if that was even possible, than it already had. It was consuming me. It felt like there was a whole set of things I really couldn't *do* with my life until *after* that event occurred. I was back at work, but I couldn't focus on the work. I couldn't be present with the boys, because some part of my brain was always thinking about the upcoming service.

During this time I really felt like we—me, my boys, and everyone else around me—were grasping for guidance on what to do next. And somehow I felt like I was supposed to be the lead on defining what to do for others. Understand, I'm not bitter or angry with that, but it would have been nice to have had something laid out beforehand, for me and everyone else. Think about it—for weddings and births, there's a pattern we all generally agree to. Not every wedding happens the exact same way, of course, but at least in our Western framework, our mostly Christian culture, there's a process to follow. There's an engagement; there's the shower; maybe you get pictures for the newspaper; there's the announcement in the paper; and the announcement goes out to family and friends. Depending on your faith, you might meet with the minister. You might go through some pre-training classes about marriage. Then there's the ceremony itself. People walk down the aisle. There are bridesmaids and groomsmen. Rings are exchanged. Vows are exchanged. There's a kiss. Then you celebrate. So there's a process to these things. There's a pattern to follow, even though it may not be exactly the same every single time. Even receptions have a pattern. You introduce the new bride and groom. There's the food. There are a variety of ritual dances. There's cake cutting. And you send them off with a shower of rice or birdseed. You can even hire a wedding planner if you want.

That's marriage.

Now let's talk about death. Is there a death planner? I don't think it works that way with death. Someone gets sick, or is hurt, and dies. Maybe they linger, maybe it's sudden. There's a service, a burial, and people come visit and help. But the details are missing. Grief is not linear. It's all over the place. What is the structure for the grieving process? Not only for the aggrieved family and friends, but also for those around them?

So where was the ritual I could lean on for support? What if I had been an Orthodox Jew or devout Muslim? They have provisions on how and when the body is handled and buried, don't they? I guess they've developed some accommodations for these horrible and unique situations. But for us? Having to wait *seven weeks* for the memorial service? When I could finally honor her—what?—her *ashes*? I didn't even know yet. It felt like we were all stuck until that could occur. Our need to grieve, need to respond, need to help, need to act, were malformed, undefined, it seemed. Hadn't there been a time in our own culture when this wasn't the case? It seems only recently that we've pushed the experience of death and grieving so far away from us that we've made it foreign. And now, looking back, I find myself sickly fascinated with comparing the way this experience unfolded for my family and the way another family in another culture might manage this. Why isn't this figured out for us in modern America? We've been dying for a long time; you'd think we'd be better at it by now. But I wonder if all our modernity has set us back in this. I've heard stories from early America— how people were "closer to death" back then. Bodies were often kept in the home parlor for the wake. Death, really, was simply a part of life, back then, a part of what was sometimes a very harsh life. Life now is better and easier, thankfully, but death still waits for us, and maybe we should have held on to some of that wisdom from our grandparents and their parents. For us, in the aftermath of Amy's death, it felt like we were winging it.

For example, the poor aggrieved woman who'd felt compelled to approach me at the elementary school—in another time and place, she might have seen something I was wearing, a black armband, for example, or she would have seen the smudge of ash on my forehead, or that my hair was cut particularly short, signifying that I was in an early part of the grieving process, and if she'd wanted to approach me, she'd have had to do it in a very particular way.

But even with all this thought of ritual and tradition and getting it "right," as we were coming up to the day of this large service I started thinking that I needed to forget about perfection, about carrying this thing off. I just wanted to get it over with. It had been *seven* weeks.

Then a friend of mine found a reference in, I think, *The Tibetan Book of Living and Dying*. The Tibetan Buddhist tradition has the concept of "bardo," which is an in-between state, or transitional state, between lives. I think there are six bardo states, or maybe it depends on the particular variety of Buddhism. They define a time that's between living and dying. So if you've taken that last breath, there is this moment of transition from the living world and the dead world. That moment would be a bardo. There's another bardo between once you have died and once your soul is freed for reincarnation. As I understand it, in the Buddhist tradition, that's an important bardo period, perhaps the most important, because that's a time when your soul can learn a lot on its eventual path to enlightenment.

In the Buddhist tradition, during this time, daily prayers help the soul of the person who died through his or her transition. These ritual prayers occur during a forty-nine-day period to help guide the deceased through the spirit world in preparation for the next life. On the fiftieth day the deceased is relieved of earthly obligations, and their soul can move on.

Forty-nine is important. Seven is a powerful, magical number; forty-nine, obviously, is seven sevens, seven weeks. I was curious and so looked at the calendar. As it turned out, the community service for Amy was on that day, the fiftieth day. It just happened that way. When I realized that, I thought, well, of course, now this day makes sense; this is a perfect way to let her know she's relieved of her earthly obligations.

It brought me some peace to think of it that way. That the date fit within some existing ritual, even if by accident. Then I had some purpose for having the public memorial service so many weeks after her death. And of course there would be some release on my part, too—another milestone to reach and pass.

Now I remember that day as if it happened a long time ago, or maybe it didn't happen at all—I'm not sure. Did it really happen, or did I dream it? I know it happened because I have the program that Bonnie made, the one with the purple ribbon and Amy's picture from our wedding on it.

My family came in to town. I wore a new purple shirt. We drove to the church. People gathered. Many people. Someone said they'd have to open up overflow space. The boys were by my side. Music started playing. We walked to the front row of chairs. Everyone watched us. We sat down. Tears stung my eyes. I held my boys. Our boys. Our minister talked. Other people talked. Sad words. Beautiful words. Then it was my turn. I walked up to the pulpit. I unfolded the pages with words on them. My hands shook. I started talking. I started to cry and had to pause. I continued talking. I looked at my boys curled up in their chairs. I thanked everyone for coming. I walked back down. I cried some more. I hugged our boys. A few more words. Music. We got up and walked out and everyone watched us. We waited at the door. The minister joined me. People. People I haven't seen in a long time shook my hand. Hugged me. People from work. People I'd never met but who knew Amy. Her friends from college. Neighbors, relatives. A long-lost friend from high school. More crying. I couldn't talk. Someone gave me a bottle of water, and I realized I hadn't had anything to eat or drink. The line ended and I moved to our community hall. Food had been brought in from the Middle Eastern restaurant that had catered Amy's fortieth birthday. Was that my idea? I couldn't remember, but it was a good one. I sat down and a wave of fatigue passed through me. I just wanted to sleep. I thanked more people as they said goodbye. Then I was home.

In the hours and days after the service there was a shedding, or a release, maybe even a letdown. I had built up the service so much in my mind. I was becoming more aware of how I felt physically—exhausted, completely wrung out. I felt more in touch, perhaps, with what my new life was going to be like, my life without Amy. I felt a little more at peace with her death, perhaps. Not really at peace, but I found myself with moments, sometimes fleeting, when I thought it would be possible to continue on. I was still distraught, of course, missing her and feeling desperately lonely, but there would be these brief moments of clarity or strength. Then complete despair and loneliness. Then I'd play games in my head, or maybe with God. I wondered what I would sacrifice to spend another day with Amy. Would I give up an arm or a leg? For one day? Probably. Would I sacrifice the house? Sure. One of the children? No. Definitely not, but the question, as grisly as it sounds, was there. What about my sight? Would I give up my eyesight to be with her but not see her? Not sure. Maybe. For one day? What about for a week? Maybe I'd jab forks in my eyes to be with her for one more week. These gruesome fantasies would start running through my mind without warning. Just in case, you know? Just in case I came across the lamp with the genie inside. If some magical force offered me a trade, I wanted to be ready.

And then I'd shake the thought out my head and be lonely again, or maybe I'd have one of those fleeting moments of clarity, gone just as I became aware of it.

Yet it was also in the days after this public service when I started feeling a sense of: Now what?

Now what?

I didn't have the just-gotta-get-through-this-next-thing feeling anymore. Up until then there had been that whole litany of events to focus on: our family service, Mother's Day, Adam's birthday, Bryan's birthday, Father's Day, our wedding anniversary. There were also all the "firsts": first day, first day back to school, first day back to work, first month, and so on. The public memorial service for Amy was the last in that line. That day I walked out of there I was no longer saying to myself, I have to get through this next minute, day, month, birthday. Instead I remember saying to myself, "All right, now you've just got to get through … life."

I *really* was going to have to figure everything out all over again. I would have the support of my friends and family, Bonnie in particular. She and I had been leaning on each other for strength from the beginning. But I was starting to see that no matter who might have been around to help me with the boys, or with household chores, or to just hold me as I wept, I would have to figure out how to press on by myself. Alone.

And I don't do well with alone.

With Amy, I had signed up for a life partner. We realized we were on a path together as early as our second date, on Valentine's Day, 1999, when we each confessed our brief but failed marriages, our mutual desire for creating a family now, and for a long-term partner to grow old with. That was my deliberate choice, and I think for her, too. The first time I got married I wasn't mature enough, nor was my partner, to really be explicit about the choice. I didn't really say to myself, I'm *choosing* to commit myself to another person for the rest of my life for specific reasons. My first marriage hadn't gone that way. We just fell into it. And after my first marriage there was my other serious relationship, but that ended, too. I think I was fortunate to have gone through both of those. By the time I met Amy—and I know it wasn't exactly the same for her, but it was similar—we were able to enter into our relationship deliberately. I think we both could say to each other, "Okay, we're going to commit to each other for the rest of our lives."

At that point we assumed that we would be together until we were seventy, eighty years old, with forty—if we're lucky, fifty—more years together. Actually, we didn't assume it—we talked about it. We talked about what it would mean to really commit to each other for the rest of our lives.

We talked about how it was going to be difficult at times. We had seen just enough to know that marriage was both wonderful and difficult.

There would be times when we would question if this was the right thing to do. We didn't know how things would work—we assumed they would, but I think we understood that this truly was a commitment that required work. I think we both realized it for ourselves—going through those life challenges with a single other person was the path for us to reach a deeper understanding about ourselves in life, and we wanted to do it with each other.

We hadn't shared our feelings in those exact words when we met in 1999, but as life unfolded for us we knew we could circle back to what brought us together. We knew, for example, that there may be times when we would need help; maybe we'd seek out coaching or personal or marital assistance, or maybe we'd need time for reflection. Back in the summer of 2008, or maybe it was 2007, we attended a workshop called "What Buddhism Teaches Us About Love" in upstate New York, at the retreat center called the Omega Institute. It was a special time for us to be together without the kids and to be able to reflect on our relationship and what was important. We had planned to go again a month ago, to a weeklong retreat. My brother was going to watch the kids while we were away, but, well, it didn't happen that way.

For us, those times came from a spirit of intentional relationship and personal growth. We weren't going there because we felt that our relationship was in trouble or on the rocks. We were going there with the attitude of: "You know what? Things are going pretty good now, pretty good indeed. But let's not get too comfortable here. We've been together for ten years. We have two kids. We could easily plateau right here, and that might be okay. But that's not what we want from life."

Because both of us had been married and divorced, young, then met each other when we were still reasonably young, we felt special and lucky, in a way, because we'd see other couples around us, getting divorced, resentments building up over time, and so on. We'd see couples bicker in public settings, or we'd hear a friend talk ill of a spouse in a group setting behind his or her back. We'd get home and discuss it. We vowed we'd never impeach the other in front of a group, either in public or behind the other's back. If we had a grievance, it must come to the other first.

Did we have doubts about our relationship? Yes, of course. But we would address it. One of us would say to the other that something wasn't working right. We would step back and look at things. We were pretty clear when we started to feel a separation, an emotional distancing. When we got married we were both certain we'd have two children and have them about two years apart. We intended not to be too old while still actively trying to parent teenagers. But after Adam was born we had a really rough time with it. We discovered we did not actually agree on parenting. How would we have known before? I thought she was too soft with him, and she thought I was too dismissive of her style. One time she confronted me and told me she felt that I thought she was a horrible mother and how bad it made her feel. It was really hard to hear, in part because, I hate to admit, she was right. Part of me did question some of her mothering. I felt she was trying too hard to be a perfect mom and wasn't just going along with who Adam was. And through this she forced me to look at how I was as a dad. And guess what? It turns out I am not a perfect dad, either. It seems almost silly now, to talk about it, but back then this was deadly serious. This stretched over several months for us, and it started to threaten our plans for having two kids. We started to doubt ourselves. I never told her outright, but I questioned our marriage. Were we right for each other? All that stuff. It was not a happy time for us.

One day we had driven Adam to day care and were parked in the lot near the Metro, about to head to work, when it all came to a head. We had practically lost confidence in ourselves as parents. I forget what got us to that point, but we just sat there arguing at first, then crying, and then apologizing and hugging each other. Adam was about eighteen months old and really hard for us. If we were going to stick to our original plan we had to get on with trying to have a second child. But I couldn't do it. She couldn't do it. We decided that we could wait, after all. We figured out that in spite of our prior self-assessment of being amazing parents—having read all the books and taken all the classes—we were just making up this shit as we went, like everyone else. I honestly can't say what got us to that awareness, but we got there. And it took what seemed like a long and painful time to get there, but once we got to that point we then decided, what the hell, let's try for a second child. Enter Bryan.

For a couple years running we would plan a quarterly date, a weekday date. It was actually easier to do this than to get a babysitter. I would take a weekday off on a day she didn't work, and we'd spend the whole day together. We'd get the kids off to school. We'd go to breakfast together. There's a restaurant in town, Mark's Kitchen. We'd usually start there, and she'd order pancakes, coffee, and orange juice, and I'd order an omelet and coffee. Sometimes we'd go catch a matinee in Silver Spring or in Bethesda. Sometimes we'd go to a park and just talk. We'd go to lunch, maybe something a little bit upscale, and have a glass of wine, then come back home, and make love. Do other couples do that? Maybe other couples do that. I'm sure they do. But I say this because I know *I* didn't do that in my first marriage. I think in my first marriage I just assumed it would all work because, you know, we loved each other. In my first marriage if I wasn't happy about something I would wait for it to just go away, which, of course, it never did. And I know Amy felt differently about what we had, compared to her previous marriage. She didn't talk about it much, but there was a similar sense that the big issues, like whether to have children, hadn't come up until later in her first marriage. We both learned we had to be deliberate about it, and that was really important and special to me in our relationship. We were deliberate about creating those opportunities to set aside time for ourselves, to have conversations, and to have difficult ones sometimes, too.

So after that community memorial service, I realized I hadn't just lost the woman I loved; I'd lost the future we had been designing together, and all its layers. I wasn't just denied a future with Amy; I was denied the experience of a lifetime partner. A partner with whom I can join and together create children, raise them, then explore what a life of growing old is like. In this life, I don't get that. I don't get the experience I thought I signed up for, which is a single, primary, long-term, committed relationship for the purpose of having a shared life, and, in that partnership, through the slings and arrows, creating a deeper, richer experience for my mate and me. I'm denied that now.

I still have this sense that there are certain things in life that are only learnable over a long period of time, measured in decades. There are certain things about who I am and about love and relationships and life that are learnable only through that long process—the process of living with someone—and now I was not going to be one of those people to have that experience.

In the weeks after the public service I remember thinking that if, magically, I were to find somebody tomorrow and we both lived healthy, lucid lives until we were ninety-five, then maybe I could say, "Yeah, it didn't happen the way I expected, but I got that." But the probability of that happening isn't much greater than zero. I have to be realistic about that. I am not entitled to the experience of a long-term mate in this life. Whatever comes next, I can't say, but it won't be what I thought I was signing up for.

So, coming out of that service, I was beginning to realize that I was mourning not only the loss of this woman and what we had but also the future we were supposed to live into. And that was difficult to grapple with. But it was helpful to be able to identify it, call it out that way, to look at it for what it was, as painful as it was.

And now that the public memorial service was over, I could, at last, shift my focus from my own grief to the boys'. I had been taking care of them, of course, but really, what do I do about the boys? What now for my boys?

—

John paused and said, "I'm beat."

I reached to turn off the recorder. "We covered a lot of ground."

"It feels like it," John said. He laughed. "Is it supposed to be this tiring?"

"It can be," I said. I gathered up my equipment and put everything away in my writing bag. "It depends on the person, and what they're talking about."

"How did I do? Are we doing okay?" John was asking earnestly. By now I'd come to realize he was asking these same questions, almost as if it were a performance for him. I imagined him wondering if he delivered his lines well, if he covered his material effectively. As if anyone in his position could be "assessed" this way. I almost asked him if he asked his shrink "How did I do?" at the end of his therapy sessions, then thought better of it. I knew he was being sincere.

So I replied with sincerity. "You're doing fine. It's good. We're making good progress."

"How is this going to turn out?"

"I think," I started, then stopped myself. I looked at him. "I'm not exactly sure, John." He looked a little disappointed, a little hurt. "But that's okay. It's all part of the process. This is what it is, John. We're talking; you're telling what happened to you and the boys. I'm taking my notes. I'm asking questions. We'll keep talking."

"When do you want to meet next?"

"Next week, just like we said."

"And after that?"

I was done packing up. "After that we'll see. I'm thinking sometime in the fall. Maybe once or twice. Let's see what we can do."

"After that?"

"After that in the winter. And then—" I stopped.

We looked at each other.

I smiled at John. "Let's get through this next one," I said.

John grinned and nodded.

And it dawned on me that our sessions were now also milestones for John to pass through. They served as "markers" of him emerging from the paralyzing trauma of the days after Amy's death to now and the continuous aching of both his loss and the search for answers to unanswerable questions. And now I was part of it, his journey.

He walked me to the front door. It was a peaceful, late summer evening. The light was just fading beyond the tall trees lining the street. We said our goodbyes and hugged.

On the drive home I thought about what John had said—"How is this going to turn out?"

I didn't know. How could I know? How could any of us know how any of "this" would turn out? I suspected some of John's questions had to do with questions I had, too. This was still to become a book. Something others would want to read. That was the intention all along. But this was unlike anything I had thrown myself into, and the path forward, beyond the next step, was hidden. The beautiful answer was that we couldn't know. None of us was meant to know. That's what made the answer frightening, too.

When I got home I went online and looked at a calendar, for 2010 and for 2011, counting out the months from Amy's death to these, our first interview sessions in August, then out to the fall and into the winter and spring of 2011. I jotted down notes, ideas, questions. I'd have to talk with John about timing. That could wait until we met next, for our final summer interview session.

One week later, it was another Saturday morning. The boys were downstairs with their cereal bowls and the TV, a typical American way to spend a childhood Saturday morning. I went to set up in the living room, in my usual place. I was surprised how normal this felt to me already, grabbing a dining room chair for my gear, getting set up in his living room, taking out my notepad and pen. I'd always enjoyed conversations with

John. I suppose, I told myself, I was getting to feel this was just that. But when John came into the room I knew otherwise.

He seemed tired but also determined. I asked him how he'd been, how his boys were. We talked some small talk, but he quickly told me he had some ideas about what he wanted to talk about.

"Some things are weighing on me," John said. "Talking with you these past couple of weeks has really loosened up my mind. I think it's been helpful. Even the past couple of days I've been thinking about what I wanted to talk about this time."

"Okay," I said. This was great, I thought. "What is it?"

"I want to go back to the beginning again. I was thinking about some specific things."

—

That first morning after Amy died, maybe when I was lying there at something like four in the morning with my sleeping boys in a cold, wet bed, I realized, somehow, I'd have to get out of this paralysis, and do it fast. I mean, here I was, lying on a gurney with a sucking chest wound, but with these two little people needing me. It sounds like it was hard, but in a way, looking back, it was almost as if something else took over. An automatic pilot. If it weren't for those two boys, I don't know if I'd have had the will to do much of anything. I never really thought seriously about killing myself. The thought crossed my mind, but I'd shake it out. I had my two boys to care for. I don't know what I would have done without them. I'd like to think I wouldn't choose to kill myself, but I get it, I get it now, how a person could be driven to that point.

I was thinking about how it has been an advantage for me to have gone through a divorce in my twenties, because it taught me the value of professional help. I'm talking shrinks, psychotherapy, counselors. So, right away I knew I needed to get support in place for our mental health, how we managed our grief and our physical health, particularly for me. A few weeks after Amy died, a couple people, other widows in my community, reached out. I didn't know them, but they had heard what happened. They became good resources for me. We'd get together from time to time, and one thing I learned from those who had been in my shoes, especially younger widows with kids, is that it's like what they tell you on airplanes: "In the unlikely event of a cabin depressurization, oxygen masks will drop from the ceiling. If you are traveling with a child or someone needing assistance, put the oxygen mask on *yourself* first, then take care of the kids." And it makes perfect sense, even though the instinct is to help the kids first. But while you are struggling for oxygen you won't be in a good place to help your kids and be a father and provider. That awareness came pretty quickly to me—that I needed to get my shit together. Fast. I needed to figure out how all of this was going to work going forward.

First up was to figure out how I would manage my job. I went back and forth with how I should get back to work: Should I take a whole month off? Should I drop down to a part-time schedule? Whatever it was I knew I had to get some agreements and understandings in place, quickly, especially because I'd been at this job only since October. Fortunately, I felt about as comfortable as one could in a new employment situation. I'm really blessed with that environment.

But I also knew I needed a shrink—the counselor I had gone to for help with my divorce had since retired. So I asked a friend, a child psychologist, for a referral. She referred me to a psychotherapist in Bethesda, and, luckily, she was able to see me the following Friday, a week and a day after Amy died.

As I drove to her office that first time, I was nervous the whole way, but just tried to focus on driving. What would I say? What could I say? I got to her house, where she has her office, and I walked down a stone path to a side door with a cipher lock. She had given me the code over the phone, and my hand was trembling as I punched in the numbers and pushed open the door. I sat down in a waiting area and stared at a table with copies of *The New Yorker, Washingtonian,* and *Psychology Today.* I stared at the artwork but didn't really notice it. Then another door opened, and she came out and greeted me and motioned for me to step into her office and sit in a chair, a comfortable black leather recliner, facing her as she sat in a similar chair opposite. She started by telling me how very sorry she was for my loss … and I just started to cry, uncontrollably. The rolling sobs continued, and I could feel those black tar balls starting to grow again. I grabbed a fistful of tissues from the table next to me and tried to calm down enough to say hello, but I couldn't. I brought pictures of Amy to show her. I forced myself to calm my sobbing just enough for me to pull those pictures out with a still-shaking hand. And then I read what I had written for our private family service. Somehow I felt I really needed to show her how beautiful Amy was and the depth of our love and my despair. I don't remember what else I talked about. I've been seeing her every week since then. Having that place to go to, to explore the depths of my despair and anger, has been important. It's hard to admit being resentful, but that's part of it, too. Just being able to name something for what it is—that, alone, removes some of its power. It's been important for me.

Psychotherapy hasn't been the only thing I've sought for care. I don't know why acupuncture came to mind, but I knew I needed a centering, settling … something. I had worked with an acupuncturist five or so years earlier for a shoulder ailment. I can't say how much it helped my shoulder, which did improve, but the process was very relaxing. My acupuncturist's practice was near my office at the time, so from time to time I'd go during lunch. Then my office moved, and I stopped going.

Now I looked her up on the Internet and found her website. She had started a new practice on her own, close to my home, and she had "grief response" on her list of treatments. So about a week after Amy died I gave her a call and left a message: "Hi. You may or may not remember me. I'm one of your former clients. I saw 'grief work' on your website, and I'm going through that right now, and could you help?"

She called me back and said, "John, I am so sorry for your loss."

Now here's the thing: I hadn't told her exactly what had happened in my message, at all, just that I could use help with grief.

I asked, "Do you know what happened?"

"Yes, I've had some patients come in because of Amy."

It was another one of those moments when I realized Amy's reach in the community. "Oh. Wow."

So I started seeing her regularly.

It quickly became apparent that Monday mornings were particularly troubling. The kids were back to school, and I would have to take a deep breath and figure out how to be a semi-functioning adult.

I had started going back to work after two weeks. The first day was a half-day, maybe. I went in for a couple hours, mostly sat there, shuffled some papers, turned around, went home. That's when I realized I couldn't function on Mondays. So I started going in for acupuncture before heading to work.

I'm not sure I believe in meridians, and chi, and that there are these certain points, and that certain chronic ailments are created by blockages of chi, and then if you stick needles in and manipulate those meridians at those points it somehow unblocks the chi. I don't know if I believe that or not. I think there's been research to suggest there is some clinical benefit, but I don't know that they've looked into the matter of meridians and chi, specifically.

What I do know is that, for me, this particular acupuncturist is a healer. It's not just the acupuncture itself, but her whole approach. The way she talks, and the way she listens. There's also the process of lying down and having somebody insert needles into your body; you have to be very body-aware, focused, and calm. It isn't a meditative state, exactly—but I have to get myself centered. So if the needles create that, or the anticipation of needles going into my body allows me to create that, I don't care. Maybe chi energy is being unblocked and restored. Cool, that's great. I don't care. All I can say is that when I leave I feel different than when I entered. I feel better but that's not the right word. I feel more even. Sturdier.

My acupuncturist is really good. Each appointment is a little different, but she follows a pattern. She'll start by asking me what is going on with me, and then check my pulse, and a few other things. Then I get on the table and she starts sticking needles in me. Then she usually leaves me there for, I don't know, fifteen or twenty minutes, just lying there by myself.

A few weeks ago, something different happened. I started crying on the table. I'd been worrying about crying during these treatments, because if I have needles in my body and I start to cry or convulse, it might actually hurt.

Usually the process of having needles placed in my skin helps me, almost forces me, to become very relaxed, very still. But this time, just when she began, a profound sorrow came through me, and I began weeping. I tried to hold it back, but I couldn't, and my body, chest, and stomach began to convulse with my sobs. There was no way to hold it back, so I just let it come out. I never know how long these spasms of grief will last. Seconds? Minutes? In the moment it feels like forever. But I know this one passed after a short while.

My acupuncturist resumed with the needles. And I became calm.

Then I became aware of myself in a different and strange way. My sense of self started to descend. Descend into me. It moved down through my throat, and then into the top of my chest.

She paused, then said, "Tell me what's going on. What are you aware of?"
I told her.

She did some needle stuff and then left me.

Then I became very aware of my consciousness, my self, perhaps my soul. It was my essential "me," moving lower and lower and lower. It was the opposite of an out-of-body experience; it was an *inner*-body experience. It kept going lower and lower until it reached its lowest point, where I could feel my awareness curled in a fetal position in the lowest part of my abdomen, in my bowels. And then, suddenly, I bounced back up and reinhabited my body. It was as if I had been reinflated to refill my physical body.

Then all of a sudden that trance or spell broke and I was back to having "John" awareness back up behind my eyes and nose, like where it is right now. My sense of self is where my brain is, not in my stomach. My stomach is part of me. But it's not *me*.

And then I felt calm. At peace.

The other treatment I've been doing is relaxation massage and body work. I've always loved massage. I think most people do, but when I tore my plantar fascia playing basketball and had neck surgery to repair a herniated disk a couple years ago, all the muscles in my upper back and neck were very tight, and it took a long time for that to settle down. In addition to doing physical therapy, I went to a massage therapist, and she worked on me a lot, and I think that helped get me back faster than I otherwise would have. There's a physical component to it, of course, but there's also the "laying on of hands" aspect, the healing aspect of it, from a psychic perspective. It works for me. There's something about the human touch from a massage. So I get one weekly now as well.

Acupuncture, psychotherapy, massage, exercise. All these things together have become so important for me. Essential, really. Combined, these activities are "putting the oxygen mask on."

Once I had built these into a routine of sorts, I had a conversation with my employer. I said, "Here are the things I have in place. I'm going to start gradually weaning myself back to work part-time over the next two weeks. So by the time a month has passed, I hope to be able to be full-time again, but here's what full-time looks like for me. I'm going to work from home on Fridays, because that's the day I see my shrink and then my massage therapist. I'm going to be in Mondays by noon, after my acupuncture. And I will do the best I can to make up this time on weekends or evenings. Otherwise, I'll take a combination of sick leave and personal leave."

I was lucky my employer accommodated this plan. I also have a dedicated team who were able to step in for me. And it makes me think now that this *should* be the way to treat people in situations like this. I think about people who are in positions where they don't have benefits, or sick or vacation leave, or whatever their situation is. Tragedy shows up when it does, and if your work life can't accommodate it you have to stifle that grief. Put it aside until lunch break or when you're driving home. Not everyone can just say, "Boss, I gotta get out of here for a couple hours because I'm about to lose it," or "I need to work from home on Friday and not get into work until noon on Monday." And how that must affect, or interfere with, their abilities to grieve, and work through their grief. I get the feeling a lot of people are told, "Oh, I'm sorry your wife/husband died. You get three days of bereavement leave. See you next Tuesday."

How do you do that?

How do you do that?

———

Besides the "formal" therapy and treatments I've sought, I've found that music and poetry are a form of therapy. Music has always played some role in my life. I've dabbled with playing the piano and guitar. I love listening to all sorts of music. And I like the lyrical poetry of Rumi. Right away certain music and songs began to resonate. And then some specific songs not only resonated but also took on new meaning. It all happened very quickly and without conscious thought, as I was grasping for anything that might provide some comfort and meaning.

Besides new music I was rediscovering older stuff. One day I was listening to old Santana, and I stumbled across some of his newer stuff. I knew he'd had a resurgence around 2000, but I'd been listening to different music then—techno, down-tempo, and electronica. That's when I stumbled across the song "Into the Night," in which the lead singer of Nickelback performs with Carlos Santana.

I started listening to this song, which has lyrics that describe a down-on-his-luck guy who meets a dancer—the way it's written, it's almost as if this dancer descends out of heaven. He meets her, and they dance, and everybody watches them dancing. It made me think of those movies when they show a couple dancing and they're lost in themselves; it's just the two of them dancing, and they're spinning, and everything spins around them. That's the way the lyrics, the imagery, of that song work for me. I'm not a big Nickelback fan, but this song was really speaking to me. After I heard it I went to YouTube and pulled up the video, watched it, and thought, "Wow, God, this is our story, right here in this song." Okay, maybe I hadn't been such a miserable loner like the guy in the video when Amy had descended into my life, but the metaphor of life as a dance really hit home. So I added the song to one of my exercise and running playlists.

I listened to it a lot during the summer. I'd go running, and I'd listen to it, and I'd cry. I'd be driving and I'd listen to it and cry. I'd be at the gym working out, lifting weights, and I'd listen to it and try not to cry. The song somehow conjured up both my first memories of that day we met at the cheesy nightclub in Tyson's Corner and the searing pain of losing the promise of that night.

And, of course, physical activity has become extremely important, more so than ever in my life. By the third day after Amy's death I started running, and I mean running pretty hard. Before, I never would have called myself a runner. I was, at best, a jogger; it wasn't my thing. But I started to feel my own body energy, my life, through running. It was the movement, the feeling of the wind passing over me, and listening to music at the same time. The anger, the fear, all of it would sweat out of me as I pushed myself to the point of exhaustion. Exercising to a new level of physical exhaustion was important—it still is important, but then, it was almost about survival. And as those first days started to drift into weeks, hard physical activity— running, or splitting wood in the backyard, or lifting weights—remained vitally important.

Within about three weeks I had these basic things in motion, with regular therapy appointments and exercise time. It was helpful in its own way. It created a weekly pattern, a ritual—Monday morning acupuncture, Friday psychotherapy, followed by massage, and so on.

Amy was killed on a Thursday, and that became the new way for me to mark the progression of time—as if Thursday were the first day of the week. The first Thursday, the second Thursday, the third Thursday, up until the fifteenth Thursday, when I lost track, when it was no longer present in my mind, when I didn't actually say to myself, "Oh, it's Thursday."

I don't know what it was about that particular Thursday, but I noticed I wasn't going through my normal Thursday ritual. It's kind of weird to think about it, but those early Thursdays, and still, many Thursdays, I think the same things at the same time of the day. This is when we got up. This is when I said goodbye to Amy. This is when Adam got on the bus. This is when she must have dropped Bryan off. I know at 10:20 she got hit by a truck while I was in that meeting, unaware that Amy was now dead. Then I had my lunch. Then I went to this recurring meeting I have every other Thursday. She was dead while I was in that meeting, but I didn't know it yet, but now there was a police officer waiting for me near my office. And so on.

Even now, when I walk back from that same regular afternoon meeting, back to my office, it's surreal; it all comes back to me, and it's like I'm coming up to the last moments of knowing Amy was alive on that Thursday, up till about 2:45, 2:50, 3:00. That's the bell-tolling moment for me. That's the anniversary. I don't count it so much from when the police report said she was killed. For me, it's when I learned.

—

When is it a good time to die? I mean, no time is really better than any other, but the timing of all this just seemed to make it worse. Mother's Day, May 9, was ten days after Amy died. Adam's birthday is May 25. Bryan's birthday is June 3. Our wedding anniversary is June 9. Father's Day was June 20. The family memorial service was May 4. The community service was June 18. There were a couple events created for or modified around Amy's death. There was a fundraiser for the birth center at somebody's house, and there was a book signing where authors had agreed to come and speak. There was an event that Amy had set up to celebrate the passage of a new law in Maryland to change some of the licensing requirements for midwives and how they're able to practice in Maryland. Within a month and a half of her death there were eleven events or ceremonies we had to deal with, the first being Mother's Day, of all things.

The night after Amy was killed, Bryan came up to me and said, "Daddy, for Mother's Day"—and it hadn't even occurred to me, but, my God, *Mother's Day*, it's a week and two days away, so the boys must have been doing some sort of project at school for that day—"Daddy, for Mother's Day, we're gonna have Spirit Mother's Day."

It broke my heart.

Holding back my tears I said, "Yes, of course. Of course we're going to have Spirit Mother's Day." What else would we have?

I later learned that Bryan had asked Adam what we would do for Mother's Day. I imagined him asking his older brother, "How can we have Mother's Day if we don't have a mom?" And Adam was the one who told him we could have Spirit Mother's Day, and then Bryan brought that to me, which I think is remarkable, on a number of levels.

Adam and Bryan, like many brothers, I suppose, are best friends and worst enemies. One day a year or so ago the boys were playing on a playground after school with a bunch of other kids. Just being crazy little kids, playing tag and swinging and jumping off the swing to see who could jump the farthest. And the occasional kid conflict. Bryan was playing by himself with one of those big red bouncy balls you use for kickball. Another kid I didn't know, maybe a year older than Bryan, came from behind him, whacked the ball out of his hands, took it, and ran off. Adam, from across the playground, saw this out of the corner of his eye and came running straight toward this kid. This won't be good, I was thinking, but I just watched. Adam ran up to the kid and punched the ball down out of his hands. The ball bounced up. Adam, the taller boy, jumped, grabbed the ball as it came down, then ran over, gave it back to Bryan, and went on about his play. No words were spoken.

That's how it is with them. And I imagine that when Bryan went to Adam and asked him how we'd celebrate Mother's Day without Mom, Adam somehow came up with an answer for him, and then Bryan came back to me with the plan.

It just broke my heart.

Fuck.

Mother's Day.

How do we do that?

How do you do "Spirit Mother's Day"?

Like a lot of things, I had to trust we'd figure it out when we got there. At that first psychotherapy appointment, I relayed this story to the therapist.

She said, "Some people release balloons." It's symbolic, and it's not an uncommon tradition. For the boys it would be a letting go—consciously letting go.

So I told Amy's mom that this was what we were going to do. Bonnie seemed to grasp the symbolism right away and thought it sounded right. I asked her if she could go to a party store and get one of those little helium tanks and a bunch of purple balloons and ribbon. Bonnie and her husband, Donald, came over that Sunday. So it was the five of us.

Then I had to decide where to release the balloons. Here at home? There are a lot of trees, and I worried we'd get the balloons stuck. That's not what I wanted. Amy loved the zoo, especially the panda exhibit. I thought of going there, but then dismissed it as perhaps a little too public. Or maybe the park at Sligo Creek at the end of our neighborhood where we'd taken the boys and thrown rocks in the creek or played on the playground equipment. But there were too many trees, again, and that made me a little nervous. In the end we decided to go over to the middle school, not because there was any sort of real significance about the place—it was just a large, nearby open space.

There's a huge hill there where we sometimes go sledding after a snow. It's where they shoot off fireworks every Fourth of July; at the bottom of the hill is the large field where kids play baseball and soccer. It's part of the center of town. We had about a dozen balloons. It was really windy, and even though the space is pretty wide open, there are trees around the edges, so I was still a bit nervous they might get caught.

We climbed the hill. We let them go. It was beautiful, and so sorrowful. The wind carried them out, quickly, carried them up and out of sight, which seemed right, because that's how she died. She was snatched from us. She disappeared. Right there on that street corner, she was snatched off the planet.

That's how it is for me—she completely vanished. I mean, I have her ashes; I've seen her ashes, and I trust that it's her, her remains. I hadn't gotten a goodbye, though. I hadn't been allowed to see her body. It was hard because I had been denied that, but I was also haunted by the knowledge of why I had been denied that. Too often I imagined that image of her getting run over by the truck and how it must have destroyed her.

Then came the birthdays and anniversaries, one right after the other. In some ways it helped to focus on the next thing. Adam's birthday. Then

Bryan's birthday. Then our anniversary. Each one had its own sadness, but each one forced me to focus on the specific task at hand. The logistics and the planning of these things helped take up my mental power so that I didn't dwell on death for a while. But the energy and stamina to maintain that focus while holding the paralyzing grief aside was enormous at times. Sometimes the basic mechanics of life completely shut down, and every-day things could quickly become near-consuming, bewildering, existential crises. For Adam's birthday, not even a month after Amy died, I really had to reach down deep.

We—Amy and I, that is—had actually goofed and scheduled a birthday sleepover with his friends on the same day as a group baseball outing to see the Nationals play, which I had scheduled and organized for our church, before the final game times had been announced. But what could have been a major conflict turned out to our advantage. The game was scheduled to start at four o'clock on a Saturday afternoon. So Amy and I decided that, because we had a few extra tickets, we'd drag these boys to the game, and then we'd have them all over for the sleepover.

All that preparation had happened while Amy was alive. I had no clue what to do now. I wasn't even sure who had been invited. Amy handled those details. I didn't dare cancel, but I was worried how I could manage the logistics of a fairly involved birthday event like this. And not only that, but Amy had been killed coming out of the Navy Yard Metro station, the same Metro station we would usually go to for baseball games. So the thought of going to this game, and being at *that* place, or near it, even momentarily, had been weighing on me. I had not yet been to that intersection. I planned to go down there someday—maybe next year we'd put flowers down there, or something like that. But not yet.

I had never driven to the stadium before; we'd always taken the Metro. But because we had this group of kids and had to get there early, we loaded up a couple of minivans and drove down. I drove the lead minivan, and my friend followed in hers. It's easy to get lost in DC. Even having lived in the area for twenty years, I still get turned around, but the layout of the city has a certain logic to it, so it's usually easy to figure out how to get somewhere, and I had a general idea.

As we drove down South Capitol Street toward the stadium I started thinking about where we should park. Should I try to find street parking among the townhomes and apartment buildings to our right or try to find a garage under one of the office or government buildings on the left? As we got even closer I noticed that some of the streets were blocked for game-day traffic management purposes, and suddenly I noticed a traffic cop motioning for me to turn left. I would have no choice but to turn and drive down M Street and right over the pavement where Amy had died, less than one month before. I hesitated, and he motioned more urgently. I took a deep breath and I turned left. I felt myself grabbing the steering wheel as tightly as I could, and I could see, just ahead, the intersection a block away. I started to panic. I had a van full of kids, and I felt myself about to shut down right there on M Street, because I was *not* going to drive over that patch of road.

It's a major road, three lanes in both directions, but fortunately, because we were so early, the heavy game-day traffic was still to come. I noticed to the right a small street, almost an alley, really. Van Street? Had that been part of the original L'Enfant street plan? Streets in the north-south orientation should be numbered. I abruptly turned right, drove about a hundred feet, and then pulled over to the shoulder. And as it turned out, this little side street led right to the closest stadium parking you can get; it's forty dollars a car to park there. My friend in the other minivan pulled up behind me.

I got out of the car and walked back to her and said, "I'm sorry, I cannot drive any farther down M Street. We have to park here." I continued matter-of-factly, pointing to the lot, "It's forty dollars a car. I have maybe ten dollars in cash, and they only take cash, but we're going to spend eighty dollars and we're going to park right here because this is really the only choice because I cannot drive down M Street any farther."

She just looked back with an expression as if to say to me, I can tell that there is nothing on this planet that will change your mind. She said she had enough cash.

So we parked.

As we were getting everyone together and walking out of the parking lot I could see to the intersection. Part of me, for a moment, wanted to go see it up close, see where she had died. But mostly I needed to set that aside so I could chaperone this mob of young boys to the game. The intersection would have to wait for some other day.

As it turned out, the father of one of Adam's friends had a connection, and he'd arranged to get us on the field for batting practice. I hadn't told

Adam or any of the other kids; it was a surprise. We went into the stadium and passed an inner layer of security where we met a representative with the team, someone in the marketing department.

The marketing woman who escorted us down to the field knew our story. I don't know if the players had been briefed; some seemed like they knew, but it could have been just my imagination and wanting to believe that. The coach came over with some of the players, and they signed the boys' caps and gloves and stood and had pictures taken with them. It was pretty cool. After autographs and pictures we made our way to our seats for the game. Then we came home for the sleepover.

That was Adam's birthday. Nine days later it was Bryan's birthday. Five years old. Amy had also scheduled Bryan's birthday, made the reservation at Chuck E. Cheese's, and invited everyone. I was able to recruit a couple parents to help haul the dozen or so boys to the party. And then I found myself standing in the middle of this Chuck E. Cheese's, kids running around, playing arcade games, asking for more game tokens, and all I could think was, "Where's Amy?" This was her event. She'd set this in motion a month or so ago. And then we were eating cake at one of the big party tables. And then this big mouse came over and gave Bryan a high-five and put a crown on his head. I was overcome with this disoriented feeling and all these questions. Were these kids having fun? Was Bryan having fun? Was anything fun? Amy doesn't exist in this world, yet here we are participating in something she had planned, and it looked like they were having fun. How was that possible? I tried to make sense of it all, but it was all I could do to not break down crying in the middle of my son's birthday party at a Chuck E. Cheese's.

—

After the boys' birthdays and all the other events, into late July, I was starting to notice a greater distance between those really difficult, paralyzing, emotional moments—those moments that reminded me of the minute-to-minute shock of the first grief. Then August came and it was hard. It was really, really hard. Unexpectedly so. My birthday is August 31; I would be forty-four. August 29, just two days prior, would mark four months since Amy's death. I could feel it coming; those waves of grief became more frequent and intense again. I knew intuitively I needed to do something on my birthday, but I didn't know what. Not that I wanted to celebrate it, because it certainly was not a celebratory time for me. But I didn't want my birthday to just pass by. The feeling conjured on that date, the twenty-ninth, was the same low, deep, convulsive grief that had been so incapacitating in the first days after Amy had died. I could feel those black, tarry balls starting to form again.

I thought I had been doing better. I thought I was going to work through this. But I started to get scared. There was still quite a bit left, and I was not looking forward to the next round of deep grief.

I reached out to a few friends and said, "Look. My birthday is coming up on August 31. I've got to do something. I can't sit at home. Could we just go out to dinner?" I just needed to mark the date, put a stake in the ground and keep going.

On my birthday I got home from work a little early and changed clothes. I got back in the car and headed out of the neighborhood. I'm a creature of habit—there are a few different ways to leave my neighborhood, but I always go the same way. For some reason I took a different street out. No particular reason. Just did. On that alternate route I arrived at a stop sign, and that's when I saw that someone had spray painted graffiti on the sign to make it read, in dripping white paint: "Never STOP Dancing."

Never stop dancing? Did it really say that? I just sat there at the intersection and stared at it. I was blown away. I was sitting there, looking up, kind of talking to myself, but also talking to Amy. "You've *got* to be kidding me. On my birthday, you're writing graffiti on stop signs?"

I stopped the car, put it in reverse, parked along the curb, and got out. I took a picture of it with my phone.

Amy had been a dancer. We'd met at a dance club. We'd danced four days before she was killed. The way we held each other in bed, when we made love, the way we played with the boys, swinging them around by their skinny arms—we were dancing right up until she died. Tears filled my eyes as I got back in the car. I took a deep breath and exhaled. My hands were shaking as I uploaded the picture to Facebook. I had to show others to make it real. I was shaking as I put the key in the ignition and started the car back up. I had to get to the boys, but I was trying to just take it all in. "Okay, sweetie," I said out loud, looking up through the windshield. "I get it. It is really, really hard to dance just now, but I get it."

After another moment of staring at the stop sign, I drove off, picked up the boys from aftercare, and from there, drove to the restaurant—Fire Station One, in downtown Silver Spring, which had recently opened. I wanted to make sure I got there before everybody else to settle things with the wait staff and give them some instructions. I did not want someone, well-meaning, to stealthily go up to the hostess and arrange a surprise birthday cake. This was not a celebration. We were not going to have a birthday cake. We were just going to have dinner on my birthday—that was it. And I didn't want anybody to pay for the meal—my friends would be doing me a huge favor by being here, so I wanted to cover it. I wanted to get there early so I could warn the waitress to say no if anyone tried to pick up the tab, and if they persisted, to say they had to honor the birthday boy's wishes.

So we parked and walked to the restaurant. And as we walked in, what song was playing?

"Into the Night."

You've got to be fucking kidding me.

That same Santana song with the Nickelback dude I'd been listening to all summer that reminded me of when we'd met.

Yes, I know the odds. If you flip that coin enough times, it's going to come up heads a dozen times in a row. It could happen. But you *gotta* be kidding me. *That* song! And *that* message on *that* sign within forty minutes of each other? On my *birthday*?

I just looked up and shook my head, "Yes, okay already, I get it. I get it! Never stop dancing."

Fall

And you? When will you begin that long journey into yourself?
— Rumi

I wanted to meet with John before the holidays, and then during the holidays, to track his progress, see where his new life was taking him. As the time approached we exchanged some emails to set up the specifics. We scheduled a session for Saturday, November 13. I phoned John the night before to make sure that we were still on for the following day. I knew, having been a divorced dad of three with the ex-wife gone, that children very much drive a parent's schedule. We spoke briefly on the phone. John assured me we'd have plenty of time to talk. His boys would be spending Friday night at a sleepover at some friends' house, so we'd have the whole morning to ourselves. We could talk just about as long as we'd want, about anything.

I think we were both recalling our tearful breakdowns in his living room in the summer. John asked if I wanted to do the interviews outside on his enclosed porch. I said that might be great, but let's start in his living room, as we usually did, and see how we progressed. I wanted to keep us to our routine.

He asked if I had my questions prepared, if I knew how I wanted these new interview sessions "to go."

I thought to myself, "What a strange conversation to have." It was almost a meta-conversation: a discussion *about* a discussion. I told John I had some ideas for our conversation but that I wanted to share them with him in time, on the spot, so that we could simply talk them through, naturally. I was remembering how tense I'd been, how challenging it had been for me, as an interviewer, to set the pace and tone for the interviews, to ask the questions when he was hesitating, to nudge him in the right directions along his narrative, all while trying to keep it together for John. I was exhausted driving home after those sessions, and I questioned myself each time. Why am I doing this? Why was I pressing John so? I shook those questions out of my head and asked John if he smoked cigars.

"Why?" he asked.

"Because," I said, "if you like, I could bring down some cigars, and we could sit on your back porch and do some of the interview there. Have a cigar, too."

"Oh," he said. "How long have you been smoking cigars?"

"For a while now." I explained to him how I had gotten back into the hobby after my divorce, when my teenage son bought me a cigar as a gift while we were vacationing on the island of Saint John in the U.S. Virgin

Islands. "I smoke a few a week now," I said. "It's relaxing. Things slow down." There's a saying in the cigar community, I wanted to tell him—*Enjoy the moment*—but telling John that, there on the phone, seemed absurd to me.

I could almost hear John thinking. He laughed. It was a genuine laugh, and it was good to hear him laugh. "I haven't smoked a cigar in a while," he said. "I think the last one I had was at my bachelor party. I think it was pretty nasty. But, why not? It sounds good. Let's do that." He added, "I have an excellent Armagnac we can have with it."

I told him that sounded great. "I'll see you tomorrow," I said.

On the drive down I was excited, and apprehensive. The memories of our first interview sessions were fresh in my mind, not from months ago but real and raw and immediate—literally. Soon after we'd spoken in the summer, I'd had the audio recordings of our interview sessions professionally transcribed, and I'd been reviewing them that week, before our first fall session, to see what sort of material we had produced in our conversations. I couldn't get past a few pages without having to stop reading to cry. It was so painful reading John's recollections of that first day, the first few weeks. And it was embarrassing for me to share my experience with John about this. I mean, here he was *living* what I had a difficult time *reading*. So I'd never read completely through those transcripts. I thought I could do what I'd done then—let our conversation develop naturally. I had no real questions to ask beyond, "How are you doing?"

We hugged at his door.

John said, "Okay, let's see these cigars."

I showed him my carrying case. "Nice ones," I said. "We'll have a choice. Let's talk first."

We exchanged pleasantries. But not really. There was nothing "pleasant" about it, except that we were there, together. I got myself situated in the living room, in my usual chair, with John on the couch.

Then I asked, "How are you doing?"

John said he was a little rattled. "I've had a shitty week," he said, "and don't have my thoughts together like I wanted to. Do you have questions?"

I put it back on John. I told him that, maybe with the distance from the event of Amy's death, he was able to think about that differently, talk about things differently, in a way that he couldn't have in our summer sessions. Maybe there were things he and his boys were going through now, because of that distance. Or because of where they were now.

He told me again it had been a rough week for him and his boys.

"Start with that then," I said. "Talk about that. What happened, where you're at."

"I don't know," John said. "I'm not sure how this all fits. You know, with these interviews."

"I don't know that I know, either," I said. "But what was it about this week? I'm imagining all your weeks are shitty now—why call this one out?"

"It might be worth talking about all the bullshit around this," John said.

—

It's my "Shit to Do Now that Amy is Dead" list. How do you like that? But before I get into what's on *that* list, let me rewind.

For a while now I've had this morbid joke running through my head: *I never realized how complicated the paperwork was to die.*

Let's walk through this. There was a dead body on a street in the District of Columbia. Because of that, certain things spun into motion: police, detectives, investigation, witnesses, body collection, medical examination, toxicology, autopsy, identification. The list of what had to happen in this "machine" seemed endless. I'd never really thought of this before. I'd never *had* to think of this before.

And if I weren't so angry this would be hard to talk about. They wouldn't allow me to do a visual identification of Amy. They never came out and said exactly why. But you know why, right? I don't have to tell you; you know why. She was destroyed—absolutely destroyed—on that street. So my imagination created these horrible images of her in the accident.

Right after the accident I was at once both craving information and terrified of information. They said it happened quickly; the initial report said, "Died instantly." But what exactly does "instantly" mean? Heart stops, brain function stops, breathing stops. That could take a minute, couldn't it? Was it a minute? Was it *four* minutes? Was she conscious? Did she know what was happening? These questions haunt me.

In the first couple days I was having trouble getting information from the officials, and so I found a local blog, written by someone who had witnessed it. Apparently, it was a gruesome scene, but the writer had taken down the post, at the request of some of the commenters. All that remained was a secondary reference to the original blog post being removed because the original had been too graphic in its description of the scene—something about hosing down the cement where she was hit.

Oh.

Fuck.

Why did I need to read that?

And that image, the one I created from the police report and what I read—the gruesomeness of it all—played like a loop in my brain

And then there were the DC police.

A couple days after she died the detective had phoned me and said, "I have Amy's personal effects. Would you like to come down and get them, or would you like me to stop by your house?"

I said, "If you can drive them over here, that would be most helpful."

The next day I was home with some neighbors, and someone pointed out the DC police car out front. I stood up and looked out the front door and saw him get out of the car. I watched him as he walked from his car up our front walk carrying this—this pale red plastic bag. It looked like a red trash bag, and as he got closer I noticed the biohazard symbol on the side.

What was I supposed to ... what do I do with *that*?

I let him in, and he walked into the living room and set this thing on my living room rug, and I just stared at it. I took a deep breath and let it out slowly to compose myself and sat down on the couch. He sat in a chair across from me. Then he started to explain to me what was going on with the investigation, the process. He was explaining the process of how things work when someone dies. There was a preliminary report filed, he said, but it could take some time for the final report because they had to wait for toxicology results, and that could take a couple of weeks or more. He was explaining all this stuff, and he was very polite and respectful, but I couldn't really hear anything he was saying. I was just staring at the red plastic trash bag with the biohazard symbol on my living room rug.

You would've thought by now—I don't know—*some* compassionate soul downtown would have said, "Look, when you gather up her personal effects, if you need to keep them in the biohazard bag, please put the biohazard bag in another box, because when you bring it home to the family, it's going to look really bad."

And it did. It looked really bad.

Then he handed me a copy of the preliminary police report and started walking me through it. I was trying really hard to focus on what he was saying and not just lose it right there. Here, finally, was some of the information I was craving. How could this accident have possibly happened? The report had the basic information: cause of death, time, and so on. Then there was a page with a diagram of the scene of the accident. The report had her exiting from the Navy Yard-Ballpark Metro exit on the same side of M street as her office building, crossing M Street south to the other side, walking half a block west toward her office, and then crossing M Street again north, in the middle of the street, to get to her office. It showed her crossing M Street *twice*! They were speculating that she'd had her headphones on, completely not paying attention, and crossing in the middle of the street the second time rather than at the crosswalk. I thought, "That's crazy." Why would she have crossed that way? And twice? A big part of Amy's career had been spent on the subject of traffic safety. Photo enforcement at red lights, railroad crossing safety, that sort of thing. I was trying to remember if we'd *ever* crossed *not* in a crosswalk. Amy was just like that. And I was very sure she would have exited Metro at the *other* exit, *closer* to her office. The same exit most people take to baseball games. His explanation just wasn't adding up for me.

I tried to ask lucid questions, but couldn't, really.

The detective was sympathetic, but he just sort of wrapped up by saying, "You'll just need to trust the information and the report."

I was dumbfounded.

He finished with something about a positive identification and how someone would be in contact with me. He got up to leave, again offered his condolences, and motioned to the red trash bag on the rug. He said, "Now, when you go through this, you might want to be careful, because there's some blood here." Then he left.

Everyone was speechless.

I was numb; I couldn't think of anything to say. "There's some blood here." What did that mean, exactly? I had a pretty vivid image from what little I'd known *before* about the accident, and now *this*? My mind started racing. I didn't know what to do or say. I was freaking out. I took the red trash bag with the biohazard symbol down into our basement office and stuck it under her desk. I couldn't deal with it, and I didn't want to see it. It would have to wait for later.

The next day I got a call from the DC medical examiner's office. They told me they were still trying to do a positive identification. Said they were trying to do it with fingerprints, but that they might have to use dental records. That was all. Just this "status update" call to let me know that they may need more time for a positive identification. I was so confused by all this, and I didn't really know what to say so I just thanked them and hung up. A couple days later I got another call from their office, from a very polite woman, and she asked, "Were you able to get her dental records?"

I was dumbstruck. I said, "I thought you were trying to use her fingerprints."

She said that they were having a hard time getting her fingerprints.

I said something about how she had been a consultant at the Department of Transportation. She wore a federal ID badge. She'd been fingerprinted, somewhere, to get that job. Can't you call the DOT? Or the FBI? Or whomever the investigative authority is in all this? I've been through this myself several times, just because of my employment history around the DC area. I must have my prints all over the place, right? She must, too! *Everybody* in this town has their prints *somewhere*. Why are you asking *me* where to find them? I mean, we are in Washington-fucking-DC, and you're telling me you can't consult some database *somewhere* to find a federal contractor's fingerprints?

Then she returned to the issue of the dental records.

I was holding the phone now, and my mind started to wander. Amy had been dead less than a week, and now I was getting this request to track down her dental records. I wanted nothing to do with it. I didn't want the task, and every time I thought about it, that dental records were the only way to identify her, it just triggered a replay of how bad the accident must have been on that street. Who gets identified with dental records? Burn victims and decomposed bodies they find in the woods. I just couldn't handle it.

This was all going through my head, and I was getting resentful that they were assigning me tasks. I was in no mood or state of mind to be getting assignments. I started to really get agitated on the phone. *Dental records!* Are you *kidding* me?

The woman from the medical examiner's office started in again. "Can you tell me who her dentist was?"

I cursed under my breath. So here was the other thing: Amy hated dentists. She was a habitual dentist "shifter." I didn't know who her last dentist was. And if she had that information anywhere, it would've been in her address book, and her address book would be sitting in the basement, in a red trash bag with a biohazard symbol, and I'd be goddamned if I was going to dig through that right now to find out who her last dentist was.

So the woman from the medical examiner's office said she'd keep working on fingerprints, but it was clear this was not going well. Certain things couldn't happen until we had that positive identification. Like issuing a death certificate. And I needed that certificate for all sorts of things, like life insurance and Social Security survivor benefits for the boys. All these little boxes needed to be checked for the benefit of the machine. I was okay for now, but I was going to need that certificate soon. Without it, The Machine believed she was still alive.

And in the back of my mind, all this time, I was thinking that if they can't positively ID her, then who the fuck else is it? Who's the impostor who is carrying my wife's purse, wearing her clothes, wearing her wedding band, her work identification badge, *everything*? Who is this impostor dead in your morgue? And what have you done with my wife—my Amy?

I said something to this effect.

"Sir, we have our procedures and—"

Fuck!

If this had been fifty years ago? A dead body with a driver's license—Amy Polk. Amy Polk hasn't shown up at home yet. Seriously, who the hell else could it be? It was just mind-boggling to me.

But it was more than just me freaking out. I was starting to get the sense that something was not right. This had started with the initial report that had Amy crisscrossing the street. I was getting this feeling that maybe I should lawyer up here, if only because I couldn't have a rational conversation with *anyone* right then, and they needed to be able to talk to somebody who could have a rational conversation, and I was not actually helping the situation, because I was *freaking out*.

It was at the beginning of this ordeal that an attorney friend from church told me that he didn't really want to advise me on this, but he'd seen a number of situations like this where people needed advocates. That is, someone who's watching to make sure things get filed when they need to get filed, and the paper gets put in the right place, in the right folder, at the right time, and all that sort of stuff. Because people make mistakes.

Clearly, I was seeing evidence of this, so I felt I had to get someone on this shit *immediately* to protect me and my boys, because this could turn into a disaster. And I was glad I did. I feel horrible for people who go through this without that support. I mean, how many people die in the District of Columbia every year without the means to have somebody do that, and they're at the mercy of the police and the medical examiner and all these other pieces of the machine to conclude whatever they conclude? Because in my case, the conclusion in the original police report turned out to be wrong. Very wrong.

So about this time, I was still wrestling with whether to hire a lawyer when I got yet *another* call from the medical examiner's office.

"Have you found the dental records?"

They were *still* asking *me* who her dentist was.

Well, no. I said, "What about fingerprints?" I mean—remember the conversation we had *last* week? *Remember?* Federal contractor, background checks, DOT, can't you find that?

And the woman from the medical examiner's office—I don't blame her, I think she was trying as hard as she could, given the system she was working in, and I don't want to go on a DC rant here—started giving me one of *those* answers. I could tell, because I've had to give that kind of answer before, too. She was trying not to put blame on another part of the system; she was trying to protect the larger unit. She said, "We don't have the prints yet." As if to say they can't *locate* the prints.

I said, "You mean the FBI or DOT can't find the prints?"

"Um, well, no," she started mumbling in a vague way. "We don't have the prints from Amy yet."

"Wait a minute," I said. "Has someone *not* printed Amy's fingers—her body's fingers—yet?"

"No. We don't have those yet."

I couldn't believe it! "Well, why the fuck not?" Wouldn't that be the *first* thing you'd do?

She explained that the medical examiner's office was different from the police department, and all that other stuff. She said something that, to me, sounded like she was trying to not shift blame, but which made it clear that this was a responsibility of somebody over in *another* part of *another* office. You know, we're all one big happy machine here, but it's that *other* part of the machine that's broken down, not us.

"Fine," I said. "The next call you receive will be from my attorney, because I cannot have this conversation with you. Get the fucking prints. Just get the fucking prints." I hung up.

I knew they'd never get the prints.

I had to figure out who her dentist was. I still had to deal with the bag of Amy's personal effects. Thankfully, a good friend of ours from church went through the red biohazard trash bag for me and inventoried everything, and it turned out that it wasn't nearly as bad as I thought it might be.

When she was done she said, "John, you have the most active imagination."

Maybe she said that to protect me, and if she did, that's fine. Maybe she had thrown away a couple of soiled items of no importance. But if that is the case, what is up with that *goddamned* biohazard bag?

Thanks to this friend, now I had Amy's address book. And with it I had the dentist. At least, *a* dentist. I called the dentist, who, it turned out, Amy hadn't seen in a while. It was not her most recent dentist, but they had records. I put them in contact with the medical examiner's office, and so, eventually, they were able to make a positive ID, about two and a half weeks after she had died.

While this was going on I told my lawyer that none of the police report made sense to me. No charges had been brought against the driver yet. It looked like Amy was "at fault" for crossing in the middle of the street. I now had Amy's wallet from the biohazard bag, and in it was her Metro card. I thought maybe if we provided Metro with her card, we could confirm which exit at the Navy Yard-Ballpark station she had used that day. I figured there was some database they kept that tracked that information. You know, which station and gate she had swiped her card through. It was worth checking, I thought. So my lawyer asked the detective to check with Metro. And the detective said, and I kid you not, he said, "Why would you do that? That station only has one exit."

What?!? Are you kidding me? Are you *fucking* kidding me? Are you telling me that this DC detective was not aware of the exit for the Metro station that everyone takes to get to a Washington Nationals baseball game?

Finally we caught a break. Turned out Metro didn't need to look in a database; they had video. It was a Friday, late morning, a day back in June. I had just gotten back from my shrink's appointment, and I was walking with my neighbor and friend, Mark, on the Sligo Creek hiker-biker trail. It had been raining earlier, the sun had come out, and it was starting to steam up. The air was heavy and damp. My cell phone rang. I stopped right at the edge of one of the footbridges that crossed the creek and pulled my cellphone out of my pocket. It was my lawyer. He'd just reviewed the Metro video with the detective, and he told me that, sure enough, the video showed Amy leaving the station just where I thought, and it showed her stepping off the curb, with the green light, in the fucking crosswalk. The truck driver hadn't seen her, made a left turn into her, and ran her over. She was found in the middle of the street because the truck had dragged her that far down the street before the driver stopped.

I was speechless.

My lawyer gave me some instructions on how to proceed. I swallowed hard, thanked him, then hung up and started to cry. I told Mark what had happened, and he gave me a big hug. We just stood there, and he held me while I cried. I can't even begin to tell you what a big deal it was for me to learn that. That information brought my Amy back. The responsible Amy. I had been beating myself up. I had been so angry *at her* for crossing in the middle of the street. I couldn't believe she would have done something so terribly stupid as to cause her own death.

But I'm talking about paperwork, right? Just as the whole ordeal of dealing with the immediacy of Amy's death, and the identification, was ending, things really started getting complicated. I mean, *a lot* of logistical stuff started to kick in, like Social Security, life insurance, stuff that you don't think about having to deal with as the survivor. There's a lot of paperwork surrounding someone's death, and I never imagined having to do it—*ever*. I guess I'd always thought that I was going to die before Amy. I'm a little older. I'm a man. She's got good, long-life genes on her side of the family. I assumed she would outlive me, so I thought she'd have to be the one dealing with all this crap.

It was a lot of work. Or, at least, it was work that was really hard to get my head wrapped around and motivated to do. Sometimes it was "fill out a form," and it took five minutes. Other times I'd have to call up any number of institutions and tell them, "My wife died."

And you know what's going on, on the other side. They get these calls every minute of every day. They're looking at their little call script for "dependent death," with the little pause as they search for the name to plug in. "I'm so sorry to hear about your loss and the passing of your wife … Amy Polk. Please accept our condolences." They're just reading a script. I'm not blaming them—I get it, it's their job. Except the use of the term "passing." I think we need to get rid of that. My wife died. She's dead. She was killed. She was hit by a truck. It's important for me to just say what really happened to her on that street. She didn't "pass." No.

Anyway, it was difficult for me to gear myself up for each of these encounters, because after that first call, and then a second call, I began to understand what to expect. I was going to have to speak of this thing, and speak of it in a clinical way to get a task accomplished, close an account, or transfer something, or whatever it was that I needed to do. Each time I did this it was a reminder of her death, and it was exhausting.

It all had to get done, but I couldn't think straight to put together a coherent plan to tackle it, so I'd wait until something would nudge me. It could be a piece of mail or a comment from a friend or family member. Whatever the task was I'd somehow get the courage and I'd tell myself that I was ready to call her employer's benefits office, or whatever it was. So I'd call them and say, "I know Amy opted out of all the benefits because she was part-time and she was on my benefits plan, but I need to confirm that you don't have some type of life insurance policy on all of your employees." And then I needed to ask, "Please give me the contact information for the 401(k) plan administrator." And then I'd call the 401(k) plan administrator and said, "Hi, 401(k) plan administrator. I'm John Robinette, Amy Polk's husband."

"I'm so sorry to hear of your wife's passing. Please accept our condolences."

I went through this every single time.

I went to the bank: "My wife died. What do I need to do to close out this account?"

"I'm so sorry to learn of your wife's passing. Please have a seat and someone will be with you."

So I sat.

Then someone called me over and said, "We need an original death certificate and a document from the courts showing you are the legal heir."

Well, I didn't have the document from the courts because I'd never heard of it until just then, so I thanked them, cursed, and left knowing I had to come back to the bank and do it all over again.

Here's another one. For some reason we titled our VW Passat in her name only. I went to the MVA and told them that I needed to retitle the car into my name. And the nice clerk said, "According to our records, there is an outstanding loan on this vehicle. And we can't do a title transfer with a lien on it." Except we had paid off that loan several years ago, but somehow we, or the bank, had forgotten to notify the MVA, so now I had to contact the bank. And it happened to be a credit union we used to use, but after we paid off that loan we cancelled our membership. So now I had to make a trip to the old credit union and then go back to the MVA. Or the auto insurance. The auto insurance still had Amy on it, so right now I'm paying auto insurance for *two* drivers on *two* cars.

And I know exactly what they're going to say. They're going to say, "I'm so sorry to hear of your wife's passing ..."

It's not the chore itself so much that bothers me—but each one of these chores reminds me that Amy is dead. And for each one I almost always have to have a conversation with them and mention her death for a seemingly innocuous transaction. Each one is a little different, but each one is draining. And after each one it's like I say goodbye to Amy again. I'm on the phone with someone, and I can barely keep it together, and then we hang up, and I lose it and grieve Amy's death all over again. It's exhausting.

Which gets me to this past week.

I thought I was through with a lot of the stuff I had to do, but once school started for the kids I discovered a whole new set of shit just waiting for me—stuff Amy handled that I only sort of knew about but didn't really pay attention to. The boys' school lunches? They don't take money to school anymore. They all have a card or a PIN, connected to an online account with a credit card. With Amy's credit card. The kids swipe their card or punch their code in the lunchroom, and the account is debited. When the account drops below some level, money gets added to the account. Amy had it all set up with auto-pay so that it would just keep going. I sort of knew this but I'd never had to deal with it. She always did it. It was set up, running, charging her card—a credit card I really ought to cancel. But that just adds to my "Shit to Do Now that Amy is Dead" list. And some days I'm just not up to it.

The other day I was wondering how much undone paperwork is lingering in the world. If I was seventy, if my kids were all grown up, I wouldn't feel compelled to act quickly on some of these things, because a lot of it is to make sure resources are in place for the kids' benefit.

So then I started thinking about how shitty, how vulnerable, it feels to suddenly be a single parent. Our whole setup was geared for a two-parent system. I never really thought of it as such, but that's what it was. When you have two parents, you've got redundancy. If somebody can't drive, the other person can drive. If somebody gets sick, the other person picks up the slack. That's just how it works. Now? Now I'm the single point of failure for my family, and that's really scary.

So beyond all the paperwork to let the world know Amy died, I have to rethink our family system from a one-parent perspective. What happens now if I die?

Our will stated that, in the event we both died, my sister and her husband in New Jersey would take care of the boys. Well, we aren't both going to die now, are we? And I look at what we just went through, and are going through, and think that I've got to keep these boys in this community. As much as I love and trust my sister, if I die, the added trauma of pulling these two boys out of this community—this community that kept us alive in that aftermath—would be too much for them. So I decided to redo the will. One more task on my list. But, unlike last time when we did our will and death seemed hypothetical, it's now very real.

So I contacted another lawyer to help with the will. I thought all I was going to change was who would take care of the boys, but he also advised that I shouldn't have children under the age of eighteen as beneficiaries. You know, you can't leave a house with a mortgage and two automobiles to an eight-year-old and a five-year-old. You need to set up a trust.

A will is one thing, but a trust? Really? I'm a reasonably smart person, but now I'm in very new territory. "Trust." That sounds like something for wealthy kids. But it turns out with a house and life insurance and a little bit in a 401(k), if I die, then there needs to be something set up to handle all that on behalf of the boys. It's one more task, and it also requires that I set aside the emotions connected with it. This isn't like calling up the credit card company and having *that* conversation. This time, to get this done means we talk about what happens when *I* die.

And that thought is what really keeps me going with all this paperwork. My life goal used to be that I'd like to live long enough to see my kids graduate from high school, then college, hopefully see them get married, and so on, so then one day I'd meet the grandkids. Now it's simply this: live long enough to get the paperwork done for my boys—my will, the irrevocable trust, the guardianship, and my life insurance. Once that's set, and the documents are there, then I can actually die. It sounds morbid to say it that way, but it's true.

And that's just part of it. There's so much day-to-day stuff I used to take for granted that I now need to deal with, alone.

Amy worked part-time so that she could deal with all the kids' stuff, driving them here, picking them up there, going to the many events at school. I can't keep up with that. Amy's mom is coming over next week to help with some of the school stuff—running errands with the boys, haircuts and whatnot.

That's one example, but there are others. Mundane things.

Take last Saturday. It was a nice day. In the past I'd wake up early. I like being the first one up. I would have gone for a run that morning at, like, 7:00, 7:30. I can't do that now. Legally, Adam can stay here by himself. He's eight years old. But Bryan's five, and I can't do that. And I also don't *want* to do that. So I can't just go for a run like I used to do. I need to plan for it. Make arrangements. The day before I had called one of my neighbors and said, "Hey, could you come over tomorrow morning and sit on my porch while you read the paper and enjoy your coffee, because I'd like to go for a run." And he gladly did it, because he is amazing.

Sunday afternoons were when I'd go grocery shopping. I liked going by myself. It's a lot easier, and it's a lot faster, when you're by yourself, not dealing with two young boys. But that doesn't work anymore. So now I've arranged to have a teacher from their day care bring the boys home Tuesday and Thursday nights and stay with them and make them dinner, so I can go to the gym and then go grocery shopping or pick up the dry cleaning. It's so helpful. I've received an incredible amount of support. But then when I get home, after the teacher leaves, I'm the only one. I have to put them to bed every night. I've got to get them up every morning. I've got to get them breakfast. I've got to get them out the door. And all the thousand little things around that.

This is really a two-person job. I used to look at single parents in the past and think, "Goddamn. How the hell do they manage? How do they do that?" I certainly didn't know. Not before I had to take care of my two children on my own, I didn't. So how do single parents do it? When there are two parents, you work it out together. But on your own? You just figure it out as you go along, because you have to. And now everything has sped up. The game is a lot faster, and now I'm always on call. I can't say, "Amy, I'm really tired. I just need to go to bed early tonight. Do you mind taking care of the kids? I'll do the dishes in the morning." And sometimes she'd need that break, too. We could do that. *I* can't. I can never really, completely relax.

At least they're old enough now that they can mostly dress and bathe and feed themselves. But they need attention; they need a shepherd to keep them moving in the right direction, constantly.

It's tiring, and I've slipped into a routine that is unsustainable.

Part of it happened over summer. Things were just a little slower then. And on a Tuesday or Thursday when I had someone watching the boys I could go to the gym, or I could use that time to go to the grocery store or run an errand. Then I'd get home around 8:30, and I'd be starving, because I don't eat dinner before I exercise. So I'd say goodbye to the sitter, make myself dinner. And all of a sudden it would be 9:15, and I'd be wrapping up dinner. And the boys would still be watching TV, even though I should have turned it off an hour ago. Around 9:30 I'd tell them it's time for bed. God forbid if I wanted to give them a bath or shower. By the time I'd get the TV off, get them upstairs, get them in their jammies, sit them down, read a story or two, or they'd read to themselves, it would be 10:30 before they'd be asleep. I'd finally have time to myself in my house, alone, and I'm tired. Now, I could choose *not* to go to the gym. I could choose to be home earlier those two nights. It's a choice. But exercise for me is so important for my physical and mental health. I cannot *not* do that. I think I would go crazy. So for now, this is the routine—this is how it works, but it means some nights the kids aren't in bed until 10:30. Then I'm so tired, but I'm wired, too, and I can't even go to bed, because I've got a list of things to do. There's the laundry. There's a stack of mail in the dining room. There's all this lingering financial and legal stuff from Amy's death. And while part of the frustration is that it's going to take me time, mostly it's a mental block. And it seems like everything I touch leads to ten *other* things to add to my to-do list.

Early on I called the Omega Institute to cancel the weeklong marriage encounter we'd scheduled. That was a $2,500 trip. I needed the money back. So I called them to get a refund. I told them we needed to cancel, and I was saying to myself, "Please don't ask me why I'm canceling. Please don't ask me why I'm canceling. Please don't ask me why I'm canceling." And I knew they were going to ask me why I was cancelling, because they wanted to know why someone would cancel. From their end it's pretty simple. There is probably a check box on the computer screen she's looking at, and she needs to check a reason. If they are doing effective analysis on customer satisfaction, they probably keep data on that because they want to know. I was imagining all this as I was on the phone.

Then it came: "May I ask why you're cancelling?"

Shit. "My wife was killed in an automobile accident. That's why we can't come to this couples' retreat."

"Oh, I'm so, so sorry."

I was forced to go through this conversation with someone I didn't even know, at a time when I just wanted to close a financial transaction. And there have been *dozens* of these.

She had a Macy's card—you know, just one of those cards you get when you go shopping and they offer you the ten percent discount that first time if you sign up for the card? It's not like there's a balance on it. There isn't. She didn't owe money. But there's an account there. And I get an Old Navy statement every month, with her name on it. But now each one, because they are connected to her, carry all this heaviness. So how long do I let that go before I finally call them up and say, "Shut this down."

But I know how that call will go.

"Hi. My name is John Robinette. My wife, Amy Polk, died last April. I'd like to cancel her credit card."

And the nice person on the phone will tell me, "I'm so sorry to hear of your wife's passing. Please accept our sincere condolences. Please wait while I pull up her information. Okay. Here's what we need you to do. I'm going to send you a form, then you need to send back a copy of her death certificate, and I need you to notarize something."

We go up to Jersey to see family fairly often, so Amy decided to sign us up for an EZ Pass device for the car, to avoid stopping for all those tolls. The boys and I just took another trip to Jersey, we were heading up I-95, and we passed through the Baltimore Harbor Tunnel, came out the other side, and cruised through the EZ Pass toll lanes. I was just driving, not really thinking of anything else, when I saw the "Thank You" indicator light up as we went through the toll, and it hit me. Shit! There is *another* thing! Fucking EZ Pass is in Amy's name! I cursed the addition of one *more* thing to that list. And I was reminded, again, that Amy's dead. Fucking tollbooth brings up my grief as I'm driving up I-95 with my boys. And every time I passed through a tollbooth all the way to Jersey I thought about the new chore and that Amy was dead. At one point I started to worry a little. Was there enough money on the EZ Pass account? Then I remembered that it was connected to her credit card. Then I realized I was using her credit card each time I passed through a tollgate. I started thinking about how this would play out. There's probably an online account for EZ Pass. I probably could figure out how to hack into her account. I could probably guess the password she used, or use her email to reset it, or I could call the number, be put on hold, and get to someone in customer service, who would then have to transfer me to a special person because this is a special situation.

But I didn't want to go to that special person with this special situation, because I'd have to tell them my story.

Dying.

Who knew dying was so fucking complicated and took so much fucking paperwork?

—

I didn't know what to say. I couldn't say anything.

John asked, "How was that?"

How was that? In an interview you give the interviewee feedback on the process, steer him in a direction to topics you'd like to cover, tips on how to relax into the conversation. But this—this felt like I was just sitting in John's living room, talking.

I told him it was good, really good.

John stood and asked if I wanted some coffee.

By now we'd developed a running joke between us about the coffee, so I replied with our rehearsed line, "Only if you're going to make some anyway. Please, don't go to any trouble on my account." I smiled.

John smiled back and said, "Well, if you would like some coffee, I'm going to be making some anyway."

He went to make the coffee.

I followed.

We talked about the routine of running a household, having a job, trying to be responsible fathers. All the things that, together, make life "normal." Listening to John talk about how his life had unraveled after Amy's death reminded me of my own unraveling after my divorce, when my children had come to live with me in the house Gina and I had bought together, one with a finished basement for them. The cause was different, of course, but the results were similar in both households: sadness, anger, confusion, chaos. I felt a bond with John in fatherhood that I'd never felt before, and I wanted to explore that more with him.

We took our coffee back into the living room and sat down. I told him that it seemed to me we should return to the time we were just discussing, and how it impacted other parts of his life, too. The most important part of his life now. His two boys, Adam and Bryan.

—

When the school year began, we started family counseling at a grief center. I think it's going to be a very long and slow process. Part of it is just getting an eight-year-old and a five-year-old comfortable with family therapy. That can be tough for even a grown-up. Then add on to that what it is we're talking about, the event that brought us there.

Family therapy sessions are Mondays at five o'clock. I leave work a little early to pick the boys up from their aftercare at about 4:30. At 4:30 they are running around on the playground, having fun with their friends. Most of the parents don't start showing up until after five, and, normally, if we weren't going to family therapy, I'd be getting there just before six. So on the last couple of Mondays when the boys saw me show up early, they knew what was going to happen. They were going to have to leave their friends, who were still having fun on the playground, and drive with Dad to the grief center to talk about their mom who isn't with them anymore. The last time I went to pick them up I could see them having fun, running around, and then Adam saw me and started to cry. A friend saw him and asked him why he was crying, and Adam tried to hide it and said he had something in his eye.

I was crestfallen. I thought, what am I doing? Is this the right thing to do? Is this really helping them? I wasn't sure then. I'm not sure now. It occurred to me that it must almost feel like a punishment for them. And I wondered if they were thinking somewhere in the backs of their minds that if their mom were still alive they could spend more time on the playground with their friends. But because their mom died, they don't get to play on the playground on Monday afternoons.

So, yes, we have our therapy where we talk about Mommy and losing Mommy, but we talk about Mommy other times, too. When it comes up for us. And sometimes it hurts, but I think it's sometimes better than talking about it during therapy. And I'm wondering how much longer our therapy can go this way before something changes. So I've started to find opportunities to talk about Mom with the boys outside of therapy.

For example, I told them the story about our honeymoon. In 2001, Amy and I went to South Africa and then to Zambia as part of a tour group to see the total solar eclipse. We had actually scheduled our honeymoon first, and then calculated a wedding date from it. The boys like me to tell that story; they think it's really cool. And there are other moments between the boys and me when I like to reminisce with them. And instead of talking about Mom and what her death means to us in therapy sessions, these stories feel different. I don't want the subject of "Mom" to be scary or frightening. Talking about her in a normal way, telling stories about her to each other, is how we can keep her alive in our memories, I think. I hope.

One night, a few weeks ago, it was getting kind of late, and I scooped Adam up in my arms. He's sixty-plus pounds, and he's getting really long and lanky, and picking him up is getting hard to do. So I was holding him in the living room, and I said, "Boy, this is hard to do now. I remember when you were little and you used to cry a lot, and sometimes the only way your mother and I could get you to stop crying was to pick you up and dance you around the living room. For *hours*. You'd finally calm down and start to fall asleep on our shoulders. We'd put you down, and then you'd start crying again, and so we'd start dancing around the living room again with you."

That got us all into a nice "remember when" sequence, and the boys started volunteering their own memories. "Remember when Mommy would read us stories? Remember when Mommy would take us to the park? Remember how much Mommy loved to take us to see the pandas at the zoo?" We were having fun with the storytelling.

There was a little pause, then out of the blue Bryan said, "Daddy, next time you should run out in the street and get Mommy and not let her get hit by a truck."

Silence.

I felt the blood drain from my face. I looked at Bryan, and he was just looking back at me so matter-of-factly, with his little five-year-old round face, blond hair, blue eyes, innocent—no maliciousness or anger or sadness. He could have said, "Daddy, look, there's a squirrel on the tree."

Silence.

I sat there thinking, almost wanting to believe there could be a "next time." Yeah. That's exactly what I'll do. Next time. I swallowed hard and said, "I wish I could do that."

Bryan was standing there, and I could tell he was thinking this through. He said, "But, Daddy, what if we build a machine to bring Mommy back to life on her birthday? Let's do that."

And, for a moment—for just this most surreal of moments—I was ready. For just this slimmest moment I too believed it could be true, that we could do it. I could feel the words forming in my mind to say to him, "Let's head out to the hardware store. Let's get what we need to make that machine."

Adam started crying, and that broke my fantasy. He'd been standing there the whole time listening to it all, then he started to cry, and then he ran upstairs into my room. Bryan was watching all this, how his brother had reacted, then Bryan went off to his room crying. Now I had one boy crying in one part of the house and another one crying in another part of the house.

One thing that's difficult for me is that both boys try not to cry much about this. I kind of wish they could let it out, even though our therapist tells me that they will each go through it in his own way. Bryan—he talks about Mommy, how he misses Mommy. He draws pictures and writes her letters and things like that. Adam has a lot of anger and a lot of sadness. Sometimes it comes out, but I can tell he often holds back.

And because Adam, at least now, is more expressive than Bryan, and lets his sadness out, I'm self-conscious about comforting Adam when he's crying. I want to comfort Adam. I need to comfort Adam. But I also want to comfort Bryan when he's *not* crying. I don't want Bryan to think something is wrong with him if he isn't crying. I need both boys to know that they are both equally right in their response.

But that night, Adam was off crying, and Bryan had run to his room crying, and I started to cry, too, sitting there by myself. I went after Adam. And as I did I started thinking about what I could say. How could I comfort him? I couldn't say it's going to be okay, because it's not going to be okay. This will never be "okay." There is no "okay" in all of this. It's rotten. It sucks. Life is not fair. That's the way it is. Somebody took my toy, somebody pushed me down; life's not fair. That's an important lesson to learn.

And boy, oh boy are they learning about unfairness.

I got to Adam and put my arms around him, trying to comfort him, crying myself, when Bryan came up and said, "Guys, you should draw pictures of Mommy. It'll make you feel better."

He showed us his drawing of the time machine, and there's dead Mommy on one side, then the machine, and then live Mommy on the other side. He called it the "January 22" machine. That's her birthday. January 22.

What do you say to that?

It's magical.

I didn't want to destroy that—that child's innocence and belief that magical things can happen. But he needed to understand that there is no magic, no technology, no time machine. Mommy is not coming back no matter how hard we may want it to be so. I tried to remind him, gently, that as much as I want that machine, too, Mommy couldn't come back.

So Bryan had shown us his drawing, then Adam went quickly to "I miss Mommy," then went running off crying. On the one hand, when I see him cry it hurts; it hurts to the core. On the other hand, I'm relieved to see it, glad to see him cry, because it's so important for him to work through it.

I followed him into his room and told him, "Cry. Get it out. It's good to cry."

I told him what I'd wanted to share with them about how precious life is, and what we have we don't have for very long, so we should appreciate it. I hoped for a response, but Adam curled up in his bed. I think it will sink in, but how can I know?

Part of me sees now—and I *have* to see it this way, not only for the sake of my boys, but really to honor Amy and to find *some* meaning out of all this—that what we think is meaningless is really important. If there's one outcome from this, if we can pull it off, it is the life lesson of all life lessons, I think. And that is simply that we are in "it," right *now*. That is, that we are in this one life right now. It's not that the purpose of Amy's death was to teach us about the importance of life. It's the other way around. That we will somehow better appreciate the simple fleeting life we are given because we are now confronted with the truth of death.

These two boys will have a different awareness of it, just because of their age differences. But if Adam can launch out of here when he's eighteen with a different appreciation of life and love and the preciousness of it, even with all the anger and questions about why we are the ones who have to go through this—if there's a chance he can leave with that understanding, and if Bryan can be sent off with his own understanding, then I have to make that happen somehow. I have to do whatever I can to help them take this event and incorporate it into their lives in a way that can help them be more confident, more aware, more alert. When I say "alert" I mean being mindful of life, being aware of what life can offer, and how to learn from what life offers. That now feels like a purpose for me, as a father.

I think back to when I was eighteen, heading off to college: I didn't have that awareness, that mindfulness, of what was around me. Looking back I can say that I was very narcissistic, though I don't think that's so uncommon at that age. I think I have a rare opportunity now to create a broader awareness—of meaning, of life—for these two boys. I don't even know what that means yet, completely, because I'm figuring it out, too. But as they see me go through this, I'm hopeful that they can somehow incorporate it into themselves, so that they'll have this experience in them as they become adults. That's encouraging for me.

I'm cognizant of them watching me go through this, and seeing me trying to create opportunities for them to work through whatever it is they need to work through—the confusion and anger and sadness and loneliness, all those things. I was a work in progress until I was well into my thirties, before I really had a level of comfort in my own skin about who I was and being on my own and by myself, and now that Amy is no longer here I can see that I'm still very much a work in progress. It isn't that I felt I had it all figured out when I was in my thirties—all I'm trying to say is that I had just enough figured out so that I could function as a thirty-something man.

I had to get through my twenties first, though. Those were difficult years for me. Maybe they are for a lot of people. For me, I was battling feelings of not belonging, not being accepted, not being loved. I had gotten into drugs and alcohol in college, and then replaced them with a relationship that ended up being unhealthy for me. I wasn't really able to experience joy in my life until my late twenties. I hope my boys can experience those early adult years differently. Maybe I'm being too optimistic and creating expectations that aren't achievable, but I think there's something that these boys can take from this that will give them strength and courage and guidance, things few people receive early in life, me included. That gives me hope, and it gives me something also of their mother to impart to them, to imprint on them.

Along with my attempts, some of them desperate, to make sense of all this, are rituals, and their importance for me. That memorial for Amy in the living room grew for the first month and came to include pictures and veils from her dancing, books that she liked, some of her jewelry, all sorts of things. And when we finally, *finally* got her ashes, those went on the mantel, too.

And then there came a time when I felt that we needed to move on. Ritually. It was time for the next phase. The living room space had become a bit unwieldy, and it no longer served its original purpose. I talked about it with the boys.

I said, "You know what? I'd like to move some of these pictures."

The mantel was overflowing with pictures, and after a few weeks I was starting to become a little self-conscious of this shrine. At some point, having her hairbrush on display, honestly, goes from "missing you" to "creepy." Regardless, I felt that many of these things needed to find different places in the house. Bryan took some of the photos of Amy and hung them in his room, and Adam put one on his door. I think it helped them to take ownership of some of these artifacts, and gave them a way to incorporate their memories of Amy into their spaces.

For me this was an activity to make me feel busy and purposeful. Deconstructing the shrine—this altar—fulfilled a similar purpose for me, I suppose. One of the things that figured prominently was her collection of scarves, which she'd used for belly dancing. Her dancing had always been a big part of her personality. She was a very strong-willed, very smart, independent, and career-minded person, but also not afraid to express her sexuality and femininity through dance. It was one of the reasons I was so attracted to her. And now, I want my memories of her to include who she was as a belly dancer—someone who was confident in herself and very sensual and sexy. I've taken two of her scarves and laid them out on the mantel so that I can set other things on them in a decorative way to fit in with the room. And I've taken some of her other scarves and draped them over a piece of art, a framed Japanese calligraphy print, we have in the living room. They're spread out a little bit more, and they're incorporated into the room's décor. It's as if they've been absorbed back into the living room. They don't have an in-your-face quality to them, I don't think. They've simply become a part of the environment.

Her ashes are still in the simple linen-and-cardboard box her mother and I got from the funeral home. We aren't sure what we want to ultimately do with them, but I've put them on the mantel for now. At first I had her on my dresser, because it was important to keep her just for me, and private with me, in our room. I'd go into our room and see the box and pick it up and hold it and cry. I'd hug her and lie in bed with my hand on the box. Some days I'd confide in her or ask for advice. Some days I'd curse at her for dying or I'd just sit on the edge of our bed and cry. But then, after a couple months, I wanted the boys to be able to see where she was. So I put her on the mantel along with the pictures. That little medallion necklace of hers she had been wearing when I met her? I took our wedding bands and added them to the leather lanyard holding the medallion, and some days early on I'd wear it. For a while I'd put it on in the morning and take it off when I got home as another little ritual. Then some days I'd forget to do it. At first I freaked out. "Oh my God, I forgot our wedding rings!" But, now, I don't feel so compelled to wear it every day.

Also in the living room is a stockpot from the kitchen, which sits by the fireplace. Our religious education minister created a ritual for us based on a children's book called *Tear Soup*. In the book, making this soup requires the tears from those who are sad. Next to the stockpot is a little glass jar with pieces of blue paper cut out in the shapes of tears. Occasionally, one of us will take a paper tear out, maybe write on it, or not, then put it in the stockpot, just to mark any special moment. It might be as simple as one of us saying, "You know, today was kind of a hard day. I'm going to put a tear in." We were doing that a lot more, earlier on. It's faded some, with time, but it's still there, the stockpot of tear soup, by the fireplace.

Bryan uses the tear soup the most. He's still writing notes to Mommy, and he seals some of them up in an envelope. For Bryan, that's an amazingly important activity. He's created his own ritual to stay connected to her through writing letters and writing on the tears. And it also keeps it out in the open, at least for us. We can see that we are each sad and acknowledge it, silently, when we either drop in a new tear or see someone drop in a new tear.

I recently reread the eulogy I had written and read at Amy's memorial service, the celebration of her life. I didn't have any real intention behind it; I just wanted to reread it. Afterwards, I realized how important it is for me to read it from time to time—maybe even read it as part of a ritual time to mark her death. I had written about our fantasy for when we retire, when we'd travel around in a Winnebago and drop in on the grandkids from time to time. I'd forgotten I had written that into the eulogy. It's interesting because I thought that dream was gone, but since then I've had moments when I realize that I still have that dream. I still want to do that for myself, and I don't know how or if Amy will experience that in the afterworld, or in my memory. I'll figure that out when it happens, I think. Will I have another companion who joins me? I don't know. Maybe she'll have her own grandkids. But Amy and I had our children, and part of our fantasy involved them, or at least their children, should we be so blessed. So I can still honor Amy's intentions with that fantasy because they include our grandchildren. The mechanics will be different, though.

But I think it's time now, several months after Amy's death, for me to start thinking about how I can be more thoughtful about the rituals I create for my boys and me. Early on it was ad hoc and chaotic. Now I can ritualize our experience of grief through something like the reading of the eulogy. I think that's going to be important, going forward, to try to honor her, and our grief, in some way.

There is something else I don't think I have adequately described. It's painful to admit to myself, let alone say it out loud. It's the sheer, over-whelming totality of what I've lost—my lover, my partner, the mother of my children, the shared history we were creating and the future we had still to live. It feels like, as time unfolds, I am becoming more aware of more things I've lost. It's as if her death is expanding. I can never be with her again. I can never make love to her again. I can never dance with her again. We should have made love and danced for forty more years. We were just getting started. And now what has filled in the vacuum of her death is so much grief and sorrow and loneliness.

There was so much going on in my head in the immediate aftermath of her death that I had to get it out somehow. I had, and have, my therapy and conversations with friends, but then came my writing. I had dabbled with journals before, but now the words just started pouring out with my grief, and I needed a way to catch them. So I started a blog. I named it *Hole in the Sun*. It's what a solar eclipse looks like—almost an optical illusion that there is a literal hole in the sun. Astronomers use the term sometimes. Amy and I took two trips to see the solar eclipse—once in 1999, our first big trip together, then again on our honeymoon in 2001. Being public with a literary expression of my grief felt necessary—it was what I had to do. Getting those words out and in public was its own therapy. Then people started reading it and commenting, which felt good. It felt good that others could see my grief in words. And it felt good because other widows and widowers, and anyone, really, could notice. I guess, partially, there was some boost to my ego about my writing, but also that others found some comfort was comforting for me, too. It was the first sense that somehow my suffering had any purpose at all. Then I discovered an online community of widows and widowers. Misery loves company, I guess, but it is amazingly comforting to know there are others out there surviving.

But in the midst of all that pain and misery there has also been a rushing in, an outpouring of love and compassion that is, unto itself, practically as overwhelming as the pain and suffering of Amy's loss.

The outpouring of love and compassion from my community has been powerful medicine. Grief is lonely business. Learning of the community of others who have come together to share their pain and suffering—the deaths of loved ones, husbands and wives, lost children, disease, marital difficulties, betrayals, and pain of all sorts—changes that. The commonness and commonality of our human suffering is more present to me than ever before in my life—no longer academic and theoretical, but real and raw and present. Others have been through this hell, and they know what it is to walk this road. I see them, standing in front of me, with wisdom I hadn't noticed before. And I see them, standing in front of me, and I see that they have survived, which means I can, too. And there are others who may not have had this type of experience yet, but I see them compelled to express their love in various ways, whether it's picking up and doing my laundry, or bringing food, or just comforting me, or bringing bottles of Scotch. And some people don't know what to say at all, but that doesn't stop them from trying. I had a neighbor come over to my house about a week after it happened, and he was so tongue-tied he literally could not form two words. He came into the house and mumbled for about a minute and a half before he hugged me and left. And I still recognized it as a profound act of love.

I never realized how hard it is for people to say the word "death" or "died." I would hear people say things like, "I'm so sorry Amy passed," or "I am sorry to hear of Amy's passing." It's so strange. Amy didn't "pass." She was killed. I use "died" or "killed." When someone says "passed," it sometimes pisses me off. *Passed?* Or "passed on" or "they are not with us anymore." What the heck is that? I don't like it. I don't like it because euphemisms hide the reality of the situation. To me, by calling out its name, by calling out death, we can diminish its power over us a little bit.

Let me say it: Amy died. Or let me say it this way: Amy was killed. A guy driving a truck ran her over in the street and killed her. Someone who *dies*? People die from cancer or heart attacks or accidents, too. She was *killed* at the hands of somebody else. I am certain, yes, it was an accident, with no malice or forethought, based on what I know. And I don't really want to know much more about that horrific accident. The driver must be in his own hell. But she didn't pass. She was taken. She was killed.

There's a connection I have to other young widows and widowers. And by "young" I think I mean someone around my age. In their forties. We have a shared experience that communicates hundreds of thousands of words. For example, when you say, "You lost your husband/wife to cancer/heart disease when you were forty, and you had a little girl," with that sentence comes an entire body of knowledge and recognition between two people who have the shared experience of losing a spouse. We don't have to say anything else. We understand.

Now, even the most empathic person can only be so empathetic. They can't *really* know exactly what this hell is like. I imagine it's like any particular hell that somebody has to go through. No one can know it, really, except that person.

Before this experience, before Amy's death, I think it was easy for me to be judgmental, or to look at somebody else and what they were doing, and question their motives and wonder why they weren't doing something differently. Maybe it would be parenting. I'd look at friends or even family and how they were being parents to their kids, and I'd have some judgment about it. Or we'd be out and see another couple at dinner in what looked like a confrontational conversation, and I would just assume something like, "Well, they must not have a very loving relationship." The unstated comparison, of course, was, "They must not have a very loving relationship like *we* do!" Stuff like that. Of course I would just keep all that to myself, but it was there. We are all going through some struggle, right? I'd like to think now that the judgmental part of me has washed out. Completely? No. It's still there, at some level, but now I see it differently. Amy's death has given me a view on life I'd otherwise not have.

And maybe I've swung too far the other way. I'll bristle sometimes when people question my motives now because it feels like they're judging me. There have been a few times when people will gently question, "Is that the right thing for the boys? Maybe they should see a different therapist. Are you sure you're ready to think about dating? Are you really sure?"

I want to say, "How dare you! Fuck you for even suggesting that this is not the right thing. Fuck you!"

That's what I want to say sometimes. Come to me after your wife is hit and killed by a truck, and then tell me what the "right thing to do" might be. I'll be here. I'll be right here waiting. And then you can tell me.

Sometimes it can be smaller things. Simple things we are all just used to saying to each other. "She's in a better place," or "There's a plan, you know, God has a plan," or "God only gives you what you're able to handle." That last one, that's a beauty. So if I were a weaker person, my wife would still be alive? Is that what you're saying? I'm sorry I'm such a strong person that God decided to take Amy because apparently I am just barely able to handle it.

Those "words of comfort" don't really work for me. And having shared my experience with other widows and widowers, from what I've heard from them, there is a similar feeling for them, too.

And this experience binds you into a community, the widow community, in another odd way. It's one of those insider/outsider situations. I grew up in New Jersey, so I can make fun of New Jersey. But if you grew up somewhere else, you can't. Right? I can make fun of my family, but you can't. You don't dare. If you're inside the circle, we can talk that way, because we share an entire world of understanding. If you're *not* inside the circle, if you aren't a widow, or widower, you'd better be careful how you talk about it.

That sounds harsh, but that is what would run through my head. I understand that people are genuinely showing love and compassion, and trying to be comforting or sympathetic, because I've had an amazing amount of that. After all, everybody has suffered something. If you have lived long enough, you've lost something. I think the ability to recognize loss, the feeling of loss and the feeling of hopelessness, is the starting point for empathy.

It can be simple things. People don't need to say much, really, but there's a different language I would like us to use, even in our greetings. We say, "Hey, how's it going?" instead of "Hello," or "Good morning," or "Good afternoon." We say, "Hey, how you doing?" That's how we say hello. That's our greeting in our culture. But we aren't genuinely interested in wanting to hear how the other person is doing.

When somebody says, "Hey, how's it going?" you're supposed to say, "Fine. How you doing?" Then it's "Great." Then the parting exchange is, "Well, nice seeing you." That's our normal, social exchange.

But those words come out heavy now, and I see people catching themselves sometimes.

"Oh, hey, John. How's it—umm, how *are* you?" Or when somebody asks me how it's going, I can't just give the standard reply: "Oh, good. How are you?" I can't say that anymore, because it so obviously doesn't apply. So I say, "We're managing," or "It's day to day," and then they know.

But I think we could say something different when we greet each other that wouldn't create that awkwardness. Something more genuine. Like:

"Oh, hi. It's good to see you."

"It's good to see you, too."

I think that would be a better greeting.

Or:

"It's nice seeing you today."

"Well, thank you. It's nice seeing you, too."

And then you could toss in a "How's it going?" if you really feel like it.

If you do it that way, we would know that there's a sincerity about really probing the "How are you doing?" question, or not, because we've already established the genuineness of our initial meeting.

So what's my point in all this? Maybe it's that this experience of death for me, for my neighbors, for this community, for those who knew and loved Amy—this experience rips back the façade. We have no choice but to face the reality of my loss, our loss. And we have no way to carry on in the way we did in the past. The social graces and superficialities have to melt away, but it's hard to know what to replace them with. We've lost all the traditions and conventions for how a community handles death. We just don't know. But what I do know is this: I wouldn't know how to get on without them, without my community.

—

John sat silently for a moment, then I said, "I could use that drink about now."

John laughed and said, "It's not even noon." After a brief pause he added, "With the cigars?"

I laughed and nodded. I packed up my gear and cigar case and followed John through the side door and into his backyard. It was what you'd call "cozy." There was a paved patio across the back of the house, nearly the entire width of the property, then a stone retaining wall about thigh-high, so you could sit on it, then a gently sloped and wooded lawn of about thirty feet to the back fence. Behind and to either side the neighbors' lawns were heavily treed so that little light fell down onto the ground still wet from mist. It was a cool November morning in Maryland. Birds were singing one to another. Very close and clear. Like heralds of the new day.

John's screened-in porch had a view of all this.

I started setting up my gear, and John said he'd be right back with the drinks. It was becoming normal now for me, these planned conversations. It felt reassuring and odd at the same time. Reassuring that we had a plan to do this project; odd that we were even doing such a thing. Going through with it. What if no one wanted to listen to what we were talking about? Amy died, yes. But people die every day in similarly tragic circumstances. Thoughts like these were intruders, and I had to push them down to be able to focus on the work. I got out my pad and made notes to indicate dates and times of interviews, topics we'd already covered, and things to discuss—the mechanics of the interview.

John came around the stone path on the side of his house carrying a tray, and on the tray, as promised, was a bottle of Armagnac and two drinking glasses. He beamed, looking like the best host.

"That looks like a treat," I said.

John smiled. He said he'd found this particular brand in the store after talking with the shop owner, who explained to him the differences among the many types and brands based on growing varieties, regions, and distillation methods.

"Cigars are the same way," I said. I grabbed my cigar case and opened it to show him the four cigars bedded there, and I explained the different quality of smoke expected of each based on the manufacturer, the soil conditions, the type of wrapper.

We made our choices and settled in for the smoke and drink. Our conversation was easy and enjoyable. After a while I asked John if he'd like to start recording again. He said sure. I knew where he wanted to pick up.

—

After Amy died, after the initial shock and dizziness and paralysis of the event had started to subside, two, three, four months later, I became aware of some old personal demons that I hadn't had to really confront in a while. I used to think those demons had left for good, but I'm now starting to see that they have always been with me. It's just that I didn't really notice them. They had never left but had simply gone to sleep and were waiting for the right time to wake up. And they had awakened slowly, and then, after a couple weeks, with a vengeance—loneliness and the need for acceptance. The seeking of acceptance from others, that is. But it starts with loneliness, for me.

Back in the summer a widow friend of mine had come over to check in with me. She'd lost her husband a few years earlier and had since remarried. During our conversation, sort of out of the blue, she said, "It's all online now, you know."

I said, "What are you talking about?"

"That's how people meet each other now. It's all online."

"What?"

It seemed too early and confusing, just the thought of dating again. I mean, in honesty, I was feeling very lonely, and I had started wondering if I'd find someone again, but still. Online dating? And how would I manage all the grief and loneliness and fear and even the guilt? I still felt committed to Amy, and it seemed almost like cheating.

I can't say I was ever really that good at dating. I'd sort of found my groove just before I met Amy, but back then the online world didn't exist. Not really, not like it is today. Today, that's how people meet. Amy's brother met his wife online. It used to be if you met online, that was kind of weird. Now it's like, "What? You met in *school*? Oh my God. You didn't meet online?"

When I questioned my widowed friend more about online dating, the appropriateness, how it works, she simply said, "Whatever. It's good for window shopping," and brushed if off.

By August I started to really wonder about what it might feel like to date again. I struggled with the notion. It had only been four months, you know? Then one night I was feeling sorry for myself, and I'd had too much Scotch, and I said, "Fuck it, I'm just gonna see what this is about." I went to one site and started to fill out the form, but it was way too complicated. I thought, I don't have time for this! There were a couple of simpler sites, so I picked one and just threw up a profile. I'd done photography in the past; I had some self-portraits around. I think they looked okay. I was up until two or three in the morning, and I was reaching this fanatical, maybe even manic, zone: "I've got to get this done! I don't care what it takes!" I was drinking my Scotch and writing. It was the writing, I think. I was writing about myself, getting it all out—the "Who I am" and "What I want from life" stuff. Getting out my emotions and sharing them publicly. I had my blog, yes, but this was different. It felt scary and cathartic and necessary. And what I was now writing in this silly profile became an extension of all that. I had nothing to hide, so I just put it out there. In the back of my mind I imagined I was probably breaking a dozen unwritten rules about what *not* to share in a dating-site profile. But I just let it come out.

As I finished my profile I sat there staring at the screen and thought, "God, I'm putting myself online! *Now?* I don't know about this."

I hesitated, and then said to myself, "I'm not going to initiate anything, but I'm out there, and if someone wants to contact me, so be it."

I was very straightforward—I either checked the box or explained in my profile that I was recently widowed. My situation was complicated. This wasn't for everyone. I wouldn't want to get into *anything* with someone who didn't understand that. So I just tried to be as honest as I could be—I'm widowed, I never thought I'd be where I am now, but I've experienced amazing, wonderful things and unbelievably horrible things, and I want to experience life fully and without regret.

So I did it. I clicked submit and put myself out there.

The next day I woke up slightly hungover and regretted it. I hid my profile. I felt guilty. It felt like the walk of shame from my computer to my bedroom. I felt like I was betraying Amy. I didn't know what the hell I really wanted. Maybe I just wanted to get laid. I went through this phase where it felt like I was peeking through a window into some other world. I could almost see it, but not clearly.

I felt so conflicted. Then a couple nights later, I put the kids to bed, poured myself a Scotch, and went online. I made my profile active again and waited.

And nothing happened.

And I started getting depressed about it. But then after a few days a couple of women reached out. And when somebody would contact me, I'd reply back and say, "Full disclosure: I'm recently widowed, so this is fresh for me. I don't even know what I'm looking for. If you're interested, fine, and if not, I understand."

Amy's death had caused a shift inside me—I'd become very aware of the uncertainty and unpredictability and finiteness of what we're given. I quickly realized I have no idea how much time I have left. Maybe it's fifty more years; maybe it's five. I don't know.

And honestly, there was something exciting about the thought of meeting someone new. But then I'd think about Amy. She'd meant everything to me, and part of me still wanted her back, and I felt guilty about my desire to be with another woman, but I also knew she wouldn't want me to be sitting around feeling sorry for myself, either. She would expect me to get on with my life, and I knew I'd need to do that at some point. At least for the boys' sake. If I have another person at my side, that would be nice.

It's funny, the other thing that started happening around this same time was that a couple of friends started trying to hook me up.

A coworker said to me, "Hey, did you ever think about so-and-so? She's really nice. She's single. She has this and that in common with you." All those sorts of things.

A coworker—that seemed like trouble, at some level. She was a lovely, attractive person, this prospective date, but I couldn't.

Then an old friend of mine from college said to me, "I don't know how to ask you this question, so I'm just going to ask you. There's this friend of mine—would it be okay if I arranged a meeting between you and her?"

I said, "You mean a blind date?"

She laughed.

I said no.

But those offers helped me feel okay about dating again. It was as if I needed some level of approval that others wanted to see me happy again. So I started thinking that, yes, maybe a date would help. Again, for me, the feeling of loneliness—just being alone—is difficult under the best of times. I've felt lonely and alone before, and now it's colored with the grief and the way I *became* alone. The suddenness. The awfulness. It has been rough. Very rough.

It was actually not long after Amy died when I let myself think about what another companion, or lover, might look like. I'd be driving to work and see a woman in the car next to me. We'd stop at a red light. I'd peek at her. Attractive. Young. Then my mind would wander, and I'd wonder if she was single. Then I'd start to fantasize about how I'd meet her and ask her out on a date. She'd tell me she'd been waiting for me all along and would throw herself at me, and we'd make wild, passionate love. I'd think back on my life and consider that I never really "played the field." Now was my chance! I'd play out fantasies of several different women, or younger women, or even more prosaic fantasies, like what it would be like to simply go on a date again, or have sex again, and get married again. Then I'd shake it all out of my head. "What are you talking about?" "It's too soon." "You're crazy." "*This* is crazy." Then the light would turn green. I'd drive on, thinking, I don't even know how to date. I don't know that I *ever* knew how to date. Maybe some people did; I wasn't one of those people. And it's all online now. People don't meet wherever they *used* to meet. So I left my profile up, and I tried letting go of my anxiety about it all. "I'm just curious," I said to myself. "No harm in looking, seeing who's out there."

I also recognized that at this point in my life, I'm pretty particular. I kind of know what I want, I think, in a companion. Smart, outdoorsy, environmentally mindful, has to like to hike and camp. Athletic. I tend toward brunettes. Not materialistic. Socially and politically liberal. My Unitarian Universalist church is very important to me, so she'd need to be onboard with a liberal theology. I'd want her to be settled in her career and know what she wants out of life. And, perhaps most important, she'd have to live nearby. Like maybe even walking distance. I can't travel very far. It would have to be simple, logistically.

But I wasn't getting much attention from the dating site, so one night I thought, rather than just wait for them to contact me, let me see who is out there. I hadn't really actively searched yet. So I went online, logged in, did the little check boxes for all my preferences. All of them—politics, environment, religion, height, weight, small radius from my house, all that stuff. I put in my criteria and ran the search. Zero hits.

Zero fucking hits.

I sat back in my chair. "You've got to be fucking kidding me. This is really depressing."

And that really fed the loneliness, because I thought, not only am I alone *now*, but there's *nobody* out there for me, *ever*.

So I decided to set online dating aside, and I tried to focus on other things. Friends were still stopping in, keeping me company, and then there was work, and the boys. So it's not like I was idle. But having stepped out, at least ever so tentatively, into the dating world, I could feel my loneliness even more. I wasn't with someone. I wasn't getting laid. And one night after the kids were asleep, when I was sitting on the porch, sipping my Scotch, I realized what had happened.

There was one old companion I hadn't counted on showing up. And I didn't even notice at first. His name is Larry. Larry Lonely. He's my loneliness demon. Being alone is one thing, but being lonely is something else. There's a lot connected to this. In particular is my feeling of not belonging, not being accepted, not being loved. Fundamentally, if you're lonely, I think you feel there is an absence of love.

My relationships before Amy each felt good in one way or another, but looking back on them now, I can see that I was still lonely on some level, because the love I was able to create with those other people was somehow incomplete. The feeling of love I was getting from my partners somehow did not fill me as I wanted, as I needed. And my ability to be fully in love was somehow also incomplete. So there was a difference between the love I needed and the love I was getting. And this worked the other way, too—I wasn't able to really give the love I needed to give. And those differences resulted in a feeling of loneliness, even within the relationship. But there was still some love, and that love, though incomplete, was far less scary than what I imagined would be the feeling of complete loneliness, or the complete lack of love, if I were to *not* be in that relationship.

So I look back at my early relationships and I see now that my fear of *total* loneliness kept them from ending when they should have. That fear could be so intense, at times, that it seemed it was better to be in *any* relationship, even a really unhealthy, painful relationship, than experience that total loneliness. So I'd rather accept that pain—or dysfunction or baggage or neurosis, whatever you want to call it—because the depth of complete loneliness is potentially *so* profound that I would accept being in incomplete love to avoid it.

In my teens and early twenties the feeling of loneliness had been very strong. Why? I don't know with certainty. I was the oldest of five kids. Had I needed something more from my parents? Maybe. Though blaming them seems too clichéd. Adolescence sucks for the best of us. Maybe mine had been a little worse? Maybe it was Catholic fear and guilt. Maybe it was just my peculiar DNA. Maybe it was a little of all of that. Starting in my teens, when I'd begun to want to be in a relationship, to have a girlfriend, I felt stuck. I was scared to ask girls out for fear they'd say no, and then what? I'd see my friends dating and would feel a sense of jealousy and sadness. I wished I could be like them, but just couldn't summon the courage and risk the rejection I imagined. And during that part of my life, my late teens,

I found new friends who could make the loneliness go away, at least for a while: alcohol and drugs.

I remember being a kid and my dad would let me sip his beer, which tasted nasty. By thirteen or fourteen a couple friends and I would sneak a beer or liquor from our parents' liquor cabinets. Usually it was during a sleepover or something like that. It started out pretty innocently, but by sophomore or junior year in high school we were drinking regularly on the weekends. Back then we didn't call it binge drinking, but that's what it was. Then, off to college and I discovered marijuana, psyche-delic mushrooms, and LSD. I only tried LSD once—at a Grateful Dead concert, of course. Once was enough. Alcohol and pot were my drugs of choice. A few times I tried what we called "crank"—methamphetamine. That was a particularly wonderful high. I can see how easy it would be to become addicted to that. But it was also a little *too* much. And coming off it made me sick, and constipated. I remember once not being able to take a dump for a week.

By the end of my sophomore year in college I was not doing well. My grades were poor and I think a shrink would have diagnosed me with depression if I'd been seeing one. I confided in a friend that I wasn't happy, that I felt I was drinking too much, and that I was smoking too much dope. I don't remember what he said, but I do remember he really cared. I went to a guidance counselor on campus and decided to switch majors. Junior year started, and I was still drinking a lot and smoking dope, but there was a difference. I was starting to feel more confident. And then I met my first real love. She was not a big fan of the drugs, and it was easy to give them up for her. Looking back, now, I can see that I was replacing my friend, my addiction, for another. Eight years later, when that relationship, then a marriage, was unraveling, I landed in therapy for about five years, and that changed me.

From my late twenties to my thirties I went through another serious relationship, and then when I met Amy I was thirty-two, and it wasn't as scary for me to be alone as it had been when I was younger. Over the years, as I've become more aware of myself and my emotional needs, my desire for love and acceptance have become less crippling. I was learning to love more, and I gradually moved away from incomplete love relationships to a more fulfilling one. It's a cliché to say, "You have to love yourself first," but there is some truth to that.

Then Amy died. The nature of that loss—the suddenness, that immediate and intense sense of loneliness—reawakened that demon.

Larry.

What can I say about Larry? He's that old friend who just shows up. Larry brings the booze. Larry comes with the Scotch. Larry *loves* his Scotch:

"Come on, John!"

"Larry, oh man, *no*. I gotta get up early tomorrow."

"Oh, come on. Just sit outside with me on the porch and have some Scotch."

And I have to say: It's comfortable, and it's nice. Larry's a buddy. We go *way* back, Larry and I.

But Larry's one of those friends who's not really good for me. I've really become aware of that. For the first time in my life, I can actually name it that way. I have always known that Larry—as helpful and as fun as he is, and as much as he keeps me company and makes me feel good, for a while—always overstays his welcome and becomes needy. But now I've come to know it like never before.

Maybe if I were able to force myself into solitude—you know, like Superman's Fortress of Solitude—I could gain some inner wisdom and would be able to confront Larry, tell him what I really think of him. "Larry, you know what? I know we've been buddies a long time. I know you come by, and we've shared plenty of Scotch. But you know what? I think it's time that we part ways for good this time."

I haven't said that to Larry, but I think I might need to.

Then sometimes I think I should just resign myself to it, to him. So instead of the great confrontation, I would say to him, "Larry, I get it. I get it. You're just gonna be here forever with me. You've been a friend forever. In high school you taught me to drink. In college we got high together. Okay. Fine. But you know what, Larry? I can't be your drinking buddy, not every time. So if you want to hang out, fine, but you and I need a new understanding. Don't expect me to do shots with you anymore."

And Larry's response? Well, he says he's cool with it, but then he starts to guilt me. "Just one shot, John, just one for old times' sake."

Then I'll tell him I don't want to get drunk with him and that I'm going to bed and he should go home.

He says again he's cool with it, but I can sense he isn't, not really.

I tell him goodbye and to go home, and I go to bed.

I wake up in the morning and find him sleeping in the living room. "Larry! Are you *kidding* me? You slept on the couch last night? I thought you were going home!"

Larry's just scratching himself. "Oh, well, you know, it was late already, and I didn't think it was safe to drive, and the last bus had already left, and it was two o'clock in the morning, so I just decided to sleep on your couch. Is that okay? Can I borrow a towel and take a shower? Got any leftovers?"

"Larry, you really need to go home, man. You've been here a long time."

"Oh, come on. What's the big deal? Oh, and I could use some coffee. Are you going to make coffee?"

That's who Larry is. He means well, I guess. And I can't really hold it against him. He's just who he is. Which is why it's hard to tell him to stop visiting. Truth is, I kind of like Larry. And I don't really want to piss him off, because sometimes it feels like he is my only friend.

It's taken me until now to understand who Larry is and to accept him on his own terms and not want him to be someone else. I have to say this about Larry—back in college when he and I were into drinking and smoking dope, it was fun to hang out with him. And he seemed popular. For a while. I felt good hanging out with him. But then I started to see there were other things possible in my life, and I couldn't stay friends, at least close friends, with Larry and also do well in school and fall in love with a woman. So when I met the woman who would become my first wife, as difficult as that relationship was, it was better than hanging out with Larry. Looking back I know I stayed in that marriage longer than I should have because I felt my only alternative was to go back to hanging out with Larry.

By the time I met Amy I thought Larry had gone away, but I realize now that he never really went anywhere. We never said goodbye. He was just biding his time. And with Amy around he knew better than to just show up, unannounced. Because if he had I would've had to say, "Dude, I've got a wife and kids now. That's not cool." And it might have been over.

But now Amy's not here, and he knows it.

I often think of how when Amy died, a part of me died, too. And it's not just that she died, but that she was *ripped away*. It felt like she had been physically ripped away from me, and it had pulled a whole hunk of my skin off. That's literally how it felt in the days after she died. It was as if my chest was burning where she had been pulled away, and there was this exposed, raw flesh there, leaving things exposed in me, physically and emotionally. I could see inside myself in a way I'd never been able to before, because my chest had been ripped open, my heart had been ripped open, revealing my fear of loneliness and the pain it caused. They had been there all along. The love Amy and I had shared had successfully treated them, but now, with her gone, I could see it again. "Holy shit!" I thought. "*That's* still inside me!" I had never really seen it that way before—why would I need to? It had been covered up. But with her gone, and now after these few months, I think I can best describe it that way.

So now I have this open chest wound. How do I treat it? Therapy, exercise, acupuncture, being with friends. And alcohol. Alcohol is strong medicine for me right now. It slows the bleeding, calms me down, helps sand down the rough edges just enough. And I'm aware of it, very much aware of it. Just like my son Adam is aware that when he plays video games he doesn't think about Mommy.

Seriously.

One night he'd been playing his video games for a long time. It was time to stop; he'd played enough, and I told him to turn it off.

He said, "But I like playing video games. Because then I don't have to think about Mommy."

I was startled. At eight, he has an understanding of how he medicates, which I think is good, actually. He just medicates with video games.

I can't really get on his case too much about playing video games as his medicine if I'm going to drink beer or Scotch to medicate my evening away. That would be hypocritical.

It's just where we are.

—

I looked at John and smiled. I wanted to hold it together, for his sake and mine. I wanted to make light, for his sake and mine. "Cheers," I said and raised my glass. I know it must have seemed ludicrous to John, but I didn't know what else to say.

He laughed.

I puffed my cigar. "It's a great way to deal with our addictions, isn't it?"

John laughed again and said, "You know, I could really work out my addiction to alcohol if I just had a stiff drink first."

Now I laughed. Hard. I knew John was joking, and I had to joke, too. Sometimes gallows humor is all you have; it's what gets you through, sometimes. I thanked John for being so honest.

He sat smoking his cigar and nodding and after a moment said that he didn't feel he was being honest so much as he was simply explaining and exploring where he was right then in life.

I asked him what he meant by that.

———

Time. I spend a lot of time thinking about time. The passage of time. I've been talking to my shrink about this and about the expectations that come with time. Part of it is wrapped up in what I imagine is our societal, and even individual, expectations of the grief process. There's something heavy and symbolic about getting through this first year. I've talked to other people who have lost someone.

"Oh, yeah, that first year." "You just gotta get through the first year." "The first year is really tough."

I think there are some truths here. One of the truths must be attached to our long-held customs associated with the first year of mourning—customs handed down over generations, in the Jewish tradition, among others. I don't know how old that tradition is—a couple of thousand years, easily. So I'm sure that sense of how time unfolds after a significant loss has worked its way into other traditions besides Judaism, as well.

All those recurring points of our lives—birthdays, anniversaries, holidays, recurrent feasts, and festivals—are another part of it, too. These are markers for us, and you'll go through one of each during the first year, obviously. I've already lived through the first Mother's Day, the first birthday for each boy, our wedding anniversary, the first Fourth of July, and my first birthday; now, coming up, we'll have the first Thanksgiving, the first Christmas, the first New Year's, and then Amy's birthday. Each of these milestones becomes a new "first" without Amy. It's almost as if there is an equivalent sorrow on the first Thanksgiving without Amy that balances out the joy of the first Thanksgiving with her. So I'm thinking that the theory around "the first year" is that you lived through each of those moments one time without this person, so you're better prepared with some sense of how it is the second time around. It shouldn't be as traumatic. So the first year looms large, and getting through this first year has been a focus for me. Maybe an obsession.

At the six-month-minus-one-week point, I was seeing my shrink, and I was remarking that the following Friday would be October 29, six months. I said, "Next week when I'm back here it will be six months."

My shrink said, "You're halfway there."

And, yes, I had meant that next week would mark six months into this and that six months was somehow a measure of progress. Now, I'm not sure she intended it to come out that way, but when she actually put words to it—*You're halfway there*—it sounded preposterous. Halfway to *what*? I wanted to ask her. Halfway to *what*? Halfway to a *year*? It sounded ridiculous when I heard it from someone else, like there was some *where* to get to! Yet this is what I was nearly obsessed with—getting through the first year.

Halfway. We just lingered on this thought, she and I, and the more I thought about it, the more ridiculous it seemed.

"Halfway." It could be halfway to *forever*.

And yet, on another level, I'm halfway to nowhere. I'm either halfway to nowhere or halfway to infinity. I think she intended it to be comforting, but the way I heard it reminded me of how arbitrary these things can be.

We talked about it a little bit more. I had just turned forty-four. I'm sure I could find some actuarial table that shows me dying at eight-eight. Of course, anything could happen, but statistically, I'm probably about as close to the halfway point of my life as I've ever been.

A friend of mine gave me a book called *The View from the Center of the Universe*. I'd gotten about halfway through it when Amy died, and I set it aside. The book explains our modern understanding of the beginning of the universe, cosmology, and how our post-Newton/Galileo knowledge of the universe has left us lacking in a human connection to that new understanding.

For example, most faith traditions describe a universe with humans in the middle, at the center. The sun revolves around the Earth. The gods are holding up the firmament, and whether it's the Egyptians or the Christians or whomever, humans are at the center. And however you imagine God, as a spirit or person or force of nature, holding it all together, we humans are in the middle, in the center of it all. Well, Newton and Galileo dispensed with that understanding. Now, not only are we *not* the center, we revolve around the sun and the sun revolves around the center of this galaxy. And we're not even in the center of the Milky Way—we're off in some outer hick arm, far away from the center of the universe. It's weird. It's not only that we're *not* in the center, it's that we're *way* the hell out in the sticks.

So our sense of self, not as individuals but as humans, as a species, has been lost because of our disconnection from that center of creation, from God, from whatever the "greater-ness" is and how we conceive it. The authors try to create a new mythology, based on recent scientific discoveries, about the nature of the universe, its creation, and our understanding of how it may end. They explain that the universe—if you consider the Big Bang the starting point—is thirteen or fourteen billion years old. When the Big Bang occurred, the first elements produced were hydrogen, helium, and lithium. Elementally, that was it. It was only after many, many years that the clumps of hydrogen started to coalesce into stars, and the fusion engines of stars fired up. In that fusion engine the elements necessary for life—oxygen, carbon, nitrogen—are created. Then when stars imploded or exploded, they threw off those elements and created others that coalesced into other stars and then planets. In other words, a whole generation of stars had to be created and destroyed before even the basic elements of life, these organic compounds, could even be possible.

So there had to be a cycle of cosmological life and death just to create the preconditions necessary for human life.

Our sun is a second-generation star, we think. We may have another thirteen or fourteen billion years left. So we're actually now in the center of *time*. We are sitting here, miraculously, somehow, living, breathing, based on this series of events, and it's about halfway over, as far as we know. It's a cosmological midpoint, and it's true for all of us.

Now I find myself halfway through this year of grief. Halfway through my own life. In the middle of the universe. The thought is strangely comforting while at the same time disorienting.

This past week I was at a work-related conference in San Diego. My mom came down and stayed with the boys for three nights. On Tuesday, after the conference meetings, there was a reception, an open bar, and a dinner afterwards. I lost track of how many glasses of wine I'd had. I was counting until I got to the dinner, and then the waiters would just keep topping off my glass. I had to stop them.

It was a nice dinner, and my thought processes and emotions had gotten a bit lubricated from the wine, and afterwards, it was about nine o'clock, and I really needed to walk off the meal and the wine.

In San Diego the waterfront is just beautiful. I'd never been there before. The hotel we were in was about a mile and a half from the airport, so I just started walking along the waterfront toward the airport. I became very aware of this feeling of—let's call it a variant of "sadness." I say variant; I was thinking of the anecdote of the Inuit, who have fifty different words for "snow" because their experience with snow is such that they understand it to that level of specificity.

Then it occurred to me that we don't have enough words to describe "sadness," and the tears of sadness. There are tears of joy and tears of sadness, but there are many subtle variations. I've felt it with my own sorrow. Some tears are conjured by loneliness, some by fear, some anger. But the sadness I was feeling this past Tuesday wasn't the sadness of loneliness, or fear, or anger. It was, simply: I missed Amy. A lot. It was the sadness of not being able to enjoy her company ever again. Let's call it "longing"—the sadness of longing. Mixed in with that was this pivotal feeling that my world was at a point of rotation, that there was this shift happening in my life, that I was at the axis and things were going to come out differently. Things were going to be different.

As I was walking along the waterfront I saw in my mind's eye a view of the top of our solar system, and I could see the sun spinning in the middle, and I could see Earth spinning and going around in its course with the Moon going around it. The sun was doing the same pirouette around whatever it was going around, and spinning, and then there was the dancing—that image and the lingering effects of the wine all just made me dizzy.

That sense of a transition point, a pivotal point was present with me that Tuesday, perhaps amplified by the wine and perhaps heightened because I was by myself, really for the first time in a while, without the boys, and without anyone else. I could just be with my own thoughts.

I continued walking along the waterfront, and I'd stop occasionally, and I'd cry. Not tears of sadness, or grief, or despair. It was still the feeling that I missed Amy, but as I walked along it shifted into a general release of emotions, a flooding out. Almost bewilderment. I thought I wanted to create some meaning. Some greater understanding of life and death and the nature of the universe. As if there could be an answer. But maybe it wasn't that complicated after all. I just really missed Amy. Terribly. It was comforting but also confusing. Could it be that simple? That I just really, really missed Amy?

Along the waterfront in San Diego are all these boats, private pleasure crafts and sailboats, and there are also Navy vessels, and an old three-masted schooner and a submarine that's now a museum you can go on. And then next I found myself standing there looking up at this big aircraft carrier, and what aircraft carrier is it?

It's the *Midway*.

The fucking *Midway*.

It's not the *Hornet*, or the *Enterprise*, or any of the others—it's the *Midway*, and it's a museum now, and I was standing looking right at it! I nearly said out loud, "Now you've got to be fucking kidding me!" This is crazy! I'm at the *Midway* at the middle of the middle of the middle. There's no more middle! What else could there be? There can be no more middle!

I tried to take a picture. It was too dark, and it's too big, and I think I could just get in the *way* or *dway*. Then I started thinking, all right, then, maybe all the cosmos had to do was get me to San Diego. Hopefully, it wasn't that the cosmos had to set in motion this global conflict, with a turning point in that war at the Battle of Midway, which would then have an aircraft carrier named for it, so I could stand and stare at the name six months after Amy's death. That's too farfetched.

The universe doesn't work that way. Does it?

—

John smiled, seemingly waiting for my reply.

"It depends on your worldview," I said. "What you believe."

John asked me what I believed.

He knew I was a Christian, so I asked him if he really wanted to dig into the details of it, have a conversation about God and being and purpose, because that would take a really long time, and did we have that much time? I grinned. All we were doing now was talking; we had time.

The phone rang.

John looked at me and said quickly, "That'll be my kids. Are we done?" I could tell he wanted to, needed to, be done.

I nodded. "Go, go, we're done."

He dashed into the house.

I packed up my gear. My cigar was still burning so I kept smoking and walked along the pathway to the front of his house. Gold and red leaves spotted the trees up and down the street, littered lawns and sidewalks. I breathed the cool fall air. It all seemed so normal, so serene, out here.

A minute later John came out and we stood talking in his front yard. "It was my kids," he explained. "They're okay. They're coming back from their sleepover sooner than I'd thought." He told me about the activities they'd had planned for the rest of the day. How keeping busy helped them stay engaged with the world and friends and not be at home, thinking. How it helped him.

I nodded. "I get it," I said. "We'll have our conversation about God some other time."

John asked, "When do you want to meet next?"

I said, "How about right before Christmas?"

John flinched.

"Too much?" I said.

He nodded.

I said, "I'd rather not wait until after the new year. I'd rather talk with you to see how your holidays are going." I felt strange for putting it that way to him, but I really wanted to get a gauge for how he and his boys would deal with that time. I knew it would be particularly rough and challenging, and I didn't want John to get too far away from it, in time, before we could talk.

John said, "How about in between?"

"*Between* Christmas and New Year's Day?" I was a little surprised. I didn't think he'd want to interrupt his holidays like that.

He nodded. "Can you do that?"

"Yes," I said. "If you can do that, I can do that. I can do that." I think I had to repeat it to assure myself that, yes, I'd be able to do that, without checking in with Gina first about the schedule.

We talked a little more about setting dates, the weather, raking leaves. When it was time for me to go I caught myself as I was wishing him, well in advance, a "Happy Thanksgiving" and a "Happy Holidays." My words sounded clumsy and inappropriate, even to me. I was embarrassed.

John smiled when he saw me react to myself.

I tried again and said, "Take care of yourself, and the boys."

He nodded and kept smiling and said, "I'll do that."

We hugged.

I walked out onto the street to my parked car, berating myself for being insensitive. Of all people, I thought, *I* should be the one most able to speak to John in terms of understanding. Then I thought, no. This is how it is. This is how it is now. Our clumsy way with words is how we sometimes get through life. I drove home thinking of Gina, how we would be together during the holidays. Christmas is one of my favorite times of the year. Then memories of long-past holidays started to crowd that out. A past life. Divorce. Loss comes in many forms, I thought, and grieving is a natural result. I held back my tears. I had to drive the car and get home.

Winter

The cure for pain is in the pain.
— *Rumi*

Winter. The dead of it. The bitterness and gray and cold of it.

I wrote John an email to confirm our next interview session for Wednesday, December 29. I wanted to be sensitive to his schedule, his family, during this time of year. In the best of circumstances the holidays and their attendant activities can be stress-filled. I told John we could keep this interview session brief. We did. We spoke for fifty-three minutes. I looked at the audio file later to see for myself how long we'd talked. But as we talked that day it seemed to me that there was a vacuum around us, as if we'd both been lifted outside of time, for John to share his experiences of Thanksgiving and Christmas with his boys, his family.

I drove to his house late afternoon. Cold. Gray sky.

I started the interview as I normally would, with a simple question. I was not prepared for his answer. How could I be? This was John's new life. And I didn't think about how else I might start except to ask what one would normally ask in this circumstance: "How was Christmas?"

And what was normal about this circumstance? John looked at me and said, "You're really asking me that question?"

I shrugged. His look, his eyes. Something was terribly wrong and it immediately set me on edge. I said yes, it's a common question this time of year, isn't it?

John said, "Yes, yes it is common. Well, I'll answer it for you then. It was horrible. Christmas Day was fucking horrible."

—

And I'll get to Christmas in a minute. First I want to share something that has been rattling around in my head.

The first week after Amy was killed, there were some people who came up to me—among the many who did—and they said, "God has a plan," or, "There's a reason for this; we can't know what that is, but you have to trust that there's a higher purpose served." It took all the energy and self-restraint I had in those moments to not strangle them. It's interesting to me to compare what I think and feel about that, those words, that type of "comforting" thought, then and now.

At that time, immediately after her death, when I'd hear, "God has a plan," I'd think, fuck that God—and *any* God—who has a plan that includes the violent death of my wife, the mother of our two young boys. That's a fucked plan. I don't *want* to be part of *that* plan. The God I believe in, to the extent I believe in a God, does not make plans that work that way.

And any "higher purpose" out of this? It's incomprehensible to wrap my mind around that.

Now—eight months later to the day—it's not that I believe there's a plan, or that God has a purpose. I still don't believe that. But I have to acknowledge that one of the things that separates us from other creatures is our ability to see cause and effect.

This is basic evolutionary biology. This cognitive ability separates us from most animals, and it conveys a certain advantage. Ten thousand years ago you're on the plain and you see footprints going in a particular direction. You can conclude that there must be animals in that direction; there must be food that way. So you understand the cause and effect and you make a good decision. Our ability to learn makes us better predators, better hunters. Or, you hear thunder. You know to take cover, because there's going to be lightning or bad weather. Simple things like that, which we take for granted now. But our ability to identify cause and effect is so greatly refined and such a driving part of how we behave as human animals that when there is no cause-and-effect relationship we seek one out, or even create it. I think the alignment of stars, horoscopes, and other belief structures are oftentimes created to explain the inexplicable. It's as if we crave it, this cause-and-effect relationship. It's almost as if, in a vacuum of cause and effect, we will *create* cause and effect.

Amy's death has no sense; it has no meaning, all by itself.

But I can feel this need, building in me now, to create sense and meaning of it, to create reason and purpose; otherwise, it remains senseless and meaningless. It's a post hoc cause-and-effect creation, if you will.

Now I find myself not so much believing that there's a greater purpose or plan, but that I have somehow been called in this strange, horrible way to do something that uses Amy's death as a leverage point. It's a burden, really. But also a calling. I feel called to do something on behalf of Amy that I wouldn't otherwise have done. What that is I don't yet exactly know.

I've thought about my future and my career—I have a nice, safe job, but is "a nice, safe job" preventing me from honoring life in a way that I feel I need to? I've been successful as an IT professional, but there have been many times over the years when I've wondered if there might be more fulfilling career choices. I've always had a passion for doing work for the environment.

Protecting our world. Something that has more meaning but probably pays a lot less. Or even volunteer work. But how much is really possible if I continue to spend eight hours a day, five days a week at my current job?

So I'm trying to work through what this all means, and in the end I wonder if, after the fact, I create an "effect" from this "cause," does that in fact mean there actually was "a plan" or "a purpose"? Predestination? I keep going round and round, and it's an ongoing conundrum, and it makes my head hurt.

I've had a couple of images in my mind lately, to help me sort through this, to try to make some sense of it, to help make it fit.

One image is the lodgepole pine. Lodgepole pines are long and straight, and fairly common out west. They got their name because Native Americans used them to build tepee lodges. They're a fire-friendly tree—they depend on fire to replace themselves. It's as if this tree has evolved and adapted in collaboration with fire. Its cones are so hard that the seed can only be released from the pinecone in fire. The forest must be destroyed to be used as fuel for the fire in order to create new life. And now I wonder if Amy's death is not my forest fire.

I was reading a *National Geographic* not too long ago that was just lying around the house; it was the May 2010 issue, which probably would have arrived the week before Amy was killed. There was an article on Mount St. Helens, and the area around it. It has been about thirty years since the eruption of the volcano there. What had been pristine streams and lakes was utterly laid to waste—acres and acres, square miles of trees destroyed, toxic metals spewed into the air. And what is it now? Now there are meadows, and the streams are running clear with trout, and new life has sprung forth.

None of this is surprising. We know this story of death and regeneration, especially with the fertile soils at the foot of the volcano, because all these minerals and nutrients have just been disgorged from the center of the earth. Destroying the area around it has set the preconditions for new life.

That is an image I'm holding in my mind now, at this moment, this sense that we've just lived through a forest fire, or complete destruction from a volcano. And so I wonder, what new life is created out of Amy's death? It's important for me to hold on to this, because if I don't, it means that death wins. And death can't win. Life has to win.

I was sharing this story with a friend, and he said, "There's a Zen koan that says, 'My barn has burned down, and now I can see the moon.'"

I smiled at that. I thought, sure, my barn has burned down. I don't know if I can see the moon just yet, but I get it.

I get it.

I'm confident this is how Amy would want us to view this. She was all about life, especially her later work; it was *all* about *new* life.

There's a new burden now, of having to fulfill and honor her pledge. But whatever the energy of life, or nature, that creates new lodgepole pines, or new meadows of flowers on the slopes of Mount St. Helens—the equivalent has to be the energy that comes from those of us who are still here.

It's me and the boys.

—

Now let's talk about Christmas. Which, as I said, was horrible. It was simply horrible. Back in August and September, both my shrink and the family therapist were saying to me, "The holidays are coming up. They're going to be tough. What's your plan? Who's coming to visit?" I didn't have an answer for them. I didn't know. I wasn't even *thinking* about the holidays at all back then. I was trying to survive, and they were trying to get me to be prepared.

Yeah. Be prepared.

How could I prepare?

In the circle of widows and widowers I've connected with, this is a theme—how difficult the holidays can be. I'd never understood it. I'd never had to think about it. I'd always enjoyed the holidays. Thanksgiving was always my favorite holiday. And even though the spirit and meaning of Christmas had faded for me since childhood, I would still get that warm feeling inside as the holidays were approaching, with the lights and decorations and Christmas carols. And I suppose I understood, intellectually, that the holidays could be hard, for some. But I'd never had that experience before. I'd never given it much thought.

We weren't prepared for it.

Thanksgiving was a small gathering. My sister and her family visited from New Jersey, and Amy's brother and his family. I was expecting a larger gathering, but for a variety of reasons my other family members had conflicts and couldn't make it. So that was a little disappointing, coloring my mood. Surrounding myself with family as I'd intended wasn't happening.

We gathered around the table to say the blessing ... and what do you say?

I don't remember exactly what I said. Something about how this was a difficult Thanksgiving, and the deep loss we feel is a measure of the deep love we've had in our lives. Something to that effect, and I was getting choked up as I spoke.

I noticed Adam had crawled underneath the table and was hiding. I knew he was crying. He does that when he's embarrassed or shy. He doesn't want anyone to see him. So I took him into his room, and we held each other and cried. Just cried.

What do you say? What can you say? "It's going to be okay"? You can't say that.

After a while he asked me, "Daddy, not that this is gonna happen, but what happens if you die?"

I wasn't expecting that. Not then. But I did have an answer.

I said, "That's an important question." I explained to him that I'd made arrangements with friends of ours who live nearby to take care of them, and he and Bryan could go to the same school and the same church and have the same friends.

He said, "But how will they know if you die?"

I said, "Well, my mom or dad would call, and people would call."

"But what if it happens at night?" And then I understood what he was getting at—what if no one else is around but him and Bryan when I die?

"Well, Adam, that's when you need to call 911. Call for help."

That's a heavy conversation for any day, let alone Thanksgiving day.

I had been planning to tell my kids at some point about the arrangements I had made—for guardianship care and *what if* scenarios—but I could never quite figure out how to start the conversation with them. I mean, how is that supposed to go? "Now that Mom is dead, here is what you need to know in case I die." So he initiated it. On Thanksgiving Day, of all days, goddammit. We should have been eating turkey and pumpkin pie and watching football, not talking about my death. Not crying because Mom was gone.

And then Christmas.

You know, you take that last bite of pie on Thanksgiving and Christmas starts up right away.

We got the Christmas tree. I was expecting this to be tough. I tried to gird myself for it. For us it had always started with the tree, the family, and rituals we had around the tree, and that meaning, that symbolism. When

Amy was here, sometimes we'd all go get the tree. Sometimes I'd get the tree. Sometimes I'd take the boys and get the tree. This year I ordered a tree from a guy in town who has a farm up in Pennsylvania. We went and picked it up after school one Wednesday, a couple weeks before Christmas. Got it home, put it in the stand. I pulled all the boxes out of the attic that had the Christmas decorations, the stockings, lights, *everything*.

Usually I'd do the lights and Amy would do the ornaments. She liked doing the ornaments with the boys. There's an ornament with each of our names on it. And there are ornaments that say, "Adam's first Christmas," and "Bryan's first Christmas," and all those clichéd, classic ornaments— glass balls and the homemade paper snowflakes. So now I was pulling them out of the boxes that Amy had so nicely labeled and organized and put in bigger boxes, to protect them. And as I was doing this I saw her handwriting, of course, and I was pulling out ornaments that had belonged to her grandparents, these family heirloom pieces, and it all hit me at once. I had to leave the room and go into the kitchen to cry. It wasn't so much that I didn't want the boys to see me cry; they've seen me cry plenty of times now. But they seemed happy, actually, in that moment, as we were busy with the tree and the lights and decorations. They were feeling that joy and anticipation of Christmas, and I was feeling loneliness and despair. The commingling of their joy and my despair was too much.

I think that's part of what makes the holidays even more difficult than average days. When you peel back the veneer of commercialism—and it really isn't that hard to do—there *are* these symbols of new life and celebration that we have built up around this season, what with the lights, the giving, the sense of family and celebration. Now those are all intertwined with the sadness and loss and loneliness and grief I'm feeling. The spectrum of emotion runs from one extreme to the other; it's a lot to handle. Not that I ever, ever want to feel again what I felt this past summer, but in some ways that was simpler, because it was all heavy grief and despair. There was no "season of joy" or celebration mixed in with it. The grief and despair is not as heavy now, for sure, but it is still there. Only now it's commingling with other—I guess you'd have to call them "positive"—emotions. And then there are the not-so-subtle messages from our culture and the media about what a joyful time of year this is. Trying to untangle all of it? I don't even know if it's worth doing, or even possible. I think I have to just let it all ride.

Over the years our Christmases have unfolded like many families', I imagine. There are all the questions of where to go. Whose family do we go visit? Do we stay home? Many years ago Amy's parents divorced, and they have their separate families. Bonnie and Donald are in Virginia, and Amy's dad, Jim, and his wife and daughter are in Atlanta. So we essentially had four Christmases: our nuclear family Christmas, Christmas with my parents and siblings in New Jersey, Christmas with Amy's mom and her family, and Christmas with Amy's dad and his family.

Four Christmases.

It sounds complex, but we had a fairly manageable routine. Once my siblings and I had reached adulthood, we found ourselves in constant negotiations over who was going to be around, who was going where, and when, and with whom, and all that stuff. I forget how far back it was—seven, eight years ago—when my mom finally said, "Look. Here's what we're going to do—we'll have the Robinette family Christmas the weekend *before* Christmas Day, in New Jersey. We'll celebrate then, so you can all deal with the in-laws however you want."

That was great, because it fixed one variable. We knew where we were going to be the weekend before Christmas.

It was nice to see everybody in my family. But Amy's death hung over everything. Whether we're watching the Charlie Brown Christmas special, or making cookies, or if I'm cutting out paper snowflakes with the boys for one of their school projects, there is the undeniable sadness hanging over each—otherwise—joyful occasion. Not just for me, but for others.

People, not just family, but friends, too, they'll say to me, "Merry Christmas," or "Happy New Year." It's just what you say to people. But I can sense as they're saying it they're thinking, "Shit. Is that the right thing to say to John? What do I say?"

Yeah. What do you say? It's not very merry. It's not very happy.

Now some people would say, "Oh man. The holidays. How are you doing? It must be so hard for you during the holidays."

I'd feel like saying, "Yeah, it really sucks. Thanks for reminding me."

I can't blame them, though, because there's nothing anyone can say to me right now. Nothing really works.

It stirs everything up, either way.

Maybe we could just say to one another, "Wishing you peace." That wouldn't be bad.

One friend called and said, "Hey. Just wanted to call and see what a friend could do for you during the holidays." That was good.

But we don't really have good social conventions for this in present-day America. I am now more cautious about saying "Merry Christmas" and "Happy New Year" flippantly, which is what we're supposed to say, to everyone we meet, but I now know how it is not "merry" or "happy" for a number of people.

So, we were in New Jersey. We did the Robinette family Christmas. It was the typical controlled chaos, because there are now seven grandkids, and it's pretty loud and rambunctious, but it's good. It was good to see the kids running around the way they do. As the evening was winding down, I was thanking my dad, and I was thanking my mom, and I gave her a hug. From nowhere I could feel it coming out, and I started crying, holding on to my mom. I don't know how long it went on. For a while. It was a while. Several minutes of just sobbing and holding her. She holding me.

I think back to last year and how it was my last Christmas with Amy, and I didn't know it. I didn't know that Christmas 2009 would be my last Christmas with my wife, the last Christmas my boys would have a mom.

Now I'm thinking, Goddammit, that's gonna happen *again*. Someday there's going to be another "last Christmas" with somebody I care about. I mean, I'm still young; I've got four siblings, and they're all married or partnered, and there are seven grandkids. I have my two parents. There are seventeen people right there in my immediate family. I don't know what the actuarial odds are, but one of these years it'll be the "last Christmas" I spend with *some*body I care about and I won't know it. Odds? Actually, it's a certainty, unless I have the good fortune of going first. That's the only way I wouldn't have to suffer through this again.

So part of the sadness during the holidays was this wave of awareness that came over me. As I went through the *firsts*—the first Thanksgiving, the first Christmas, the birthdays, and every other holiday—I could think back to the *last* one. And I started to wonder what I would have done differently had I known. Would I have done something differently? Would we have constructed those days, those events, differently? Then I started picking through memories of last Thanksgiving and Christmas for moments of discord or disharmony, small little conflicts, and I was left wondering whether they would have come up if we had only known that was it—the *last* one.

One popular philosophy these days is about living life now, in the moment, in the present. Seize the moment. Carpe diem. I think we say those words without really knowing what they mean. Not *really* knowing. But why don't we act that way? What if you knew? What if this was the last day you had? What if this was the last Christmas? The last New Year's Day? Is the way we treat one another consistent with that philosophy? Or is the weight of being truly awake to the thought, the mere possibility, that this could be our last Christmas together too much for our minds to handle? Would that knowledge be so great as to render us paralyzed with fear?

None of us knows our final hour, but we all know we *have* a final hour, with certainty. So we have that precognition of our own mortality. The question is: Are we fully honoring that knowledge of our own, and our loved ones', mortalities?

My mom and I held on to each other, and I needed that.

To hold her.

For her to hold me.

And just cry.

—

So Christmas Part One was done. Christmas Part Two was our nuclear family, the boys and I. On Christmas Day, in the past, we'd wake up, do our presents, and in the afternoon we'd drive over to Amy's mom and Donald's and have the next round of Christmas there, and dinner. Christmas Part Three.

Leading up to it, I was trying to imagine how it would go. It was hard to predict, because some of the most lighthearted things have turned into the most heavy. For example, I had four stockings in one of the Christmas decorations boxes, and there was an "Amy" stocking there. What do I do with Amy's stocking? Do I hang it up? Do I put something in it, or not? These were questions I hadn't anticipated wrestling with, and here they were, staring at me. Burdening me. It's just a stocking, but for a moment I was paralyzed. In the end I decided to hang her stocking, but getting to that decision was draining.

As I was hanging the stockings, I wondered who was going to buy me a present for Christmas morning. It's not that we were extravagant; I think our Christmases were pretty modest. Rarely were there big surprises under the tree for Amy and me. We'd gotten to that point in our marriage that most couples get to, I think, where we were comfortable saying to the other person, "Look, here are the three or four books from Amazon I might be interested in, and maybe get me a Kindle this year, or I need new batteries and socks." We'd gotten to that point, and it was okay. But Amy was still pretty good about finding something that wasn't on my list—not necessarily a big thing, but something nice, something thoughtful. That's how she was. And she always orchestrated whatever gifts the boys would have gotten for me.

I thought, "Man, I'm going to be sitting there watching the boys open their presents, and how's that going to feel, not having anything?" So I thought about it for a moment and then went out and bought myself a new camera, wrapped it up, and stuck it under the tree, just so I'd have something to open Christmas morning.

—

Christmas Eve, the boys and I had returned home from church; I'd put them to bed, and it was very lonely in the house. I felt very alone, and I did not sleep well. Bryan had bad dreams and crawled into bed with me in the middle of the night, so I was not well rested. When I woke up Christmas morning, it was very present with me, the loneliness. I could just tell this was going to be a miserable day.

The boys got up. We unwrapped our presents. I think the boys enjoyed what they got, for the most part. Santa brought them gerbils, which was cool. The boys liked that. But there were no real toys, like traditional toys they could play with right away. At some point Adam made a remark about it, and he started crying that he didn't get what he wanted. It was so sad, seeing him cry.

But it set me off.

There was so much going on in my head. I was fatigued from not sleeping well. I was trying to cope with my own feelings of despair and loneliness and sadness. I'd been struggling to maintain my own energy level, as a parent, for some time—to be patient and understanding and help them work through their own emotions and reactions surrounding their mom's death. Any parent can tell you the level of energy you need for kids on a regular, normal, daily basis is pretty darn high, even in the best of circumstances. And if you don't have that level of energy, for whatever reasons, you can snap at them, cut them short. You don't mean to do it; you don't want to. It's just hard. And this was one of those days when I knew I was *not* operating on all cylinders.

So Adam started up with this thing about the toys, and I got angry. How *dare* he be upset that he didn't get what he thought he ought to get? I wanted so badly to say something about his dead mother—but I knew that would be the worst possible thing, ever.

That's what was in my mind, though.

He and his brother got into a fight over something stupid. Exasperated, I just sent them both straight to their rooms. It was the "he-started-it-first" routine, and I couldn't get a straight answer out of either one of them, and I did not want to deal with it. I was frustrated and angry, and I was starting to feel bad, physically.

I was becoming aware of the lightheaded, dizzy feeling I hadn't had in months. It was that feeling I'd had early in the summer, when everything had been askew by ten degrees. Everything listing. Right angles didn't exist. Colors were flushed out of the surroundings. That feeling was coming back, that I was starting to lose it, and it was just the three of us in the house.

I was thinking, "Fuck. I am *not* gonna make it. I am absolutely *not* going to make it through Christmas day." And then I'd have to drive over to Amy's mom's house for the next round of this?

The thought of it was nearly unbearable. But I had to do it.

Somehow we made it through the morning, and I got our shit together just enough to get in the car. I was barely holding it in. Trying not to fall apart in the car, crying, driving over.

Yeah.

Goddamn.

God-fucking-dammit.

As I was driving I started doing the math: We'll get over there about 3:45. I know we'll stay for a few hours, probably until 8:30-ish. That'll give me almost five hours to get drunk, then let my body detox enough so I can drive back home safely. If I can get four or five glasses of wine in me in the first hour, we'll be good.

First thing I said at the door: "Where's the wine?" I was very much aware and deliberate of my intention to medicate. Alcohol's a convenient, socially acceptable way to do it. I'm not necessarily proud of it, but good ol' Larry can be helpful.

The boys were mostly fine. We opened gifts, had dinner, then the kids started playing. By then I'd switched from wine to coffee. I left the gathering and walked down to the basement, and there were pictures of Amy along a wall of when she had been a little girl, up through college, different parts of her life. Then from nowhere, it flooded over me: the utter incomprehensibility of what has happened.

Why must it be this way? Why had I been asked to suffer through this? Why was this my suffering? I know we all have our suffering, but this particular suffering—losing Amy—why?

I just didn't get it. Everything was confusing again.

I was standing by myself looking at the pictures of Amy when Bonnie walked up to me, and I asked her, "Why? Why is this what we have to have?" We both started crying, and holding each other. It was overwhelming, thinking about our loss. My boys can never have another mother, and Bonnie can never have another daughter. My God, what would it feel like to lose a child? And, my God, to grow up without a mom?

All those thoughts were swirling with my own feelings of anguish and despair, and I was feeling my boys' loss maybe more than my own in that particular moment. And I started thinking, how do I compensate for this? How *can* I compensate for the death of their mother? How do I structure a life so that they can come to their own terms with her death? I mean, that's the role of a parent, *period*—to create structure for children to figure out life, for themselves. We want to help them and care for them and do everything we can for them, but at some point we all know that they have to go out on their own and seek their own way. We all figure out parenting on our own, to a large degree, but I certainly didn't expect to have to incorporate this—the loss of their mother—into their understanding of life.

And I was thinking about Bonnie.

God.

How do you come to terms with losing a child? Can you? Can you come to terms with losing a child?

So we got home, and I had to get the boys to bed. I was tired, and it was getting late. Adam started up again with how he didn't get what he was expecting or what he wanted. He didn't get any toys.

I said, "Well, we've been to three of the four Christmases. You've still got Grandpa Jim." That was Christmas Part Four, with Amy's dad and his family. There could be some relief there, I figured. At that point, I didn't want to engage in anything. I felt everything piling up on me: the fatigue from lack of sleep the night before, the fatigue of the burn-off of the alcohol, and my own disorientation with everything.

But he was being persistent.

And I lost it. I looked straight at him, raised my voice, and said, "Adam, we don't get everything we want. *Ever*. Understand?"

He looked a little chilled by that.

I was angry. I continued. "It's just that way, so get used to it," I said. "I didn't get what I wanted for Christmas."

He asked me, "What did you want for Christmas?"

I hesitated, then confessed, "I wanted your mom back."

Now we were both crying.

And something must've flipped in Adam's mind, because he started apologizing, saying how sorry he was, how he didn't know, and how he was a bad kid.

It was horrible. It was just absolutely fucking horrible.

I'd let my anger take over and felt like I had laid my entire burden on him, so now he was suffering my anguish, too, and realizing the weight of what we now bore.

I knew all along, on some level, that it had never really been about the toys he didn't get. I knew that. He just cried and cried and cried. And I cried, too.

It was devastating.

—

So people ask me, "How was Christmas?"

What do you say to that? What can you say to that?

"It was fine. Kids got gerbils."

No. It was fucked. It was completely fucked up.

We survived it. And are still surviving it. Earlier today we had Christmas Part Four, with Amy's dad and his wife, who were driving from the Berkshires, heading back to their home in Atlanta. They stopped by; we had a nice lunch and exchanged gifts I don't remember. And that went fine, actually.

By this point we've all been wrung out pretty well. Amy's stepmom is having a hard time with it. She's finding things that Amy had given her for past Christmases, or on other occasions. I imagine we're all going through similar things. Amy and her mom were both good at keeping and reusing certain boxes and Christmas bags and things like that.

I'll pull out these old Christmas bags with her handwriting on them. Or the bag will say "To: Amy, From: Mom," or "To: Mommy, From: Adam and Bryan." Things like that. Goddamn, I'll think. There it is again. That was the last Christmas.

So they were right. Holidays suck. I'm glad Christmas is over. I'm glad Thanksgiving is over. And I'll be really happy to say "Fuck you" to 2010 on New Year's Day. Now I've got to get through New Year's Eve, and then January 22 is her birthday. And after that it's April 29. And we'll have completed the year.

Then we can do it all over again.

—

I sat dumbfounded, watching John, listening to him tell his story.

We talked for fifty-three minutes, barely the length of a TV show. Time enough for me to hear John's story of a holiday season shattered by loss and by grief. Time enough for John to tell me what he and his boys had gone through, were going through, without Amy, in this holiday sea-son—the season of family, the season of joy, of renewal. Worlds destroyed, worlds made new. When I got to my car I sat behind the wheel and wept for a good long time. I questioned myself again. Why am I doing this, these interviews—*this*? Why am I putting both of us through *this*? I felt ashamed for probing my friend's wounds so deeply.

On the way home I thought about the lodgepole pine John had talked about and how it needed fire to release its seeds, to make new life. I thought about Christmas and the birth of a child sent into the world to take away the sin of the world. God sending Himself in human form to die, to make new life. I prayed for John and his boys. I prayed for us all. When I got home I hugged Gina longer than I usually would have, and we talked about things we usually would not have. That was John's gift to me:

a renewed understanding of the brief and precious time we spend on earth with one another.

In a few weeks the new year had come and gone and now it was into February. I needed to sit with John for another set of interviews.

I'd been thinking about John and his boys a lot since our last session. Driving home from his house last December, I had prayed there would be renewal in their lives. I did not know what to ask for exactly beyond that—simply: renewal. I gave them up to God in my prayer to work out the details.

In late January, a week or so after Amy's birthday, I contacted John to set up our next round of sessions. I thought two different dates should do it. He agreed. We settled on a Friday night, February 11, for our first, and a week later, February 18, for our second. I phoned John the night before to confirm our session. He said we were still on, and he was really looking forward to talking. He said he had a lot on his mind, such as how he and the boys had celebrated Amy's birthday recently, and he wanted to discuss some things that had been weighing heavily on him since the new year. I said we could talk about anything. Amy's birthday, his new life, God—everything that he usually kept packed away in some corner of his mind could be spilled out for examination. Opportunities that before he might have let pass now seemed ready moments for reflection.

I told him I was looking forward to our time together, to talk. I ended the call, questioning myself again about why my concern in that moment of talking with John had been for the project, and not for him. I had to keep reminding myself why I was doing this. My hope was to bring back something of value, something that would last, for others to see. I think, in the end, we all want to be recognized somehow, someway, as mattering to someone. That's the essence of our existence, isn't it? That who we are matters, what we do matters, that it lasts. So, for myself, then, I could admit that I was doing this to prove that I mattered, that what I did could last beyond me.

Through the tears, through the laughter, through the fear, through the joy.

I walked out of my home office and into the living room to look for Gina. I needed to cry with her and hold on to her, have us be together.

Let it last, I kept telling myself. Let it last. I kept telling myself that all night and into the next day and during the drive down to John's house.

Let it last, somehow.

John and I greeted each other; we hugged. Months earlier we had dropped handshakes as a greeting and instead hugged. Our hugs over the last interview sessions seemed bursting with meaning now, particularly as we were parting. We'd often linger and hold on to each other, as if we were holding on to life itself, as if we were afraid to let go. Knowing, perhaps, that we'd never see each other again. After all, this is how John had left Amy that April morning. He didn't think anything of it; he'd just left, so *certain* that he'd see her again later that day that he didn't even *think* about another possibility. But now both of us knew—there was that possibility. I think the weight of that realization filled our meetings, our interview sessions. How could it not?

As I was setting up our space for us to talk John told me he'd been thinking a lot about God and how it had affected his understanding, his ideas, his beliefs. He said with Amy's birthday he'd been thinking about God even more.

I couldn't imagine the pain of "celebrating" Amy's birthday without her. Who would she have been? I wondered. Who would she have become?

I wanted to start there. A birthday is a marker. I reminded John that we'd talked in earlier sessions about him "marking events" during this first year—the first Mother's Day, the boys' birthdays, their anniversary. I was wondering how he and the boys had marked Amy's birthday.

—

Amy's birthday was a couple of weeks ago. January 22. She would have been forty-three. Over the year, she would have been with me to see the boys' baseball games, the birthday parties over the summer. She would have been working on her birth center activities, seeing that move along. We would have gone to our summer marriage retreat, and she and I would have celebrated another wedding anniversary. Then Thanksgiving and Christmas and New Year's. But now? Not now. Nothing, now. I was preparing myself, mentally, for her birthday, but it was the day *before* when it all actually hit us.

We received in the mail some months ago a plaque from *The Washington Post*—her obituary. It's really nice, actually. The family gets a copy of the obituary, just how it was printed in the newspaper, with the photo and all the words, laminated onto hard board. I wasn't exactly sure what to do with it, so I'd just set it on the mantel, leaning against the wall.

Now it felt time to hang it up somewhere in the house. We've got a bunch of framed family pictures and a couple pieces of kid art from kindergarten and preschool framed and hanging in the stairwell going down to the basement, and I thought maybe that would be a good place for it—along with the other pictures of her and us and family and so on. I wanted the boys to be involved so that when they saw this new thing on the wall they wouldn't be surprised or upset and ask, "What's this?"

So I called them over. "Hey, boys, do you know what an obituary is?"

Bryan said he didn't know. Adam said, "I think I've heard of it, but I don't know what it is."

I explained what it was and I showed them the plaque. "This is your mom's obituary. The newspaper sent us this to hang up on the wall, and I'd like to hang it up in the stairwell here."

So I hung it up in the stairwell, and the boys were watching me.

Then Bryan asked me, "Daddy, what happens to someone when they die?"

I figured he was asking me the heaven question—I still don't know how to answer that question for myself—and I didn't want to just tell him that Mommy is in heaven. There is no good answer, as far as I'm concerned. There's *no* answer. So I gave him the best line I could, "We believe people live on in memories and thoughts and in the deeds they do. Some people believe that their spirit continues on."

He said, "No, for real, Daddy, what happens?"

I tried again, and Adam was just watching as I got twisted in this back-and-forth with Bryan about what *really* happens when you die.

Finally he said, "No, Daddy, when my mommy dies, do I still have a mommy?" *That* was his question.

I said, "Bryan, Mom is always going to be *your* mom. She's always *your* mommy, no matter what."

Adam started to cry, and I started to cry, and Bryan started to cry. We were in the stairwell and sort of tumbled out together up onto the kitchen floor, crying, holding on to each other for support so we wouldn't fall. We made it together and just sat there, the boys curled up next to me. I missed Amy so much right then, holding our boys. I wanted her to be there with me, to help me comfort them. I know that sounds crazy, but it's how I felt.

I held on to the boys; we held on to one another, and we cried. We were crying hard.

It was weird. I was in the middle of my own feelings of loss and grief, and then that was supplemented by my sense of Adam and Bryan's loss and grief, for what *they'll* never, ever have. Maybe someday I could have another partner, but they could never have their mom again. At the same time, something else was hitting me: seeing Bryan cry. I hadn't seen Bryan cry as much, but now there were tears, actual tears, coming out. Now, part of me was starting to feel a sense of relief. Relief that it was starting to come out for him. He'd been dealing with it like a five-year-old would, of course; I mean, he has a whole different understanding and response to this event than I do, or Adam does. In some ways I think his understanding of death is much purer, much simpler, maybe even healthier, than ours. Seeing him crying was encouraging to me, to know that he was feeling that way.

It's strange. It's a strange way to describe it. The last thing you want is to see your children suffering. And yet I knew that for him to come out on the other side of this, somehow, he would have to have moments of grieving like this.

Eventually the crying turned to quiet sobbing, and we started to wipe our eyes. We were still sitting there on the kitchen floor when Bryan asked, "Daddy, what happens if *you* die?"

Here we go again, I thought. I said, "You and your brother would go live with our friends." This was part of the planning I'd done with my lawyer over the summer. "I've talked to them, and I've made arrangements, and they would take care of you."

"Would we live in their house?"

"Probably."

"Would we keep our stuff?"

"Yeah, you'd keep all your stuff."

"And Baby, my teddy bear?"

"Yes, Baby, too."

"Will I still go to the same school?"

"You probably would be able to. That's something we're going to have to look at." And I was starting to get a little nervous, because then a whole series of other logistical questions started to pop up in my head that are, quite frankly, unanswerable. Would they *really* get to go to the same school if they lived with our friends? Those friends live in a different school district. Maybe there could be some kind of approval from the school, but then what? There is no bus that would take them. Could they take a cab? Would I have to provide in my will for this? I mean, who *knows* what would happen?

Then Bryan asked, "Daddy, what happens if *you* die while we're at school? How will anybody know?"

That's when it hit me. They'd had that same period of time that I'd had, but theirs was a little longer. They had gone off to school at 8:30 in the morning and got home at 5:30. They had eight hours, or so, of what seemed like normalcy, when in reality their world had been shattered. Do they go to school every day with this thought now? This *wondering*? Do they? I don't know. Maybe not every day, but it's there now. The possibility of it. *The* question: What happens if I go to school and Dad dies?

I told them, "Somebody would certainly know and let you know."

"But how would you really know?"

I didn't know. I don't know. I couldn't say, couldn't tell them, because who really knows? There *is* no certainty.

I told them, "There are a lot of people looking out for you—neighbors, church, friends. You'd be taken care of." And they would be.

But how do you answer that question?

It's exhausting. It's exhausting thinking about it.

I wanted to tell them something comforting, and reassuring, but at the same time, what can I say to really comfort and reassure anymore?

So that was the day before Amy's birthday. By the end of the day I was drained. A fair amount of the emotion of the day had already spilled out.

We woke up on Amy's birthday, and it was cold outside—eight-degrees cold. And the house felt unusually chilly. I checked the thermostat, and the house temperature was about fifty degrees. I quickly realized the furnace wasn't working. Which makes sense, because—of course! *That's* the day your furnace breaks.

I had to do something, and fast, because I'd made arrangements to have a sleepover for my boys with a few of their friends that night, and I'd invited their parents to hang out that night, too. I had learned my lesson; I didn't wanted to be alone on Amy's birthday.

So I woke up the morning of Amy's birthday expecting five boys to be sleeping over and also a gathering of adults, and there was no heat.

I pressed two portable electric heaters into service—one in the living room and one in the basement, and they were *struggling* to keep up.

I was thinking, "We're not gonna make it. It's gonna get cold, and I need heat."

I called the HVAC guys. They said, "Well, it's Saturday, but we can have somebody there about noon."

Emergency HVAC call. Saturday. Overtime. Yeah. I'm stuck. What are you gonna do? "Sure, come on out."

We had planned to go down to the National Zoo and release balloons. We had the party helium tank, and some lavender balloons left over from Mother's Day last year. So we were going to blow those up and go down to the zoo where Amy liked to go, especially with the boys, and let those go on her birthday.

Now, by the time we had gotten ourselves up and I had called the HVAC guy and all that, it was 9:30, and by the time we got our acts together it was pushing ten o'clock.

So I said, "Boys, here's the deal: We've got to go to the zoo, release these balloons, come back here to meet the furnace guys, and get ready for everybody coming over tonight."

Adam and Bryan said, "Dad, that seems like a long way to go. Do we have to go to the zoo?"

I said, "Well, your Mom liked the zoo. And she liked taking you there to see the pandas."

Then Adam asked, "Why can't we just go over to the middle school?"

I said, "Is that where you guys want to go?"

Bryan said, "Yeah. Let's go there."

"All right."

So we blew up the balloons with the helium tank, half a dozen, and drove to the middle school. We got there, and it was so cold and gray and breezy. I was immediately glad we hadn't driven to the zoo. It would have been miserable. We walked to the playground next to the school, near where we had come for Mother's Day, to let go of the balloons. We stood there for a moment and decided that they each would let go of two, and then I would let go of one, and then the three of us would let go of one together.

It was sad.

So sad.

We were silent as we let go of the balloons and watched as the wind carried them away. And we stood there, the three of us, as the purple balloons danced in the wind and faded one by one into the gray background of the sky.

Then I just said, with little emotion, "There they go. Happy birthday, Mom."

I blinked the tears from my eyes and squinted to watch the balloons bob and weave into the winter sky. I wiped my tears from my eyes and cheeks and tried to find the balloons again, but the wind had taken them up.

We stood there for a moment on the playground, then the boys decided to run down the big hill to where the soccer and baseball fields are. It's one of those hills where your legs start moving too fast for your body and you're always on the verge of falling head over heels. It's the kind of hill you like to run down, especially when you're a kid. So they were running down and then back up the hill, and I was watching them with a combined sense of joy and dread. Joy that they were able to have some fun after a rough day and a half. And dread that one of them would take a bad tumble and require a trip to the hospital, which is exactly the other kind of thing that happens on your dead wife's birthday when it's freezing cold outside and your furnace goes out. But then I just decided to ignore the dread, and I joined them. It felt like the right thing to do: run. Run down and run up and then run back down again screaming each time down. It was quite a workout, and after three or four I was struggling to make it back to the top. I gave the boys the "one more run down the hill then we're going" announcement. We made our way back to the car and went home.

The furnace guy got to the house a little after lunch. He went into the basement, took a look, called me down. He said, "This furnace. Have you been thinking about replacing it?"

Oh boy. "Well, no. I don't know. Should I?"

"This one is an older model, and it's hard to find parts for it. Parts are expensive." He was trying to soften me up for it.

What was I going to say? "Yeah, let's replace the furnace instead." No. That is not happening today; that would take more than just today to do. I need heat *tonight*. It was the thermocouple/pilot light piece. It was around $400, plus $150 just for the HVAC guy to walk through the door.

He was done in no time.

It was easy, for him, and $550 later we had heat.

That was her birthday.

—

I thanked John for sharing that story. I checked my notes and the one I'd written to myself to ask him about God. So I asked him about God.

"What about God?" John said.

"In a previous session you started talking about God. On the phone you said you wanted to talk about God. So, what about God?"

—

Growing up Catholic, I was told of the Judeo-Christian God, the God of the Bible, the New Testament variant, in particular. The loving God, the forgiving God, the guy we pray to for help and guidance and so on. In college, at Virginia Tech, I'd go to Mass—certainly not every weekend, but they had a Sunday Mass at four o'clock in the afternoon on campus. The hangover would be gone by then, and it was before the dining hall opened for dinner, so, especially in winter, when there was nothing else to do, I'd go to church.

And I remember this moment distinctly. We were reciting the Creed. "We believe in one God, the Father, the Almighty, maker of heaven and earth," and so on. Halfway through it I stopped. I don't remember if there was one particular phrase or word or something else that caused me to stop, but it just occurred to me that I was spitting these words out by rote without even really thinking about them, and what they mean, whether or not I actually believed them, or what was behind them.

It startled me. And I think that was maybe where it began for me— starting to question what I had always assumed were truths.

At the time I was doing a little bit of volunteer work for the Newman Community, the campus-based Catholic organization, helping the priest there with a computer database, and there were activities in the evenings and on Saturdays, times when we'd talk.

On one of these occasions I asked him some questions about salvation and heaven and non-Catholics. What happens to them? Those kinds of questions.

He said, "You ought to read what Vatican II has to say."

So he loaned me a copy of a Bible, this dog-eared paperback, and the preface was this write-up about Vatican II and what it had been about. I had always just thought of the Vatican II Council in the early 1960s as when the church decided to stop saying mass in Latin. But there was a lot more, like addressing its relationship with the modern world. It was enlightening for me.

It didn't talk about universal salvation, not at all really, but it gave some credence to other world beliefs and faiths, and it had a much broader—or maybe enlightened—view than I had been familiar with. And there were other things, like how to reconcile evolution into this Bible story.

I asked my priest about this, and he said, "Well, you know, let's not be so literal about the Adam and Eve story."

Oh, really?

Cool, I thought. I could get on board with that—that this was okay within the constructs of the Catholic Church, that our new scientific understanding could coexist with faith.

So I kind of set that aside for a little bit, but I liked it. Maybe I didn't need to be so literal about the Virgin Birth, either. With that, I could still hang on to my Catholicism and reconcile it with my understanding of how the world works.

It was my junior year, and I met and fell in love with the young woman I've mentioned. We started dating, and it got pretty serious, and we got engaged. After five years of engagement we finally married, and it started unraveling right then. In the end it didn't work out. After about three years of marriage we divorced.

As this process was unfolding, a lot of my questioning about the nature of things came back up again, especially as I started to face the concept of a divorce, because we had been married in the Catholic Church. And the concept of a divorce within the Catholic Church simply did not exist.

Somebody told me, "Well, given your situation, you could probably seek an annulment."

"Really?" This was news to me.

She explained, "Marriage is a contract, and contracts are only valid when both parties are of sound mind." Or whatever it was. "And you could make the argument that neither one of you was mature enough, or were entering the contract validly."

Though this relationship was crashing and burning, to annul it as if it had never existed seemed preposterous to me—insulting, actually. We had tried to make it work; we tried really hard. Hours and hours of therapy. Individual sessions and couples counseling. Group counseling. Weekend retreats. Books. Trips. I didn't want to discredit what we'd gone through, because it mattered to me.

I was also worried about how my family would view this. There was a lot wrapped up in going through a divorce in a Catholic family. It was really hard for me to tell my parents, but when I did, they were very supportive. Whatever shame and guilt I imagined would come down from them never really materialized. I think they could see more clearly than I could that the relationship hadn't been that great.

So as I was going through that I went through a round of searching and seeking and drew some pretty grim, nihilistic conclusions about the world. A quote I had read back in college kept coming back to me: "I stick my finger into existence and pull it out and it smells of nothingness." Who was that? Sartre? Kierkegaard? I can't remember.

For a while I thought, yeah, right on, I get that. Nothingness.

So I went to the local library and starting checking out books on philosophy and existentialism and Sartre, in particular, but it seemed all so depressing. I wasn't sure I wanted to hook my world philosophy to his wagon. So I set that aside, but I was still really angry—at God—and twisted up inside with all my questions and accusations: "How could I wind up in this situation?" and "I'm going through this horrible divorce," and, "This is really hard."

I was living in Northern Virginia at the time, and one day I went for a walk. It was late spring. She had finally moved out; we'd thought that with some time to ourselves we could then come back together. I'm not sure I really bought into that idea, but there I was, in an unraveling relationship, and alone. It was kind of muggy; there had just been some late afternoon showers. I was really depressed.

As I was walking, I put out a demand. "Okay, God. Now's the time. If there ever was a time, it's now. I need something from you. A sign—*something*—to let me know you're here, because I don't see you. I don't hear you. I don't feel you anywhere. I really need a sign."

And—I swear I'm not making this up—within moments, as I was walking, I came around the corner to see an amazing horizon-to-horizon double rainbow.

Wow.

For a moment I thought I would believe again. Truly, the timing of this rainbow was nothing short of miraculous. But my bitterness would not let me. Obviously, there is a scientific and statistical probability that these things happen, I told myself. It was late spring, and we had just had rain showers. This was actually a really obvious time for a rainbow to show up. It's just optics and physics, after all.

I pointed up at the sky and said out loud, right there on the street, "Is that all you got? That's too fucking clichéd. You're going to have to do better than that." I kid you not, that's what I said. Even if that had been the work of God, I could not accept it as such. A rainbow? *Really?* Come on.

But it left an impression on me. Yet even so, in my mind, I still had to make this rainbow's appearance a coincidence rather than the act of God, out to call my bluff.

Spring passed into summer and the six-month lease my wife had signed on her rental was nearly over. I probably would have entertained the idea of her moving back in, but she wasn't interested. I was starting to grow tired of the condo we had lived in. I decided I didn't want to live in the outer suburbs anymore. I wanted to move closer to the city, so she moved back into our condo, and I moved out to a new apartment in Arlington.

I had been in my new apartment maybe a month. It was late July, early August; she came over, and we went out to dinner for "the talk." She used the word "divorce" for the first time, and we both knew that it had come to an end. Our marriage was over.

I went back to my apartment. I was thinking about the "to do" list. We had to start the paperwork. It was just a matter of time now. And then it hit me. I started feeling really, truly alone—and lonely—in my apartment. I was scared. I was in a new apartment, a new town, and I didn't really know anybody. I was lying in bed, crying, and I thought that if there was ever a time to pray, now was the time. I didn't know if it could work; I didn't even know *how* to pray. What do you ask for? And I was also cautious about being too over-the-top with my prayer, like if I asked for too much, God wouldn't even consider it. I thought maybe I should start lowering my expectations. I didn't want to fix my marriage anymore, really. But I didn't know *what* I wanted. I didn't know what I needed.

Then it came to me. *I need courage.* I needed strength, too. And guidance. I thought, I need the strength to be courageous, and I needed guidance to get me down whatever this path is. I started reciting it over and over in my mind. Courage, strength, guidance. Courage, strength, guidance. A mantra. Over and over again as I lay in bed.

I fell asleep.

My memory of this is that I fell straight into a dream.

There was a man on a barren, rocky horizon, a black and white Martian landscape. He was walking to me. As he came closer I could see that he was in color, in contrast to everything around him. He kept walking to me, and as he came into focus he reminded me of the character Tevye in *Fiddler on the Roof*: stocky, heavyset, salt-and-pepper beard, with the thick belt and the Russian peasant look. But he was also wearing a southwest Native American poncho, all different colors.

He walked up to me and took my hand and said, "Don't worry. Everything will be okay."

He started to let go of my hand, and I squeezed his hand and said, "You can't leave right now."

He looked right into my eyes and said, "Don't worry, I'll be around. Everything will be okay."

I hesitated, and then reluctantly let go of his hand.

He turned and walked away, and there was a door that I hadn't noticed on this barren landscape. He walked through the door and disappeared.

I woke up in a cold sweat, my heart racing. I had this feeling I had been cleansed, like something had washed out of me. The terrors of being alone and being lonely and going through this life transition were still all there, but had diminished significantly.

I said to myself, "I think I'll go to church next Sunday."

I thought, that was my God. And—who knew?—my God is a Jewish milkman. There was comfort in that, a lot of comfort that there was something there, something around. I've shared that story with others, and gotten into little debates about what it meant—the King archetype, all the Jungian stuff. Maybe it wasn't actually an external actor God, but the internal archetype you need to be in contact with to help you through a difficult time. Maybe my mind created that image purely out of the synapses and chemicals in my brain, as a mechanism to overcome the emotional trauma I was going through at the time. Maybe I was so afraid of being alone that my brain had to create the image of someone who was there for me, telling me that everything would be okay. The brain is a pretty powerful organ; we know that. Why wouldn't it construct something that my body might use as medicine to get itself through this trauma?

At some point I started to wonder if it really even mattered. Did it matter if there was a God or not, if it manifested itself for me this way and helped me? I could have taken that superficial evidence at face value and not worried so much about how it had been created, either through a true external God or by my own psyche. Maybe He had actually been listening to me a few months earlier when I'd cursed Him out for the clichéd rainbow. Now, visiting me in a dream? Nice work!

Through the separation I'd been in a support group, and one time I had mentioned my Catholic upbringing, my questioning of that faith, and a woman there revealed she'd had a similar trajectory. She told me how she'd found comfort in Unitarian Universalism. So the morning after my God dream I looked up the nearest one and that Sunday, I went. It was in Arlington. I met a whole bunch of great people, including a woman I would end up dating pretty seriously for a while. She and I dated for two years, lived together for a year, and then it crashed and burned.

In hindsight, a lot of good came out of that relationship for me, but ultimately it hadn't been right for me, and, I suspect, for her. But when it ended, all the same stuff returned, all the stuff about being alone. When we moved in together I was starting to think maybe she was the one I could spend the rest of my life with. I knew it wasn't perfect, but we were in love, and I still had a strong desire to create a family with someone. But in the end we were moving in different directions, and she wasn't interested in creating a family. But we didn't realize all this until we had been living together, commingling our lives, and the breakup was hard. It wasn't as difficult as my divorce, but it was traumatic nonetheless—we had spent nearly three years together, building our hopes.

One day, soon after our breakup, I was driving, having those familiar feelings. Here I was at the end of another failed relationship; I was alone; I didn't feel loved. I was driving down the road—and what did I see?

A rainbow.

I had to pull off into a parking lot. I rolled down the window and leaned out and wept as I watched this rainbow. I didn't challenge God on His choice of symbols that time. I just wept.

It was there again.

This time, seeing that rainbow, I felt like things would be okay again. I didn't feel gratitude, necessarily. It was more a sense that I'd been through this before, and I could get through this again. I had a strong sense that a God figure was manipulating events to create that rainbow.

Fast forward another dozen years, and here I am facing the loss of my relationship, but on a scale I could never even imagine, would never *want* to imagine. The reasons for the loss are vastly different than before, but all the questions I had set aside earlier in my life are now as present with me as ever. The boys have asked me—where's Mommy? Now, over the past decade, just *living*, just sort of seeing how life unfolded, I can say that we had a great life. And my thoughts about "God or not God" had moved toward a naturalist god, the god of nature, Gaia. That is, God is all; we are actually God as much as each cell in my body is me. In a similar way I see that I am a cell of God, in that regard. I would say "God is the universe" as opposed to this external, third-party actor as He's described in the Bible and the body of literature we have created over thousands of years to explain the nature and cause of our existence.

Having meditated on this over time, God, for me, took on a less personal manifestation. The God who walked in the garden with Adam and Eve was not my experience of God, even though He shook hands with me in my dream. After attending the Arlington Unitarian Universalist church, I attended the Universalist National Memorial Church for a while. Inscribed on the wall behind the pulpit is text from 1 John: "God is love; and he who dwells in love dwells in God, and God in him." That made sense to me. And it has become a simple substitution for me; when I hear someone talk about God I replace the word in my mind with "love." And it fits with my understanding of our modern, science-oriented understanding of the universe.

That's where my theology was trending; then Amy got killed.

And I had to explain this to my boys.

It's hard to explain that all the particles and atoms in our bodies were created from the explosion of stars thirteen or fourteen billion years ago and that the random assemblage of life created this miraculous human being, their mom, and now she's dead, and those particles are returning back to where they came from and will be reabsorbed and continue on in a cycle of never-ending life. And it's her creation of love that endures in the universe and is what we can hold on to.

How do you explain that to a four-year-old and a seven-year-old?

I had never completely abandoned the God of my childhood, or even the concept of heaven. And right after Amy died there was this strong tug to want to believe in an afterlife. A place where she is and where we would meet again, with a benevolent God who would look down and protect me and the boys. I wanted there to be a spirit world, a heaven, where Amy's soul was looking down. Within the first couple of weeks I wanted to give my kids a structure in their minds of something that they could latch on to; after all, there is comfort in that version of what happens after we die.

So that day, the day Amy died, the story was this: Mommy's in the spirit world. Adam has subsequently talked about how Mom's in heaven with God. Whether I believe that or not is less relevant, because that's what *I* believed when I was eight years old. And I think that's okay. He can believe that, and if he comes to a new belief when he's twelve or sixteen or thirty or fifty, that's okay, too.

And I really, really wanted to believe that Amy was in a spirit world, that she could look down on us and see us and enjoy—however the soul of a person enjoys—the growth of her two boys and grandchildren and seeing all that. Because that's what she wanted from life.

The notion of Amy's sentient spirit being somewhere would have been comforting for two reasons. First, it would have allowed her to experience, somehow, those experiences she had otherwise been denied. Because it was too painful for me to consider that she wouldn't be able to experience the birthdays and the graduations and so on. Second, it would have been comforting because I could then see our separation as temporary. Because, someday, when I die, we would reunite in the spirit world, heaven, or some other plane of existence. I could see my loneliness as being temporary.

I really wanted to grab on to that concept. Then I started thinking about it a little bit more, and I'm not sure I could think of any worse damnation for someone than to see the suffering of those they left behind. And to have a sentient spirit that can experience the graduations and birthdays and all the other beautiful times here on Earth, *and* all the times of our suffering—I think that has to be part of that philosophy. That is, if you believe that our loved ones are in heaven or the afterlife and from that place they can bear witness to our joy, then they must also bear witness to our grief. So if you have just died, and are sentient and can see us grieving, you must feel tremendous sorrow, to just be *snatched* out of life and then to see those you left behind in such pain.

I can't abide that. I cannot abide by that. To imagine that kind of suffering for Amy was intolerable. So I had to abandon that concept, because it was too painful for me to think of her that way. Of her bearing witness to our pain.

I'd mentioned this to a couple people, and their responses were something like, "In the vastness of eternity, our lives are just a blip, and your separation from her in this world will pass quickly for us and for her." Or they said, "We are in an imperfect world, and we can't apply human emotions and sentiments to *that* other place."

Well, I thought, *exactly*. Human sentiments—the sense of missing the birthdays or the graduations, or of seeing the boys, or of her being there for me when I die—don't apply anymore.

So you're going to tell me the time span of all eternity is incredibly vast. And for the spirit world this suffering is just a moment, here and gone. It is overwhelmed by that vastness of time and the great peace and light that you exist in. *And* those who have died are able to experience these earthly moments of joy and pain and suffering. If you're saying all of those things, then it is finally making sense. You can't have all of that without the other. You either have it all—the suffering *and* she's waiting in heaven for when I die *and* she also experiences the birthdays and the joys and pain and suffering *and* whatever else—or she doesn't. I don't see how there can be love without suffering, because those two things are joined together like twins. Suffering and love.

So the whole notion of that comforting afterlife, where we can rejoin each other in some eternal love or grace, must also coexist with an awareness of suffering. That "happy heaven" place can't exist without continued suffering. But you might say, "Well, the physical rules don't apply in the afterlife," to which I loop back to, "Then why did God create this place of suffering for us?" Yes, there is beauty and love, but there is lots of suffering.

So I came back around to "no God." The concept of the loving, forgiving God—not only does that *not* make sense, all the evidence is actually to the contrary. *All* the evidence. It's not so much that God does not exist, it's that the New Testament God does not exist. The forgiving God, the loving God. Now, that Old Testament, son-of-a-bitch God? *That's* my God. It's the wrathful, vengeful, fuck-you God of the Old Testament. The one who is taking bets with Satan to see how far He can push Job. Think of that story. If I believe in that Old Testament asshole God, then maybe that Job story should have me nervous now, because we know where it goes, right? God doesn't end with just one tragedy for Job. He comes back for more. And the bet God has with Satan for me—He starts this all by taking my wife at the hand of a truck driver. What's next? Will He come for my house and my kids? Isn't that it? I'm going to come home and my house is going to be burned to the ground with my two sons inside. Luckily, I don't have slaves and goats like Job, because they'd be gone next. So I have this sense of waiting for the other shoe to drop because that's how *that* story goes. I'm lying naked in the street with nothing, abandoned by my friends. It's Job's fault, because he didn't worship enough, or he didn't believe in God enough. If that is God, at best that is a petty, adolescent God.

Last year, middle of July, we took a trip, the boys and me, to the Unitarian Universalist Mid-Atlantic Community—UUMAC—up near Allentown, Pennsylvania. Whatever summer travel plans we originally had were all gone, and I felt like I had to do something at some point and not just sit at home with the boys all summer. So we registered and went. It was our first trip without Mommy, without my wife. And getting there was hard. The simple logistics of packing up and traveling solo with two kids was its own challenge.

There were times when we were driving that I'd look into the passenger seat, and there'd be a bag of food there, and no Amy, and I'd think back on all the road trips we'd taken together. She had always sat there when we traveled somewhere. And now I'd look, and she was not there, but I could imagine her sitting there.

I'd nudge her. "Which exit do we take?"

She'd be the navigatrix. "Oh, no! You were supposed to turn off at that exit back there!"

Or I'd reach over and rest my hand on her leg, squeeze her thigh, and she'd grab my hand. Or the boys would start getting into some scuffle in the back seat, and she could get them squared away and I could keep driving, or she would hand out the snacks, pour drinks for the kids, keep them entertained. Not this time. This time I had to pull off the road, or risk reaching back with food or drinks, to do those "Amy things."

We managed, the three of us, but I realized it was going to be different from then on to not have her riding along. Because that's where she was supposed to be. A year ago we had driven up to Niagara Falls, and I can still see her so clearly, sitting there with her sunglasses on, her brown hair pulled back with a hair band, probably falling asleep.

—

UUMAC was held at DeSales University, a small Catholic school near Allentown. There were a number of people from our church going, and other Unitarian Universalists from the mid-Atlantic area. The event had daily workshops and services, day trips in the afternoon, and evening meals together in the dining hall. So the week unfolded, and the boys and I were trying to make the best of it, trying to have a "vacation" of sorts. But this was a church retreat. So we'd have morning service and sing songs, and I'd think of Amy. We'd be at the dining hall, and I'd have to help the kids and not have help doing that, and I'd think of Amy. We slept in dorm rooms; we had two rooms connected by a bathroom, and at night I'd be alone in my room and I'd think of Amy. So there were all these new experiences and all these new events that were bringing my grief to the surface. Some mornings I'd wake up with the weight of our grief and wonder what would happen that day to cause it to bubble over. And through the week the whole question of the existence of God was weighing heavily on me, and I was starting to really settle with *no*—no God.

Thursday night we all gathered for a group event, a talent show of sorts put on by the kids and teens. My mind was wandering, and I started thinking of Amy and how sad I was that she wasn't here and if she were still alive, we wouldn't have even been at this event; she and I would be off by ourselves at a couples' retreat. I could really feel the sorrow and sadness. It was early evening, after dinner, maybe 7:30, and there was still light outside. A big line of thunderstorms had just passed through the area. I got up from my seat, walked to the back, and I looked out a window to where the sun was starting to sink low behind a big thunderhead, and rays were shooting out from behind the clouds. It was beautiful. I walked outside the building, through a parking lot to the edge of a baseball field, to take in the sun coming out from behind the last bit of clouds. Everything was cool and wet from the thunderstorms, but the late-afternoon July sun was reemerging from the clouds and warming everything back up. After a moment I turned around to go back inside, the sun now behind me, and there, canopied over the student center of this tiny Catholic college, was a double rainbow, horizon to horizon.

Fuck me!

You've *got* to be kidding me!

I ran back toward the baseball field, took out my iPhone, and started snapping pictures of it, but I couldn't fit it all in one frame, I couldn't do it, it was too big. The view in the little camera was too small. And I was crying, weeping. I was taking pictures and sobbing the whole time at this awesome rainbow, and I was thinking, Jesus fucking Christ. Here we go again. A rainbow. Right now. Right when I had given up hope yet again.

There were all these emotions of sadness and grief and also a feeling of spiritual awe, and I was also trying to stay focused on the technical-photography thing. I was thinking, I've got to get this whole rainbow in. I started taking a series of pictures, and I was trying to be careful about my overlap of the pictures so I could bring them home and stitch them together in Photoshop. Then it occurred to me that some joker had probably already built an iPhone app that would do this for me. I took all the pictures, then I looked on the App Store, and sure enough, there it was, a $2.99 download. Yeah, I'll take it, I thought. I'll pay $2.99 for this. Five minutes later I had a stitched-together panorama of this rainbow in my phone. I cleaned it up a little bit and then uploaded it to Facebook, then later to my blog.

I was standing there and started laughing to myself. What's more miraculous? The hand of God, painting this rainbow yet again across my life's canvas, or that now I can take the picture and stitch it together in five minutes and upload it for the world to see?

That was last summer, and I haven't seen any more rainbows. But I see other signs. Like the stop sign on my birthday last August. Or a couple months ago I was at a bookstore downtown, and there was *one* book sticking out from the shelf at an odd angle. What book was it? C.S. Lewis's *A Grief Observed*. Of course I bought it right away.

Were these signs from God? Or just coincidences? I don't know where it all leaves me now. I still want something more certain, and I'm pretty sure that will never happen.

But it was after that rainbow at DeSales University when I started to think that I have to give some credit, perhaps, where credit is due. Fine! If there is a God, it's that Old Testament guy, right? He's able to create rainbows. I guess that is something. But in my mind, as we evolve as a species, He evolves as a God. He created us in His image, got pissed off with how we kept screwing up, destroyed the planet by flooding it, but picked out Noah because Noah is special somehow, a righteous man. Though when the floods cleared, there's Noah, drunk and naked, an embarrassment to his family. *That's* the guy God pulls off the planet to save humanity? Some loser drunk who runs around naked?

Mankind-in-God's-image suggests to me that God has His issues, too. And as we evolve as a species, and God gets smarter and learns more about being a God, He's still prone to mistakes, which is why Amy got killed. Because that's clearly an error. This thinking doesn't necessarily negate God's existence, but it negates the all-powerful, all-knowledgeable God, because He can't be. I think He's struggling to keep it going, keep it together. He's like an adolescent God. He went through his whiny, selfish, narcissistic twos and threes. That's the Garden of Eden story, and some of His other early stories. The jealous God. Maybe He was a six-year-old then. Six-year-olds can be a real pain in the ass. Now He's kind of gotten over that. But just as we all lapse back to our old behaviors, He does too.

So I guess I'm at a point where I can cut Him some slack. That doesn't mean I see Him as salvation, per se. He's just trying to figure it out, like we are. Meanwhile, to tell you the truth, I'd be happy to see no more rainbows.

So that's "what about God."

—

John smiled. Then he asked me what I thought about God.

I smiled and said, "You know that already. I'm a Christian."

"Yes," he said, a bit frustrated. "I know that. But what does that mean? What does it mean to you?"

I laughed. "Are you interviewing me now?"

John smiled. He said, "What do you think?"

I told him. I said I thought I held to the basic tenets of Christianity. That Jesus Christ is the son of God, and he had come to take away the sin of the world. That the same power He evinced by conquering sin on the cross and death in the grave through his bodily resurrection was freely available for the asking today, in the immediate present.

John asked me what I thought about evil. How could I believe in a just God if there was evil in the world?

I said that evil is simply a part of the created world we're now living in, and that I believed that Satan was a real being, active to this day, going around like a lion looking for someone to devour.

I could see by John's look that he wasn't sure if I was serious.

I assured him I was.

He asked me what made me believe that.

I told him about my conversion experience in college. At that time, as I've said, I'd known John for several years, but I'd never shared the details of my spiritual awakening.

Mine was a Damascene conversion.

I grew up Catholic and went to a Catholic elementary school and then an all-boys Catholic high school. My faith in the structure of that religion, though, throughout my childhood and into my teen years, was marginal. I didn't know what to do with my life and did not enjoy it or like it—or myself—much, at all. Mental health issues were not discussed in my family; certainly "depression" was not a word we'd ever think to talk about. But that's what I had been struggling with, from about twelve years old. After high school I went to work full-time at a local foundry. I didn't know what to do with my life, and I didn't want to waste time or energy on continuing my education when I saw no hope in it. My foray into drugs helped me find some relief from my mental anguish, but not my spiritual anguish. There came a crisis point—I made bad choices, and I was forced to get the help I needed. All throughout I did hold the concept of God close in my mind and dear in my heart.

My moment with God came when I was twenty-two years old, in college and living away from home, having a probing conversation with a person I knew to be Christian. There was a Bible on the bed stand, and I pointed to it and said, "You don't really believe that, do you?" That one question cascaded into the briefest exchange; and I'd never before heard such a plain defense of faith. It was as if she said, "The sky is blue." I left the dorm room feeling haunted by something. I walked the campus feeling soul-sick, wandering and wondering at my own creation, my life up to that point, and God's hand in it along the way.

All the questions, all the essential questions—Who am I? Why am I here? Where did I come from? Where am I going?—that had been haunting me for years ... I sensed them all coalescing and being overshadowed and overcome by something very powerful manifesting itself in me in reply. I could not put words to it then; now I can look back and say that that reply sounded like this: "I am that I am."

It was as if the heavens opened up to me right in front of me.

Over the course of a few hours I began to sense a rending, a tearing away, of the fabric of my sighted soul. My worldview was shattering, and I sensed a powerful and undeniable creature-creator relationship being revealed to me. The creator revealing itself to the creature.

I'd changed. Something was stirring in me. I knew it in my heart, my soul, my mind. Something had shown itself to me, and I wanted to know and needed to know what it was. It was a challenge for me to put a word or words to it. It was as if a fire had been lit inside me and was roaring up. I sensed a new being internally, an actual presence welling up a hope and joy for life I had never known before, which was also hungry for—what?

Understanding. I needed to know what was happening to me.

I wanted to know about what had manifested itself spiritually in me. I was starving for God. That's the only way I could put it. And I consumed Him.

I told John how over the course of the next few days I bought a Bible at the campus bookstore and began to devour it, page by page. There I found the answers—in the Old and New Testaments, the Psalms, Proverbs, parables, letters of Paul—about the God-man savior Jesus Christ. It wasn't until later that I felt the desire and need to have it as daily bread, to understand as much as I could, to explain to myself why I believed what I believed, and to defend my faith. So over a couple of decades' time I determined to read the scriptures of the world's great religions and philosophies. I started with my own, I told him, back in the 1990s, reading the Bible in two different translations, from beginning to end—first the King James Version and then the Hebrew-Greek Word Study New International Version Bible—to gain a better grasp on my own spirituality and walk with God and to think critically about why and what I believed. I also wanted to get a better understanding of the world's major religions so that I could be more in tune with people, their languages and their cultures, and current events. So next I turned to Islam and Al-Qur'an. After that The Bhagavad Gita and the Analects of Confucius. Each of these helped me understand the world and myself and my own Christian faith a little better. Of course, growing up in late-twentieth-century America, I knew what people termed this event. I told John that what had happened to me was that, in Jesus' words, I was born of the spirit—in human terms, born again.

I hadn't shared this story with many people, and I told John as much. Our session had been a lot, for both of us, and we knew it was time to wrap things up for the day. We hugged and said our goodbyes and agreed to meet the following Friday. I reminded John that it would be our last interview session before the one-year anniversary of Amy's death.

"Thanks for the reminder," John said.

I smiled. Sheepishly.

When I arrived at John's house Friday evening, February 18, I was eager to learn the details about what he had to share. When we had talked the night before to confirm our meeting, he wouldn't say much, only that he had met someone he thought he might be able to be serious with. He left it at that. We set up in his living room, and John started.

—

Lately, now that there's been more time since Amy's death, it's really starting to hit me. I miss having someone to share my life with, to share *life* with. And I miss physical intimacy with a woman, too. I want that again, but I've been conflicted on this whole notion of putting myself out there, to make it happen. There are so many questions. Is it too soon? Will others think I didn't love Amy if I do this? And when is it "okay" to do this? We had created this shared experience—after ten years together we had figured out a whole bunch of things about each other. What we liked and didn't like. We had each developed a deeper understanding about how we were together, and how to be together, so certain things just flowed.

And that's what I want, again, with a partner—like right *now*. I want someone who can parachute in, who already has that shared experience and backstory that comes after being in a relationship for a decade. Knowing what the warts are, knowing how we danced, knowing that I occasionally stepped on her toes. I don't want to have to go through figuring that out all over again. Because it's a lot of work, and while the thought of a new love or lover is exciting to me, the thought of having to figure it all out again with a new person is a bit daunting. But I do want to find someone. It's pretty clear to me now that I do better in a relationship than not. For a moment, set the kids aside—I really want to share my life with someone.

Someone I can be in love with and also experience life with. Someone I can sit with on the couch and watch a movie and eat popcorn with and we'll see something and I can turn to her and say, "Remember when we stayed at that B&B in the Blue Mountains near Sydney?" And that will recall a whole set of experiences and a memory of the hike we went on, the dinner we had in town, and how we came back to the room and made love. That is what I want again.

But to have *that* somebody, the one with the shared experience? How do I do that? It starts by finding someone. But then we've got to *create* that shared experience and develop a history together. That takes a long time. I'm thinking, "Goddammit, to get to where I am *now*, or where I was before Amy was killed, could take a decade or more. I'll be pushing *sixty*." That's a little depressing. I had a whole different expectation of where I would be by sixty. I thought there'd be a whole set of things on autopilot. Not just the stories we'd remember together, but other things, too, those things that become settled affairs in a long relationship. There's a certain ease to it. There's comfort. There's precedent; we don't go back and revisit this issue or that issue. Certain roles have been established, like who makes dinner and who cleans up. It's done, and we know that, and we're cool with it. Amy and I came to an agreement on how we shared family responsibilities and chores around the house, and beyond that we also came to certain understandings about which each preferred. I wouldn't ask if she wanted white or red wine. I knew she preferred white. And if I was out picking up dinner on my way home Friday evening and couldn't reach her, I had a pretty good chance of picking up something she'd like. And when I went grocery shopping I could toss Pepperidge Farm Orange Milanos in the cart and be confident she'd appreciate them. And at night we automatically slept on our sides of the bed, and if I leaned over to her she knew to pull her knees up so I could spoon up to her and she would take my right arm in her arms and hold it against her. I knew Friday nights she was likely too tired to make love, but Saturday mornings were better. Little things like that make a difference.

And after the patterns are established, you're finding new things to share, and you keep adding to this thing that's the two of you, and that's the richness, that's the patchwork quilt of a relationship. We had a lot of things figured out, so we were looking for new things to figure out, together. Now what do we need to figure out next? What do we add on to that? What's the next panel of quilt going to look like for us?

When we get married, we all make vows that we will stick together in good times and bad times, for richer and for poorer, and in sickness and in health. The good times, for richer, and in health? That's the easy part. But bad times, and sickness, and poorer? No one really wants that, but by making those vows, that's the commitment—to see it through to the other side with that one person. You don't give up. And when you're in those places, if you don't have some doubts and questions about that original decision, you're not human. Yet getting through those times is how you add panels to your quilt.

But then there was the other part of that vow: "Till death do us part." One of us goes first. That's how it is, and we knew that, I guess, as much as any one of us can be aware of our mortality. But this? *Now?* There's *no* sense to it. It's random. It's chaos. If you want to call chaos evil, then this is evil. If your Satan is not only a hungry lion looking to devour someone but also equal to chaos and uncertainty, then Satan exists.

I didn't deserve it. She didn't deserve it. Shit, the driver of the truck didn't deserve it.

There's no purpose, no meaning, no sense at all here. None. Zero. It's the absence, the void. So that comes from the beginning, doesn't it? The universe was without form; there was chaos, and God created form. So He was trying to separate the chaos and the evil from the light and the good. So there's still work to be done in that area because there's still chaos, and that's what killed Amy.

Why did the bolt on this wing shear off on this plane, but not that plane? It's inexplicable. Why did these two hundred people die and not these two hundred *other* people? Not because they were evil, not because they didn't worship God the right way. It's independent of that because of this chaos we find ourselves in. I'm paraphrasing from Rabbi Harold Kushner's book, *When Bad Things Happen to Good People*, which I've been reading. Sometimes there is circumstantial suffering—there is no reason for it.

Recently, these thoughts were swirling in my head, and then in a moment I had the most profound sense of having lost my future. It was an important and deeply moving recognition for me in creating a distinct sorrow from losing Amy herself.

And the way it shows up is jarring.

Early on, when I was starting back to work, I overheard a conversation that included a curious turn of phrase. Amy travelled a lot—in fact, she had been to every continent—and she was big into different languages. When I heard that turn of phrase, I thought, "Oh, that's interesting. I can't wait to get home and tell Amy that." And as *that* thought was coming up in my mind this *other* thought came up and snatched it away to say, "Nope. Can't do it. Amy's dead."

It was as if that second thought had come from outside my mind and just pulled the original thought right out of my brain. That's when it occurred to me—this is my future. I was in the middle of living a past future, the past future where Amy was alive. In that past future, I could hear that turn of phrase and have the thought, "I'll share that with Amy later," and then share it with her later.

I could feel the time-fabric ripping in that moment as another thread snapped. I was experiencing something that would have happened *anyway*, and then I was being told I couldn't finish that experience. I was becoming very aware of time, and events in time. Imagine your life unfolding along the branches of a tree. When you are born, all the branches and leaves are possibilities. As we age we make choices, things happen, and we find ourselves on one of the limbs—well, there are moments when the limb branches into two new branches. I caught myself thinking, "Is this something that would have happened when Amy was alive, or not?" Are the branches completely separate now? I am now standing certainly on this other branch—the one where Amy is dead. But I'm so close to the other branch where Amy continues to live that I can still see what was possible. But now, as time is moving on, the two branches are drifting farther apart.

Take Bryan's birthday party at Chuck E. Cheese's; that experience straddled the event of Amy's death. Amy scheduled it. Then driving to Chuck E. Cheese's, having the cake, having the mouse come up to us, all that stuff—that experience would have happened *either way*, but it straddled this increasing void between my old history and my new history. It was as if there was a period of time when my past future and my new future coexisted, and yet they were slowly being pulled farther apart. As time goes on I'm becoming less and less aware of that sort of thing, those things that would have happened anyway, as the branches separate.

Today, for example, is Friday. I worked from home. I went to see my shrink. If Amy were alive, this would not exist. These events only exist in my new reality, this new future.

But some events exist in one form or another on both branches. For example, the first day of kindergarten for Bryan was last year in August. That experience would have happened no matter what. But the experience had Amy still been with us would have been different. She and I would have both gone out to the bus stop with him. So that specific experience is on this new branch.

For all those events—the birthdays, the Mother's Days, the anniversaries, even the small ones—it's the first one that is the most difficult. I can talk about it now without breaking down in tears. I remember the week after she was killed, the first time I took out the trash, I broke down in tears. It was the first time I had taken out the trash without Amy, and there was stuff in the garbage, like some tissue she had used to dab her lipstick, and other things she had thrown away, things she touched that had gone into the trash I was carrying out to the street to be taken away. I had that sudden, jarring realization—our future selves were gone—and I broke down in tears.

In the aftermath of her death it was like that the first time I did anything, it didn't matter. It could be the first time I took a bath, the first time I went and got my hair cut. I thought, Amy won't remark on my haircut. The first time I went to work, the first time I took the boys to school, the first time I went to the grocery store and didn't buy the cookies she liked. Each one of those was a step farther down the new branch without Amy, a step farther away from the one that held her.

So I can see that branch, the one I would have had with Amy, but I find myself on this branch, with only me, in my new life. And while I long to be on that other branch, the one with Amy, I am solidly on this other branch now. And among all that is different on this branch, there's really no other way but to say it: on this new branch, I find myself to be a fairly eligible bachelor. It's a strange and—I have to say—nicely ego-fulfilling thing. I think I'm being objective when I say these things: I'm a good-looking man, I'm in good shape, I've got a good job, I've got two adorable kids.

I was feeling a little more confident about the idea of dating, so I went back to the online dating sites. As I reacquainted myself with the websites I wondered how many *widowed* people were out there. I guess earlier I had been thinking that if I met someone she'd be divorced, or I had fantasies of someone young. But young women probably want kids.

Ugh.

But then I thought maybe I could just find the widows out there. So I searched. And there were a few, but they weren't close by. But it felt different. I was starting to feel okay with the idea. I was flirting with the idea of flirting, I guess.

And then, just as I summoned the courage to start considering dating again, to meet someone new, I think about when Amy and I first met at that nightclub. We clicked right away because we both wanted the same thing. We each wanted a life partner. We wanted someone to share a life with. We wanted someone to create a family with, and someone to share the joys and sorrows of life with. That was the deal. We knew this very early in our relationship, and whatever happened afterward, good or bad, that undercurrent was there for everything. So when things would get a little rough or disconnected, we could always lean on our foundation. We held on to our dream of growing old together. We held on to that dream to the end. We still talked about it that day I took a furlough day and we made love. It was still what we wanted, and I *still* want that. I still want it. And still wanting that and not being able to have it with Amy is a difficult, difficult concept for me to come to terms with. And when I think of dating, I also think of all of what Amy and I created, and I wonder how can I ever get that again.

There are moments when I can aside all of that and it boils down to something pretty straightforward. I've been missing the touch of another human being, that physical closeness of another human, of a woman, and sharing a bed with her.

I started thinking more and more what it would be like to make love to another woman. I wanted that. And I also wondered what it would be like as a father to two boys. What I mean is that I am done creating a family. Making love with Amy to create that new life stood out among all the other times. It was not only to satisfy our own human desires but to join in love and create new life. It truly was a holy act.

What could it be like with a different woman?

I was sharing this with a friend and he said, "You just need to get laid."

"What?"

"You need to look on Craigslist. That's where that action is."

"Craigslist? Really? I thought that's where you get used chairs and bags of gravel."

"No, no, no. That's Freecycle! Go to Craigslist."

So I looked on Craigslist. And there it all was—women seeking men, men seeking women, and every other possible human connection, and I got a little excited. I started window-shopping. Now, I don't think of myself as a prude, but yikes! I'd been out of the game for a while and I was amazed by what people actually posted online about themselves. The descriptions of themselves, what they liked, even photos of themselves, even a picture of some woman's shaved crotch. "New to town, petite cutie, loves to suck big cocks. Send photo to such-and-such email. No solicitations or offers."

No solicitations or offers? For real?

It was titillating and exiting, but quickly got more than a little creepy. Who really are these people? And I thought of my boys. How could I actually pull off that kind of lifestyle with two young boys in the house? Running off to some place for a blow job? Do I just leave the boys for an hour or so, or do I get a babysitter? Or maybe I take a long lunch? That wasn't going to work. How do people find the time to have affairs? Speaking of that, someone else told me about Ashley Madison. This was all news to me! People actively seeking affairs online. Hmm. Well, it wouldn't *really* be an affair for me. But maybe I could be someone else's affair. There are a lot of attractive moms around here! And that would be uncomplicated, right? "Lonely, horny MILF, discreet, etc., etc." They wouldn't be looking for anything serious. No strings attached. But then I'd realize—that wasn't really me. While there was something exciting about that fantasy, I could never really bring myself to go down that path.

I'd like to think I'm a player, but I'm not. That's just not who I am. And then I'd think of the kids. Really, who are these people I'd be meeting? I knew that I could not do anything that would even *accidentally* bring someone into contact with them. So I gave up on that pretty quickly. Maybe I was chicken. But that was that.

I was widowed, I was miserable, I was alone, and I wanted some female companionship. I didn't have the energy or wherewithal to go chase it. But I'm reasonably attractive, and I think I can write a good profile, and maybe somebody would be interested. So I did it. I put a little effort into it, updated my profile, and reposted it.

A week went by. Nothing. Nothing at all. Maybe I was impatient, but I was expecting something to happen right away. So *that* started another little cycle of depression. I kept checking each day for several days. Still nothing. No winks, no touches, no pokes from women who may have seen my profile in their searches.

I started to fiddle a bit with the searches. One night I created a dummy account as a woman just so I could do a search, as a woman, and put in the profile criteria I would expect for a woman searching for someone like me. I was curious what she might actually find. All these other profiles came up with crappy photos of guys posing in their boxers, showing hairy chests, trying to show off a little too hard that they thought they were still in good shape. I read a couple profiles. Some were okay, but some were also a little creepy, with all sorts of innuendo and linguistic chest thumping. I looked at these other guys and said to myself, "Oh my God, these guys are *losers*. Is this really who I am? Am I really one of these guys?"

Ugh.

It was a moment of two conflicting thoughts. First thought? This is going to be easy; there's no competition here. Second thought? Oh my God. *This* is the school of fish I'm swimming with?

No offense, guys, really, but at least spellcheck your profile. And maybe go easy on the hairy chest shots.

In the process of searching and playing around with the different site tools, I started to understand somewhat how the system worked, how you can see if people have viewed your profile, things like that. Women would see that I'd viewed them. So even though I wouldn't initiate something, I started to understand that they could tell if I had looked at them.

After a while people started reaching out to me.

I still wasn't planning to initiate. If somebody initiated something with me, what I was planning on doing in the follow-up message was to say—because in my profile it said I was widowed, single dad, two boys, life's been rough—that I didn't even know what I was looking for right then, but I wanted to think someday I would have a partner again. I'd tell her I was just looking for companionship, to hang out on my front porch, sip a glass of wine. That was it.

And then one day a woman reached out to me and wrote, "Hey, I like your profile."

I wrote her back: "Thanks, but you've got to know, there's more to the story. I'm not just a widower; I'm a really new widower. If that freaks you out, I get it."

She wrote back, "I'm not freaked out. Let's have coffee."

Coffee? Is this a date? Wow! Someone actually wanted to meet me. But there was this one small detail. I hadn't really thought through the logistics of going out on an actual date.

She asked, "When are you free?"

And I thought, "When am I *free*?" I'm *never* free. What do you mean, "free"?

So I wrote back, "Well, I have a fifteen-minute window of time between 8:30 and 8:45 after I drop off one son at preschool and before I need to get to my shrink in Bethesda. Or maybe I could make some time after my shrink appointment and before I get back over to my job." That sort of thing. And it made me depressed all over again. Dating? Forget about all the emotional stuff. How does a forty-something-year-old man with two young kids, a full-time job, and a shrink have time to go out on a date? How does that even happen?

She was accommodating, and we settled on a time for a quick coffee. Our date was for eleven in the morning. I got there a little early and parked in a nearby parking lot. I got out of my car and from across the lot saw her walking to the door. I could tell it was her from the profile picture. She didn't see me. And as soon as I saw her I realized that I couldn't do this. I could tell right then that I had no interest in her. There was this moment, as I stood there, when I thought, I could just get right back in the car, back out of the parking lot, and go on about my life. And only two people on the planet would ever know what happened.

I took a deep breath and went inside. We said hello and exchanged pleasantries and sat down with our coffees. She probably picked up within the first thirty seconds this was going nowhere. We were polite with each other and shared a little about where we were in life, what we did, and so on. We shook hands and said goodbye and that was that.

So as I was driving off I thought, well, at least I can check off "first date." Even if it was just coffee and a handshake at the end, it felt like an accomplishment.

That sort of thing went on for a little while. I started to sometimes use one of my Tuesday or Thursday evenings to go out on something resembling a real date instead of working out. And I met some nice women, a couple with whom I actually had more than one date. I made it to three dates with one. Nothing really panned out, though. And I was finding that it took a lot of time. Women contacted me, and I responded back, and I wanted to respond back thoughtfully. But after the first couple of responses I got tired of it; I created a form letter response so that I could copy and paste it.

But I kept at it. A few things were driving me, I suppose. On one level, certainly, loneliness drove me. I wanted adult female companionship. I enjoy the company of a woman. And, yes, I was also wondering when I'd get laid again.

After a couple more weeks of being on these dating sites, actively using them, it started to become almost an addiction for me. I was checking my accounts constantly. Is somebody looking at me? Is somebody winking at me? I was trying to reach for something that wasn't there.

Over the course of a couple of months, I went out on maybe ten more dates. I made it to a third date with another woman. She had a lot of the qualities I thought I wanted—smart, funny, attractive—but there was no real attraction, not really. And there were some contacts where I would send back my standard response—"Look, here's my situation; I'm recently widowed"—and some people never replied. And that was fine. I couldn't hold that against them.

So this went on for a while, and it all started taking way too much of my time to keep up with. So I shut down my profiles again. I kept the accounts, but hid them or disabled them. Around this time someone told me about an eco-friendly dating site. She said, "You should check that one out. It's for the nutty, crunchy, tree-hugger crowd, like you." It was GreenSingles.com.

Really? That exists?

So I copied and pasted my profile from another site, edited it, and put it up there.

The nice thing about the more popular dating sites is that there's a constant influx of single, divorced women showing up. With the "green" one I went to? Not a lot.

I started getting inquiries from women in Canada, like Saskatchewan, and upstate New York, and Maine. They were all interesting ladies, really, and they genuinely seemed like the type of woman I'd be interested in, but some were three thousand miles away, in a different country. I had correspondence from one woman who was in Zagreb, Croatia. A real knockout: high cheekbones, long blond hair, hazel eyes, full red lips. It was a professional head shot, I could tell, because I could see the square light reflection in her eyes of a light box, and I noticed the narrow depth of field with trees out of focus in the background. She could have been a model. At least her profile photo was of *someone* gorgeous. I wanted to ask her if she was planning to come to the United States—ever? This was really just frustrating. This was all the women I *couldn't* have, geographically speaking. There were already enough women in the world I couldn't have. I didn't need to know about *others*.

I was getting fed up with the whole thing. I was bored. I set the GreenSingles site aside. Then after a while, on a whim, I hopped back on and decided to do a search. I extended my radius a bit, and it pulled up this woman's profile, not too far from my home. It was a cute, interesting profile. Liberal politics, liked the outdoors, hiking and camping, liked to cook, liked the simple things in life. It didn't seem like she was trying too hard. There was something in the tone. I liked it.

Her profile was vague on what she did for a living, but she had two pictures posted. One was a professional head shot with her head tilted, brown hair, blond highlights, hazel eyes, nice smile. And the other photo? It was a picture from one of those polar bear plunge events. She was in a black bikini, and it was clear she was in very good shape, very nice body. So, yes, that got my attention. But what *really* got me was she had on one of those toboggan knit caps, with the earflaps and the little fuzzy pompom on the top and the strings that you tie under your chin. Standing next to her was an older guy in a green superhero outfit with green tights and green cape, and he was wearing a big, fake, compact fluorescent light bulb on his head. He was Light Bulb Man, or something like that.

I thought the picture was hysterical, and there was just something about it that really grabbed my attention. By then I'd seen enough profile pictures of women trying to show off their bodies. But this was different. She had this kind of smirk on her face, like: "Take the goddamn picture now, would ya?" And she was wearing this hat, and she was standing next to this goofy guy, and I was sitting there thinking, "I like the vibe of this woman who's willing to put *that* picture of herself in a bikini on her pro-file." She's confident enough in how she looks, but also doesn't take herself too seriously, posing next to Light Bulb Man. It was a completely dorky photo, and she was hot.

I thought, I gotta say hi.

So I broke my rule about no first strikes.

I wrote to her, "Hey, saw your profile, liked it, and anybody that would pose in a bikini with Light Bulb Man … I have to say hi. So: hi." That was it.

She replied, "Oh, hi. I just saw your profile, too. I really like it."

She talked a little bit about the picture on her profile. "That was the CCAN—Chesapeake Climate Action Network—polar bear plunge event in the Chesapeake. I had a great time. I'm sorry, but I'm actually in a conversation with another guy right now on GreenSingles, so, sorry, not right now. But if that doesn't go anywhere, I'll reach back out."

I thought, "Yeah, fine." Whatever. It seemed like a polite brush off. So I wrote back, "No worries. I'm not going anywhere." And I was feeling a little cocky for some reason, so I added, "*When* that one fizzles, give me a call." And I forgot about it.

Two, three weeks later I got a message from her: "Hey, that other thing didn't pan out. Are you still free to talk?"

I said, "What did you have in mind?"

We emailed back and forth and *very* quickly got into some really profound conversations over email. I started with my standard reply: "All right. Here's my deal— recently widowed. This has scared a few people away, and so on."

She wrote back, "A couple of years ago a friend of mine died from breast cancer. She was young and had three daughters, and I kind of helped take care of them."

So she had some experience with a grieving father and his children.

Over the course of a couple of weeks we had these amazing email exchanges, back and forth, about life and death and love. I felt really drawn to her, felt myself becoming attracted to this woman through email. It was the strangest thing. She lived only a dozen miles away, but I kept imagining the long-distance correspondence that must've happened hundreds of years ago, homesteaders out on the frontier putting ads in the paper back east, looking for a bride, something out of *Sarah, Plain and Tall*.

We covered a lot of the basics that often happen on a first date. She is single, no kids. We shared music and food interests. She's a vegetarian. In one email I asked about the work she does and she replied that she'd be happy to talk "shop" more, but over a beer. Over a beer? Hmm. I wrote back and said, "If you are asking me out, then I accept!" So we made a date. Her name's Lori.

It was a Tuesday, after work, and I decided to use one of my babysitter nights that I normally used to go to the gym and get errands done for the date. We agreed to meet at a nearby brewpub in Hyattsville, not far from the University of Maryland campus, called Franklins. It was a favorite of mine, and as it turned out, for her, too. Because of the extensive mailing back and forth, I felt that this first date had a lot more potential than any of the others. But I couldn't get too excited. I mean, I felt pretty confident the pictures of her on her profile were actually of her. I had googled her, of course, and found the same head shot on her company website. She had her own business as an event producer. But you can just never know.

I think we had agreed to meet at five o'clock. I got to the parking lot and parked. It was a pay lot, and there was a kiosk where you have to punch in your parking space and pay. As I was walking to the kiosk I saw a woman already there; tall, athletic build, brown hair, and even from the back I was pretty sure it was her. I walked up and asked if she was Lori. She smiled and giggled and said, "Yes, and you must be John."

I could tell she was nervous, and I guess I was a little bit nervous, too. We headed into the restaurant and got a table. It was early, and a Tuesday, so it wasn't that crowded. We got a booth by the windows and fell into conversation. We had already shared a lot about our lives in our emails, so a lot of the normal "get to know you" stuff was behind us.

Lori had a whole bunch of questions written down. It was funny. Nothing intimidating, just stuff she had thought of while reading my emails that she wanted to know more about. What I did for a living, more about the boys, normal stuff.

One conversation starter question I like to pose to people is this: "What is the best day of the year? And there is only one right answer." Most folks go through the normal litany of birthdays, holidays, and so on. Of course, it's none of those. I gave her a bit of a clue that the day would be coming up soon, and she got it! Daylight saving time—the day we fall back! We all get that extra hour and it is, in my opinion, the best day of the year, every year, for everyone. It's a silly question, of course, but she played along and also guessed it. Many people give up, and when I tell them some nod approvingly, some sort of shrug and mumble, "Yeah, I guess so." But Lori really liked it, and she had fun with it, which I liked.

The conversation went on and we ordered our food, and then we realized three hours had gone by, and I really had to get home, *fast*. So we paid, left the restaurant, stood in the parking lot, and said our goodbyes and kissed. It was a really good first date. Really, really good. I wasn't sure just yet, of course, but I couldn't wait to see her again. In quick order we figured out some schedule stuff and scheduled, in advance, our next two dates. And we're still dating.

I really like having someone in my life. I'm still nervous, I guess, but it's a funny thing that's happened to me. You know when you first meet somebody? You try to get to know each other, and there's this little dance you both do; you're both a little cautious, a little nervous about what the other person might think. You play one card at a time because you don't want to reveal too much, because you don't want to be too vulnerable, and you're trying to put on a good face for the other person. I think we all do that, both men and women. We all want to play our best cards first with each other. But at some point you've got to play your whole hand, and no one has a perfect hand. We *all* have bad cards in our hand.

The thing of it is that I didn't feel like drawing it out with Lori. I figured, I don't have time for all that. So I just said, "Fuck it," and put all my cards on the table. Here's my hand. Look at my hand. Do you see my hand? Yeah, I have some good cards over here, but over here, these are some shitty cards, some real shitty cards. And I don't care that you know about them. In fact, I *want* you to know about them, because if any of these things scare you, I need you to leave right now and not waste my time. Because I don't have time to waste. Not now on this date and also in life. I've got two young boys and a job and all of that, and also because, realistically, it's half over for me. My life is half over.

Think of it—just go by the averages. I'm in good shape now, but someday someone will be feeding me mushy oatmeal with a plastic spoon. So there's a subtle sense of urgency for me. It's like that line in *The Shawshank Redemption*: "Get busy living or get busy dying." I saw that a couple months ago, and I cried when I heard that line. I just burst into tears watching that movie. Because that's what it is. I've got to hold on to that, I've got to get busy living, because if I don't—if I lose *that*—then I might as well die, because what's the point?

So I showed Lori all my cards. I said, "Lori, here's my deal. My wife died in April. I love my wife. I will always love Amy. Her ashes are in my living room. There are photos of her in my house. I talk about her with the boys, because we're still grieving her loss. I'm still grieving her loss, and probably always will be." I said, "If you come into my life, if you come into my house, this is just how it is. We will have pictures of the woman I was married to on the wall. And, by the way, it will be a whole lot easier for you to come visit me than for me to visit you. The boys and I aren't moving. Are you okay with that?"

So far she has said she's okay with it. But more than that. It's hard to describe, but I don't get any sense that she feels threatened by it. I hope that can continue.

In the back of my mind I wonder if at some point she'll realize that this never really goes away. If our relationship continues, and over time as my grief, and the boys' grief, changes, at some point we'll be in a different place. Our grief won't show up every day or even maybe every week. It will show up as we try to get on with it. Stuff like having a cake for Amy's birthday, or me needing to be alone on our wedding anniversary, or on April 29 each year. I'll need some special accommodations to just manage that day. I imagine that's how this will unfold, but I don't know that. I can't predict it.

I told Lori, "I don't know how *this* goes." My life, that is, and my reaction to grief. I may be present now, in this moment, have my wits about me and be able to hold a reasonable conversation, be an attentive, loving companion, but there will be days when I'm going to be checked out *completely*. And she may understand being checked out completely *now*, within a year of Amy's death. But what about a year from now? Five years from now? Ten years from now? I'd like to think "checking out" won't happen as much as it's happening now, but I can't say that.

When Adam graduates from college and we're sitting there and Mom's not there, it's going to be there. When Bryan goes to the prom and Mom's not there to dote on him, it's going to be there. The absence of Amy will simply be there.

I told Lori, "If you want a relationship with me, you need to figure out how to have a relationship with my dead wife. You need to figure it out. I can't figure that out for you. And if you can't figure it out, then I don't see how it could work between us, really."

She said, "Yes, I know."

So I'm continually amazed by this woman. She's hanging in there, and I love her. And I'm surprised that I do, in some ways, but in other ways it's easier now. Being vulnerable or being open doesn't feel risky or scary like it used to.

When I fell in love with Amy, we fell in love pretty quickly, too. But I do remember feeling hesitation throughout, playing my hand one card at a time as I suspect she did. I was thirty-one, thirty-two. I was still off-balance from a bad breakup and a divorce, and I'm sure it affected my ability to be vulnerable with Amy, my ability to be fully loving to her and to be loved by her. It probably took a few years, even after we were married, to open up to the strong relationship we had and what it was becoming.

Now that hesitation has simply been *blasted* away, and if she simply decided at some point to say, "You know what? This is too much. I can't deal with it all," I would understand, because this is a lot to handle.

It's freeing. I don't feel obligated or compelled to be anyone but myself, and I actually think that's better, not *trying*, but just *being*. It's easier for me now, and I think Lori loves me for that. Maybe that's one reason she's hanging in there. It's a strange thing. There are some interesting love lessons coming out of all this that I was not prepared for.

Now when I read that line from Rumi that grief is the garden of love, I am starting to see it differently. Something about death, or the awareness of death, this experience of death, through grief, has forced me to face how little time we really have on this planet. Undeniably, we will all face it, and grief strips away what is not important. Maybe that's what it is. Grief strips away what gets in the way of love. Grief *is* the garden of love.

—

John and I looked at each other and knew we needed to break. It was getting on in the afternoon; his boys would be coming home from school soon; I had to get home, too. John asked if we were done for the day, and I said we could be, but we didn't have to be.

We kept on talking. John confessed that he had been holding back on telling me about Lori, but was glad he did. He seemed to be waiting for or wanting my approval or permission, and I told him that I didn't know what I'd be doing if I were walking in his shoes.

He smiled. He seemed genuinely excited, if not also tentative about it. I told him I was happy for him, and Lori, too. Our conversation paused, then shifted to small talk. Jobs, kids. Moved on to our partners, Lori and Gina.

We went into the kitchen for water, still talking.

It struck me, I told John, how we'd been talking about some pretty heavy topics related to Amy's death. Last week it was God. This week it was dating. I could sense there was still more underneath all that. And I was interested in how he was managing as a single father. I asked him what it was like doing the day-to-day things around the house, like he was doing right now. What was that like for him? Was a new routine setting in?

John said, "It's odd, what triggers a memory, what memories come now, where they come from." He started to talk about household tasks, grocery shopping, cooking dinner.

I asked John if I should get my recorder. He acquiesced and said, "Sure."

I got my equipment from the living room, and we sat back down at his dining room table, and we talked. There I discovered the grief in the ordinary.

———

I do all the kitchen stuff, always have. The shopping, the cooking, buying all the kitchen gear. I enjoy it; it's one of my things.

Two, three years ago, a cutting board I'd bought years before had grown old and nasty or cracked. I don't even remember. We needed a new cutting board, and I had remarked to Amy, maybe even in passing, "We need a new cutting board," or maybe she noticed it and said, "It's looking kind of nasty. We need a cutting board." I didn't think too much about it.

And then, as Amy does—*did*—she went out and bought me a new cutting board.

Now, there are two parts to this.

One thing Amy really prided herself on was buying the right gifts for people. She did not like giving gift cards, or cash gifts; those were too open-ended and impersonal. It was a source of pride for her that she would pick up on some subtle need someone might have and not even know. We were visiting my parents once, and we were having ice cream, and whoever was scooping bent the spoon or complained about how hard it was to scoop out the ice cream. Next Christmas? There was an ice cream scoop under the tree. When we had been dating for maybe a year, and I was still in my old apartment, we had a conversation about geography, and a question came up. Where was some river, or what was the capital of some country—that sort of thing—and I was looking around for a map, just to answer our question. I couldn't find one and was frustrated. I said, "Man, I really wish I had a globe." This was before everyone had a phone with Google maps on it. Four months later on Christmas, she got me a globe. I didn't even remember that conversation until she reminded me.

One day after we'd had that exchange about needing a new cutting board for the kitchen, Amy had run some errands. She'd gone to IKEA and gotten an IKEA cutting board. Now, I like IKEA, but for certain things, especially tools and especially *kitchen* tools, I go a bit higher end because I want something that's going to work perfectly and last a really long time. Even though a cutting board is more a utility item, there are certain cutting boards I like and others I don't like.

This IKEA cutting board she brought home was thin wood; it wasn't that sturdy or heavy. I like big, heavy cutting boards. This one was just plain wood; I'm not even sure what kind, but not a hard wood that would take a long life of cutting. And it wasn't perfectly flat, either. When you put it down on a smooth surface it wiggled; there was no way for it to grip the counter. Whenever I used it, it would slide about on the counter top. I had to go buy these little rubber feet from Home Depot and screw them into the bottom with little screws.

I never told Amy about it. I never said, "This is the wrong cutting board. Maybe you should just take it back, and I'll go ahead and take care of the cutting board." I couldn't do that, because she prided herself on getting the right gift. And she may have sensed that I was not exactly thrilled with it when she pulled it out, and I might've said something like, "Oh, hey … a cutting board. From IKEA."

Just the other day I was using the cutting board, and as I pressed on it with a knife to cut something—because I had put those little rubber feet on it so it wouldn't wobble and slip—it cracked right down the middle. Now I need to get another new cutting board.

Before she died, and even after, I would think about it. I'd be cutting something that required some force, maybe a large potato or something, and the board didn't quite have the mass I needed. And I'm carrying this small little resentment around. "Amy, why did you get me the wrong cutting board?" I don't think I ever said anything about it to her. But there it was—this little bit of resentment toward Amy for this little thing that she didn't get right.

I want to remember Amy as this near-perfect human being. Maybe it helps me to remember her that way, because I want to remove all mental images of whatever unspeakable horror must have happened to her on that street. I have to block it out, and the best way I can block it out is with the memory of her, perfectly formed. And when I say "perfectly formed" I don't mean physically something other than what she was, but as I remember her in a particular, specific memory:

We had been dating a year or so. We were young, early thirties, no kids yet. We were on a mini-vacation in Berkeley Springs, West Virginia. We were making love. She was astride me. That is how I remember her, beautiful as she ever was, at that moment. *That* was my visual of her when I'd be daydreaming before she died. That was the image I'd conjure in my mind, in a fantasy at work, or in the car. And that's how I remember her now.

Amy left this world a beautiful person. There was no long-suffering disease that I had to deal with, no secret lover I discovered after she was killed, no unsettled hostility. We loved each other, amazingly so. I truly felt her love toward me, and that was a first for me. It was through Amy that the feeling of being loved by another took root in me authentically.

I think we humans struggle with love. Letting ourselves be loved. I think it's sometimes easier for us to love someone else, to *think* we love somebody else, than to allow ourselves to fully feel loved by another. And Amy gave me that gift: the gift of her love for me. And in spite all that I managed to hold on to a resentment that she bought me the wrong cutting board. And when it broke the other day the memory of those resentments flooded back, and I just stood there over that broken cutting board and cried.

—

I was going through email the other day, and the announcement to sign up for little league baseball was sitting in my inbox. Little league. And just like that all the memories from last year flooded in. I was just reading email, another simple matter, and then I was reliving each moment in rapid-fire succession. The moment the police officer told me Amy hadn't made it. The kids coming up the front steps. Friends visiting, and the one neighbor who encouraged me to sign Adam up for little league. I could see his face in my mind's eye and his voice in my ears. "Is Adam playing baseball this year?"

I kept staring at the email and, again, found myself in this strange disorienting place where I could see how our lives were straddling the void between what our future would have been and what it was becoming. Because we probably wouldn't have played baseball last year if Amy had been alive. We hadn't signed up, we wouldn't have signed up, except that Amy died and a neighbor nudged us—*because* Amy died. But then again, I could also imagine taking the boys to practice, and then coming home and ordering takeout, and Amy being so interested to hear all about it. And the boys' faces glowing, so happy.

That fantasy evaporated as I stared back at the email. We don't get that now. None of us gets that part of the experience. Not in this life.

As last season progressed, Adam really got into it. He's got a pretty good glove, and he has a sense for the game, which is neat for a second-grader.

During the season I was continuously reminded that his mom wouldn't be cheering him on like all the other moms. It's almost mythic, in a way, not having Mom around. I have become acutely aware of all the references to moms in our culture, whether in books, movies, TV, or anywhere else. The trigger could be the most innocuous thing—when we are watching a sitcom, and something funny happens with the mom in the show, I wonder if the boys are thinking, "We're different. We don't have a mommy." But what really bugs me is that the dads are all portrayed as morons, whether it's Al Bundy or the dad in *Family Guy*. It's like Homer Simpson is the most mature and sympathetic, loving dad on TV. And single moms come off as heroic figures, but single dads don't know how to load the dishwasher, then hilarity ensues because dad's a bumbling idiot. It's almost as if we're allowed to laugh at the dad but not at the mom.

Disney seems particularly adept at this. It's Bambi's mom that gets shot. Or it's Cinderella and the evil stepmother. *Finding Nemo*? Where's the mom? Would there be a *Finding Nemo* if Nemo had a neurotic mother? Now a neurotic father, that's a good plot device. I wonder how it would have gone if the cold, detached Baron Von Trapp died and left his widow to care for the kids and escape from the Nazis. That doesn't seem like much of a story.

—

While the sharp spikes of intense grief still return from time to time, it's now more of a low-grade chronic sadness that's occasionally broken by moments of feeling okay. But just like with the little league sign-up, there are all these seasonal cues that take me out of the moment, tap me on the shoulder, and say, "April 29 is coming."

I had a strange, almost out-of-body experience as I walked into that recurring Thursday meeting—the one I had just before I learned Amy died. I don't know why, but something felt very different as I walked into the room. A sense of unease or foreboding. Almost as if I was imagining myself walking into that room last April 29, unaware of what was awaiting me. I tried to remember that meeting. The one last April 29. But I couldn't. I couldn't remember the experience of sitting there, *being* in the meeting. What I did remember, though, was seeing myself, in my mind's eye, from across the table—*that's* how I remember it. I see myself sitting there, taking notes, maybe slouched in the chair, checking email on my iPhone because the meeting had drifted to something I'm not directly involved with. I don't have a memory of that meeting, but I see myself from last year so clearly, sitting across from myself today. And I see myself with one part longing and one part sadness. I'm looking back at my life in those last few moments before I knew that Amy was dead and the life we had was over. The sadness is the anticipation of what was about to come—the trauma of the news—then having to call my parents and Amy's mom, and then tell the boys.

But what is also curious is that I now actually sit on the *other* side of the table from where I used to. You know how when you have a recurring meeting you fall into a pattern and sit in the same seat every time? There are no real assigned seats, but for recurring meetings each of us has our "own" seat. I actually remember the next time I had that meeting after Amy died. I just instinctively sat on the other side. I didn't even think about it. It just happened.

I remember, in every detail, what happened *after* I left that meeting on the day she died. Everything is clear: the slight detour I took to the mini-mart in the engineering building to get a big diet soda, checking my iPhone, dealing with some issue a staff member had with his new computer. Walking up the sidewalk to the building where my office was, coming up the stairs, turning down the hall, seeing the police officer come into view.

I can remember it all so vividly, all the moments just before. But then after that—after the moment I was told Amy "didn't make it"—my memory shifts into weird hallucinations, a bad dream, fragments: the police officer, the drive home, meeting the boys, the near full moon that night, my brother and my dad arriving. Little things I wasn't aware of at the time and only remembered much later. It's like my day shifted from a movie to a slide show.

And yesterday? It was nice and sunny, close to seventy degrees, and I could feel that feeling coming back, the feeling with the change in the season, from winter to spring, the expectation, almost hope. There is that day, that first day when you can feel the new warmth of the sun and smell the grass trying to break through. Who doesn't look forward to spring? I like winter, but spring? I like spring, especially around here, even though it only lasts three days. It's gorgeous. But instead of feeling nostalgic and excited for spring's return, I sensed that feeling emerging again—that feeling that the heavy grief is just below and wants to get out. I'm getting nervous, getting nervous for April 29. I want to enjoy spring, and I want to enjoy hanging out on my front porch, but it's looming.

Last Wednesday we were at the dining table, right here, and I was working with Adam on his homework. Bryan was drawing or writing something, I wasn't really paying attention, then he asked me, "Daddy, how do you spell 'mom'?"

I wasn't even thinking about it—that he should know how to spell mom—so I just blurted it out, "M–o–m."

Then he asked, "Daddy, how do you spell 'died'?"

Fuck.

"D–i–e–d."

Now I'm on high alert. I wanted to know what he was writing, but decided not to press him on it.

Then, "How do you spell 'pizza'?"

Pizza? I told him how to spell it.

He kept writing and writing, then he showed it to me. He'd written: "Mom died on April 29. I didn't know. And then we watched TV and ate pizza."

I asked him, "Really? We ate pizza?"

It made sense, of course. Somebody had ordered pizza. But I have no memory of that. I remember watching TV in the basement as we tried fitfully to sleep, Bryan with his teddy bear. But the pizza? I don't remember eating anything.

He said, "Yeah. We ate pizza after we stopped crying."

Then the day came back to me; it just came flooding back. Another snapshot memory from that day.

He said it so matter-of-factly, as if he was recounting getting on the bus in the morning to go to school. That night when I put him to bed he started crying. We talked some, and we hugged, and I tucked him in.

Now my attention and sadness and grief includes even more than before about what these boys have lost. I can see now how I can find someone else in my life; it will never be the same, of course. No one can ever replace Amy. But I can see myself with another companion, and not just theoretically, because Lori is in my life. But for my boys—they don't get another mom. Amy was their mom. She's Mom.

Last Saturday I woke up, got out of bed, came downstairs. The boys were still asleep. That's a good time of day, early morning; it's one of the few alone times I have. I was in the kitchen, making coffee, and I decided to make oatmeal. The real thing, steel-cut oats.

I said to myself, "I'm gonna make that. I've got time."

As I was going through the motions of preparing the food I became aware that I was feeling normal. I felt like myself. Not happy, not sad, just me again. It was the first time I was aware of that feeling, and it was nice. I decided to make muffins for the boys. I made these chocolate-peanut-butter-banana muffins that they like. I took my coffee out on the front porch and read the paper.

I still felt normal.

I took the boys out to run errands, and that feeling lasted the entire day and into Sunday. It felt really good, and for the first time I just felt like I could be myself again. It may not have been the first time I felt good, but it was the first time I was aware of it and was okay with it and thought that maybe I could somehow not be sad all the time.

Part of this, this feeling of being myself again, is being able to get beyond the grief and sadness, from time to time. But there's another part, and it is hard to describe. After Amy died, I suddenly felt like I stood out, was somehow different. I was very self-conscious, especially early on, and felt that I'd been marked "Widower," like it was a scarlet letter. I imagined walking downtown and people nodding at me and whispering among themselves in conversation I couldn't hear:

"There's John."

"The one who lost his wife."

"Poor John."

Shaking their heads.

I don't know if there was any truth to it, or if I only imagined it, but I'd be reminded each time someone, and with good intentions, would bump into me and ask me, very seriously, "How are you *really* doing?" Sometimes I would be glad for it, but sometimes I just wanted to be about my errands and not be reminded, and I certainly did not want to be "Poor John."

So it felt good to be out and about and to feel like I could be myself again, to feel that I could just say things the way John would say things, and I wouldn't have to pretend to be mourning, to assume the persona of a widower. Because part of it was just that. People would see me in town, and it looked like they expected me to be sad, so then I felt myself becoming sad. It's a strange thing. I wanted to be happy, but sometimes I felt there was this expectation for me to be sad.

There have been a few times when I'd be out and about and actually feeling fine—as "fine" as I could be—when I'd run into someone, and they'd come up to me with such a weighty look and feel to them. They'd say something like, "John. I'm so sorry. I haven't had a chance to reach out to you."

And it would all come back, and then I actually would be sad.

But now I can feel a shift of some sort going on inside me. Maybe it's because we are approaching the one-year passing of Amy's death. Yes, there is a sense of dread as it approaches, but I am also beginning to feel I can get beyond it and be myself again. Whatever my new normal is, I guess maybe I'm starting to feel okay with it.

So last Saturday when I got up and made oatmeal and muffins I could sense the "me" starting to come out, and that was nice.

That feeling? It lasted a couple of days.

—

Along with whatever this new normal is for me is a strong sense of what is around me. My space. And recently I've been aware of the clutter in the house.

Back in the fall I was looking at our little coat closet, and two-thirds of the usable space was Amy's stuff—coats, mostly. Amy's coats. Just sitting there, where they'd been for months. All of a sudden this feeling rushed over me, this sense of urgency that I had to clean stuff out. Now! I grabbed the collection of coats by their hangers, lifted them all off at the same time, and I lugged them all to the couch and set them there.

I sat down next to them and stared at the whole pile, and I started to cry.

After a minute I thought, "What the fuck am I going to do with these coats?" Should I stick them in a box? I can't *throw* them away. I guess I'll give them away, but to whom? And was I really ready to give them all away? Amy had worn those coats. I could see her standing there, in one of those coats, with her mittens and a knit cap, ready to go out in the cold. I wanted to hold her, so much; I pulled one of her coats to me. I was sad that I couldn't really smell her anymore in them. Somehow I sort of expected—or "hoped" is really the better word—I *hoped* that I'd smell her in her clothes. I could almost remember her smell. So subtle, the soap she used, non-perfumed, but just this smell of her hair and skin and even her breath. But it wasn't there in her coats anymore. They just smelled like coats that had been in a closet for a while.

Then I started to curse myself.

Goddammit! You have no plan for this. Dragging all these coats out here. That was impulsive!

I picked them up and put them back in the closet.

Fuck.

I sat back down again. I thought, not only do I still not have closet space; I'm going to have to do this *again*. I'm going to have to go through this closet *again* and go through the emotion and the feeling and the pain all over again someday.

I got pissed at myself for creating double the anguish with the coats.

After that experience a gradual feeling of clutter started to build inside me, and I began to really fixate on it. Not just Amy's stuff, either—clutter in general. I started feeling anxious about it. It was weighing me down, becoming a burden.

I spent a couple of weeks last fall going through all the boys' clothes. They had so much crap—things they don't even wear anymore because they've outgrown them, and hand-me-downs that have been hand-me-downs twice. I made several trips to Value Village and got rid of a bunch of their stuff. That felt good. I went through all my clothes and got rid of a bunch, and that felt good, too. I started going through their toys and trinkets and broken pieces of things—all the crap that accumulates over time. It's unbelievable. The sheer weight of stuff I was able to remove from this house was amazing.

And that was just the beginning, the obvious stuff. There were some items that took more thought. Like bookshelves.

We had lots of books. Amy and I loved to read, and we kept our books. Amy, in particular. But I was noticing how much room they took up, and I was beginning to see the reality that most were books I'd never read again. I looked around the living room, and I saw these bookshelves, and I wished I could move them out of there and move all the books somewhere else. But where? It's not like there was space somewhere else. Then I thought maybe I should get rid of them, donate them to the library or something. I resolved to sort through them. Then I just sat in front of the bookshelf and stared at it.

One bookshelf had all these travel books—Fodor's, Lonely Planet, Frommer's—from trips we'd taken. I couldn't get rid of those. Amy had hundreds of science fiction books, and I have plenty, too. And then one day it just happened. It struck me, and I thought—it's not so much that I have all these books, but that I have all these book*shelves*. It's almost the notion that I have all these books *because* I have the bookshelves. The less furniture I have to store things, the fewer things I need to store. So I started moving the books into boxes to donate and got rid of the bookshelves. Put them on the curb. Neighbors claimed some; others went to the thrift store. And I started to feel better.

Part of it was that it felt "right" to do that. The space felt better. Our house is small. But the other thing I started to realize as I was doing this was that I could make decisions on my own. Of course, I know I can make my own decisions—I'm a grown man. But it's different now that Amy is not here to consult or even argue with.

It's funny how this has shifted. Moving furniture can be a moment of reckoning for a couple, right? "Where should this go?" "Do you think it looks better over here?" "No? Should we try it over here?" I don't have that conflict any more, and it's kind of nice, I hate to say it. I was actually anticipating conflict inside myself, as if I'd somehow be betraying Amy, or somehow disrespecting her, or not honoring her somehow. Even the simple act of moving furniture. But as I was going through it, that feeling never materialized, and it surprised me.

Instead, what happened was that I was reporting back to her. I'd be going through this conversation: "Amy, I know you know how I felt about those bookshelves. I'm sorry, but I think it'll make more sense for us to clear out this bookshelf and move it to Adam's room to use for storage space. And the little nightstand that your grandfather made? It's really nice, Amy. It really deserves to be out here for people to enjoy rather than up in our room where only we could see it, don't you think?"

These conversations would go on not only in my head but also out loud, back and forth. So I can imagine the outside observer saying, "Who's this guy talking to?"

I wonder how many crazy people we see walking on the street talking to themselves are actually talking to their loved ones who have died.

Then there's the stuff from the boys' schools. The abundance of paper that comes home is simply amazing: papers to be signed, emergency contact cards, the PTA thing, the fundraiser thing, all the papers for all the field trips, and every blessed little assignment and project and notice. And Amy used to handle all of it. So when I was going through the boys' rooms and clearing out stuff, I came across these banker's boxes *full* of memorabilia from elementary and preschool. It dawned on me what she had been planning to do. She had collected all the school stuff that entered the house, stuck it in the boxes, and then at some point she probably thought, "When I have that free afternoon or weekend, I'll go through the boys' stuff and throw away the litany of work papers and keep the important ones."

Well, the free afternoon or weekend didn't come.

So here I am—there are three boxes for Adam and five boxes for Bryan.

I consulted with two single moms I knew. I asked them, what the hell do you do with all these papers?

They both laughed and said, "Yeah, it's amazing the amount of stuff that comes home. Here's my process ..." And they told me that they each have one box to keep everything in, and when they have the time, they go through it and pull out whatever's meaningful for keeping.

I said, "Well, yeah, I guess that's what Amy was doing."

But I am not that type of sorter. So I ended up throwing away *pounds* of paper. As much as I could recycle I did, but a lot of it was mixed media art projects, or laminated with plastic. I did keep a couple really nice ones, and those I am going to put on a wall somewhere.

For me, it was this sense of shedding, this sense of shedding *stuff*. It feels really good when I drop stuff off at Value Village.

Now none of that has been Amy's yet. In fact, this was all precipitated by the coats-in-the-closet episode, but none of what I've gotten rid of is hers. Not yet.

Back to the office—our home office has become a dumping ground these past six months. I mean, I can't even walk through it. There is just shit *everywhere*. Now I don't even like to go there when I need to work—and I wonder if it's about that space, because the two of us would be in the office, down in the basement, sort of parallel working. Amy on her stuff and me on my stuff. So, afterwards, after she died, I'd find myself sitting in my chair, and I'd catch myself looking over at her empty chair. I don't know how many hours we spent just being in that same space together. Then I'd be looking around my desk, thinking, "Goddammit." I've got so much crap to get rid of. I don't even know where to start.

Then I'd sit in her chair. Just sit there. I'd start imagining the work she would have been doing, day-job work she brought home, volunteer work, PTA, the birth center, and all the stuff she's got filed away for us and the kids and just—I don't know. I don't even know where to start.

I was sitting at her desk one day in the fall, and I noticed her bag, the bag she was carrying the day she died; it was still sitting there, under her desk, with whatever work papers she had taken to work that day. I had put it there in the summer after my friend had sorted through the biohazard bag. I picked it up and started going through it. There was her lunch carrier. One of those soft sided rectangular carriers with a strap on in with a zippered lid. I made lunch every morning for all of us.

What am I going to do with this? Am I ever going to use this lunch carrier again?

I picked it up. I looked at it. It was a little dirty and a bit banged up.

God, was it *always* that banged up? Did it come loose in the accident and go skittering across the street?

I unzipped it. There was an empty plastic sandwich container with a lid, and the melted freezer pack, and a spoon. So I probably sent her off with a yogurt, a peanut butter and jelly sandwich, a banana or an apple, and a sports bar. That would have been her lunch that day. All the food was gone. Probably cleaned out by the police or my friend.

Am I going to use this plastic sandwich container again? Will I use this lunch carrier ever again? Can I do that?

I'll just put the spoon back in the dishwasher, and it'll get mixed in with the others, and that way I'll never know which one it was.

Then the sandwich container—I could put that back on the shelf with all the other plastic stuff, and when I need to put something in it, when I reach for it, will I think about how this was *the* sandwich container that had Amy's sandwich in it when she was killed? Will I think about that? Do I want that in my house? Or do I want to get rid of it? And what does it mean to get rid of it?

So it's simple things like that. A simple decision of whether I should keep a plastic container or not suddenly carries enormous weight. A plastic sandwich container has a weight to it that it never, ever had before.

I sat there for I don't know how long. A minute? Ten minutes? It's hard to know. But in the end I decided to keep the sandwich container. I put the freezer pack back in the freezer. I don't know which one it is. There are three or four in there, mixed up.

But the lunch carrier itself I threw away because I wouldn't use it, ever. And that was hard to do, to throw that away. It rested on top of the trash. You can't recycle that. It was one of those soft foam cube containers with a strap handle, and it was too beat up to send to Value Village or Goodwill.

I don't remember crying when I set it in the trash. But I don't remember not crying, either.

So there are a thousand things in this house like that. I still have the same pile of Amy's dirty laundry. I've moved it from the hamper into a laundry basket that sits in my room. It's been sitting there for months. I haven't even touched it. There are dirty socks and pantyhose of hers. In the closet by the bathroom there's another hamper. Just sitting there. I'm not sure if I'm afraid to even touch them, or if it's something else.

I know when I touch them it's going to be hard, and I don't know what I will do with those. Do I wash them and give them away? For some reason, to me, those are the last remnants of her in this house—whatever is on her dirty clothes.

The clean clothes are different somehow. I don't expect it will be easier, but it's just different somehow. I know at some point I'll go through that stuff, and I'll find clothes that I didn't even know she had, so I don't expect them to conjure a memory of some thing or some time we shared.

I remember one shirt of hers. We'd taken a trip up to New York, and halfway there she realized she had forgotten her nightclothes, so she bought an extra-extra large "I ♥ New York" T-shirt, kind of as a little souvenir. "Well, we're in New York. I guess I have to get an I-heart-New-York T-shirt." So she wore that to bed, just that weekend we were there. I don't know if she ever wore it after that. So that's somewhere in her clothes drawers, and that's one I know that I cannot give away. I'll just keep that.

So I'm expecting that. That reaction.

There are other pieces of clothing that I won't remember the meaning of, until I come across them. And I'm not quite ready for that.

Amy had two large steamer trunks of belly dance and folk dance costumes she used for dancing performances. Not just costumes, but scarves and veils and jangly-bangly things the scarves looped through. Those trunks had been sitting up in our bedroom, too. There was something about those, though, that felt different. It's hard to describe exactly, but I felt ready to let those go.

After she died that was the first place I went, because it's the image of her as a dancer that I carry forward. I knelt there and pulled a few things out almost immediately, just to hold, and smell, and be close to.

I finally decided what to do with her dancing clothes. I contacted two other dancers from her troupe and they are coming over soon, and Amy's mom is coming over, too, to go through it all and take what they can. Right now I feel good about them coming and taking what can be reused. I know Amy would want that; she wouldn't want that stuff hiding in a box. It needs to get out and see the light of day, to be part of someone's life, someone's dancing life. I know that and I want that, too. I feel okay with that somehow, maybe because they are costumes, and they aren't what Amy wore on a day-to-day basis. To me that's different from the clothes she wore every day. It's hard to describe, but this'll be the first of her things I'll give away.

So we'll see how that goes. The four of us will go through them. I imagine I'll let the boys pick out something if they want to.

And even though clearing things out is easier, I'd still get stuck, so I hired a woman, a de-cluttering coach. She was great. A year ago I would have rolled my eyes at the thought of hiring someone for this. Now? Now she's exactly what I need. She came in and helped clear a couple of mental blocks I was having about certain things, things I wouldn't get rid of. Like clothes. She made me feel okay that they were better donated to someone who could use them. And she was right. And the paperwork in the office. She helped me see past the enormity of the task and to a place of de-clutter.

In reality, I know these items—clothes, books, furniture—are just that: items. Things don't *make* us. *We* make the thing. I know that. I understand that. But, still, every one of those things was an expression of her in some subtle way—what she wore, what she read, who she was. Those things were her impressions on the world. And each time I gave away one of Amy's things, I gave away a part of Amy.

—

We ended the interview there. We had to. It was late. John had to prepare for his boys coming home from school; I had to get back home. As I was packing up we talked a little longer about the things you'd normally talk about: work, family. The "getting on and through" of life. I thanked John again, at the door, and as we were saying our goodbyes we hugged. Greeting and leaving. Greeting, the hug signified our missing each other, our happiness in seeing the other. Leaving, the hug seemed heavy. It was the hardest part, now. I imagine what was going through my mind was also going through John's mind. The way Amy was killed altered our thoughts about life and death. Forever. How could it not? Our eyes met momentarily and I knew we both had that same horrible flitting thought. I could see it in John's eyes. How can two people talk about life and death and then just say goodbye without wondering if this will be the last one? I smiled at John and we hugged. Of course we would see each other again. That's what we were planning to do. I'd see him again. Just like I was now. To meet one final time, in spring, at the anniversary of her death. I was thinking about Amy and what future things she might have been planning as she left her house that morning.

I didn't want to let go of John.

Spring

"Don't be satisfied with stories, how things have gone with others.
Unfold your own myth."
—Rumi

Spring.

I remember it. So many thoughts swirling in my head: endings, beginnings, rebirth, new life springing from the old earth, always at this turn, this cycle of the year.

When I left John in February I could sense that he was on steadier ground. He seemed to be coming into a new season of his life, and I was happy for him, happy for his boys, happy that he'd found a woman with whom he might be able to share his life going forward. John and I exchanged some emails after those sessions in February, and I called to check in.

He asked me how I'd like to finish up.

I said, "One session. We should finish in one sitting. On the anniversary."

John told me he was planning on having a small gathering of family and close friends at his house on Friday, April 29, 2011, the one-year anniversary of Amy's death. He invited me, but I didn't want to interfere with that, with his family, so we planned on meeting the following day. He said he was having a few friends over that day, too, but it was going to be a much smaller party, and he'd make time away from the guests for us to talk. It would be our final interview session.

"You can meet Lori," he said.

"I'd like that," I said. "Is it okay if Gina comes along?"

"Of course," John said. "We'd love to see her."

I reconfirmed the time with him.

"Can you bring some cigars?" he asked.

"Sure," I said, "if you bring out the Scotch."

We laughed. It felt good to laugh, together, even if our laughter was tinged with the ever-present heartache.

Driving down to his house that Saturday, I had a deep and abiding sense of relief and sorrow, grief and joy. I held on to Gina's hand. Her presence calmed me, as it does. She was sitting next to me in my car; I recalled John's story about driving with his boys, alone, no Amy next to him—*Not this time*, he'd said. Simple words to describe a horror none of us expects, and few of us will experience, in life. I squeezed Gina's hand.

Driving, my mind sifted through memories from the beginning of this project, last summer, to now, this end, and everything in between.

Now, it was over, I told myself. John and I were about to finish what we'd started last summer. At the same time I knew that this was not the end but a new beginning. The time we spent talking had been recorded, yes, but now those words were waiting for us to make something from them. Waiting for us to review them and revise them and sift through them, like old photographs in a family album. Items needed placement, structuring, development. We'd need to bring order to our original, raw, spoken conversations.

Spring carries with it so many mixed meanings. Easter Sunday was April 24 that year. Death, burial, resurrection. Leavings and arrivals.

I thought of John and Adam and Bryan, now a full year distant from that awful morning of April 29, 2010, when Amy was ripped out of their lives. I remembered sitting with John last year in the summer, listening to him tell the story of that day, that morning, when the policeman had met him at work and asked, "Are you John Robinette? And your wife's Amy Polk?" I thought about John's boys, Adam and Bryan, coming home early that day from school, bounding up the front porch steps. That bright and terrible image above most others, I think, is seared into my mind's eye. That youthful joy of coming home, racing home. I can see so clearly those two young boys bounding up the steps with their school backpacks and dashing into the front room to see their father sitting on the couch.

To tell them that their world had changed forever.

My God.

So heart-wrenching.

The verse from Ecclesiastes came to me: "For everything there is a season, and a time for every matter under heaven: a time to be born, and a time to die; a time to plant, and a time to pluck up what is planted ..." (Ecclesiastes 3:1–2).

Tears welled in my eyes; I brushed them away; I had to drive the car. I held Gina's hand.

I thought of the back porch talk with John in the fall, smoking cigars and sipping Armagnac. That was a pleasant memory of our times together. I tried to linger on that before I moved on to the terrible interview session between Christmas and New Year's Day, how hard that time had been on John and his boys and their extended family.

I forced myself forward into thoughts past the new year, talking with John about God, celebrating Amy's birthday with the balloon release, learning about Lori, and John trying to get on with life.

The getting on with life.

I thought about our interview session now, coming up, this final one. One year had passed since Amy's death. I was wondering what John could say, what he would say, what he would *want* to say. And for myself, I knew I'd be saying goodbye to Amy, in my own way. Never again would John and I have this time back, this year, to talk so deeply, so expansively, as we'd done.

All these thoughts and attendant emotions were mixing and rising up in my mind, my heart, during my drive down to see John. I had a real sense of new birth mixed with feelings of finality, closure, for what we were doing within the space we were calling "this project," and for what it had done to me, for me.

This project.

This talking.

This sharing.

This record.

This view into a man's life after such an incomprehensible loss.

What John and I were doing at the end of all this was each one of those words rolling around in my head, and more. I was grasping for words to describe what we'd been doing this entire year since Amy's death—to help define it, understand it—not only for myself but, ultimately, for anyone reading what we would eventually produce.

I felt it had to be the right word, too, for me, so that I could understand the entirety of this event—Amy's death, the conversations I recorded with John. I'd learned last year from John how words matter. So much. I kept thinking, kept digging.

This book, yes, this book—but even more than that, it was a testament.

This testament.

Was that the word I should use? It seemed sacrilegious, but that is what it was, I felt. It was a testament of what we'd done as two men sitting down to talk, an account of John's grief and growth and renewal. How else would his two boys know what their father had gone through with them in such detail during that first terrible year after their mother's death? So it was a testament, a proof. Stories handed down from father to son. But not just a testament of a single person, or of two friends sharing their lives through conversation, but a testament of love and life. And, for me, proof that I counted, too, that I'd helped a friend manage a grief so terrible it's hardly imaginable, barely describable. Yet this is what we had done. Proof that I had completed what I intended to do.

I was satisfied that I'd found language to put to our shared experience. I was glad we had done it, but I was so very glad that it was coming to an end. Recalling events with John, listening to his stories, examining the wild range of emotions and their impact on him and his boys—as engaging as this process was, it was exhausting. I was ready for the conclusion.

Saturday, April 30, 2011, was a beautiful spring day in Maryland. The narrow street outside John's house was crowded with cars. Regular street parking plus the few guests for his party. I had to park down from his house a bit, and Gina and I walked up.

The party was outside on the back patio. Gina and I were introduced around. We met Lori. We shook hands and hugged. Everyone there knew about this project now; John had told them. So when the time came for us to slip away, there was no question about why. John and I sat down inside his screened porch, alone and away from the crowd.

A tray with two glasses and Scotch were set out. I showed John my cigar carrying case. We talked pleasantries while I got out my gear and set up, and we both settled in.

"What do you want to talk about?" I asked.

"I've thought about that," he said. "A few things are on my mind."

—

I should tell you some of what happened yesterday, the day that marked one year. It's strange, how much goes into one year—not just the time and activity, but even the concept of the cycle, the expectations that time carries, the weight of it, and how much leads up to the complete "first year" after someone's death. We have this way of thinking about it, as if something happens after twelve months, but not at eleven or thirteen months.

It's only been recently since I could let myself even consider what it would be like at the first year, plus one day.

I started to imagine comparing it to other life milestones, like when someone asks on your birthday, "So, how does it feel to be forty-four?" And we all know the response. "Well, it kind of feels like it did yesterday."

So I was imagining that today would feel like yesterday, and the day before, and to some extent, it does. It's not as if suddenly everything's fine and we're in whatever our new reality is, or whatever our new normal is, *now*, officially, here and in place. It's still very much evolving.

So, I think, unfortunately, I was right. Today is like yesterday, which was like the day before, and the day before that.

But in another way it *is* different. I was somewhat startled this morning as I was lying in bed. Letting it really sink it that it's a year later. I almost said out loud, "I don't have to go through *that year* ever again." And that felt okay. I was glad I felt that way. I wasn't happy, but I felt okay.

Perhaps there is something to the Jewish tradition of lifting the veil off the headstone after the first year.

I still get these feelings—they're subtler now—where I'll say to myself, "Oh, yeah, she's still dead." It's every day, probably several times a day, sometimes. I might be getting lost in whatever it is I'm doing with the kids, or at work, when things sort of feel normal, like when I've forgotten about it for a while, I'll have a moment and it snaps me back. "Oh. Yeah. That's right. Shit."

As winter started shifting into spring, something different happened inside me. There was foreboding. The anticipation of longer and warmer days, being outside, going on hikes, mowing the lawn, sitting by a pool—all that had been nudged aside by a more recent memory of long, warm days, sitting alone on the front porch in the hot summer, slowly getting drunk. I could feel it all over again as the weather started to shift. I really was not looking forward to spring because I could feel them coming back again, the memories, and I could recall the more intense feelings from last summer, the echo of the intense grief of a year ago reawakened by the changing seasons.

I have an image of a flooded rock quarry, its sheer walls going straight up, and the deep still water, and if a large boulder falls right into the center of it, the waves would cast out concentrically until they hit the walls, and then they would reflect back to the center. The waves would ripple out and then bounce back and come back in, and each time you'd feel it, but it wouldn't be quite as intense as before. The height of the wave would be a little less every time, and then the ripples would start to interfere with each other, so the big swells would begin to merge with the smaller swells, and then it would all eventually settle down. But that rock is now in there, forever, somewhere at the bottom of that flooded quarry.

It's like that for me. I get these echoes, reverberations, of last summer passing through me. One was triggered by that first warm day of early spring. It triggered the thought, "Oh, yeah. I remember the last time it felt warm. Yeah. It was when I learned my wife was dead."

It got cold and dreary in March, which was actually kind of nice. I felt almost happy for that. I actually thanked God that it was miserable outside. It was nothing like the warm summer of last year, which reminds me of Amy's death.

But then the event itself, the "event" of yesterday, the marker, if you will—I won't call it an "anniversary," because that word doesn't fit. I think I need anniversaries to be celebratory. At least, they've always been for me, until now. So with that marker coming up, I knew I needed to do something. I knew that. From the lesson of Christmas Day, I knew I had to create an event, surround myself with people. Not to necessarily "celebrate" it, but simply to be with people to stave off the loneliness.

It was just dumb luck that April 29 was a Friday this year. Once I had the boys off on the school bus, I headed to Bethesda to my shrink's office. So that was a good way to start the day for me.

It wasn't as hard as I imagined it would be. I walked in, and the first thing I did was sit down and cry. A lot of it was just the buildup to that "event," I think. If you've ever played sports, or done public speaking, it's that lead-in, the buildup, to the event. I've spoken in front of enough crowds or at meetings, and for me, it's that hour before going on that is stressful. Once I get going I'm going. It's the anxiety and tension and nerves before "The Big Game." I think there was a variation of that sort of lead-in anxiety, but I felt a calmness as the hour was unfolding, sitting there talking.

After that I had planned for a friend to come over and be my "chaperone" for a couple hours at my house. My family from New Jersey was coming down, and Amy's mom and stepdad were coming over from Virginia. I picked the boys up from school. We all met at the church at 1:30.

In our church, in the back of the sanctuary along the wall, hang seven handmade quilts. Large, tapestry-sized quilts. This is where we record the names of those in our community who've died. One quilt has embroidered names of those who died before 1985; the second has the names of those who died between 1985 and 1995. The third quilt has the names of children. And there are a lot of names on that quilt. Those three quilts are in the middle. Then the four other quilts, two to the left and two to the right, each depict a scene of a season of the year—winter and spring on the left, then summer and autumn on the right. Below each scene is a panel with space to add more names, for those who've died since 1995.

One of the women who does the embroidery met us at the church. We put Amy's name on the spring quilt. We each took turns pulling the needle through one or two times. I had cut a thin piece of fabric off the bottom hem of that sheer, gauzy, white dress that Amy had gotten when we were in Greece. I also took a piece of fringe off of one of her veils, one of the scarves she had used in her dance. Amy's mom pulled a piece of brown yarn from a doll that Amy had loved when she was a little girl. We twisted the fibers into the embroidery thread and stitched that in.

I remember sitting there, in church, before any of this ever happened, looking up at these beautiful quilts with all these names. And I remember thinking, "My God. What would I do if I had to put one of my children's names on one of those quilts? Or Amy's name on a quilt? What if maybe someday *my* name is on that quilt?"

And there we were.

I didn't know very well the woman who had volunteered to help us with the embroidery—but I found out that one of the names on the children's quilt was her son. He had been killed in a car crash when he was thirty-three years old. It was four years ago, and I just didn't know that. I thought of the grief that each one of us must bear without others ever knowing it. It's unseen, but it's in each one of us.

We do not have a big church community. There are about 350 members. But there are a lot of names on those quilts. Maybe twenty-five or thirty names on each quilt. The children's quilt goes back twenty years, and some of them are kids who died at childbirth or when they were young, and some who died as adults, but who had been children in our community. So being part of that community and history now, and seeing all the other names, gives me some comfort. But there's also a lot of sadness that comes in knowing this. It's the knowledge of joy and sorrow—now I see it. In that sanctuary where we gather in love are the names of those whose loss we're grieving.

We finished the quilt, put it back up, and we came back home.

—

Besides Friday being my shrink day, on the last Friday of each month a bunch of guys from church get together. Guys' night out. We've been doing it for about four or five years. We joke and call it Gentlemen's Club. We'll go hang out at somebody's house or go out to a bar and have some drinks or go out to dinner. It's a pretty low-key affair.

I said, "Look, you guys have been there for me a lot this year, and I need you guys one more time—let's have Gentlemen's Club at my place."

Then I started thinking about everyone else who had been there for me in the past year, and I quickly lost count, so I just decided to essentially open up the house.

It wound up being a big party. So it certainly accomplished my objective of not being alone! Probably a hundred people came through here yesterday, which was really nice.

Lori was here, too. She met my parents and siblings. There are moments when I can try to step outside of myself, out of the situation, and look at it dispassionately. Here is a woman who has not only entered my life, but my kids' lives, too, and beyond that—she has become a part of this very large circle of people, lovely people, family, neighbors, friends. And she isn't shy about it at all. It's really quite remarkable. I don't think I could do it, if the roles were reversed. I feel it's enough that she's just there for me, for us. But she also took an active role and helped plan the whole event. And everyone seemed really happy she was there, and happy for me.

I'm glad yesterday went as it did, now that it's over. I think it was good for other people, too. Being with others, seeing how this event has impacted each one of them— somehow I feel less alone. I am part of a larger community. And that is something that matters. And as the first year ends, as it all settles in, it's becoming clearer to me how certain things that used to matter to me now don't matter to me at all.

—

In my line of work, I have to deal with lots of different opinions and feelings and emotions, and there used to be a time, a year and a day ago, when if there was some disagreement or misunderstanding, or two people weren't quite getting along, I prided myself, as a manager, a leader, on my ability to bring people together, to be a good communicator, to find consensus, if it was possible, and if not, to find a compromise.

But now?

Now I just have no patience for it, at all. For *what*? It comes up all the time—somebody feels slighted or ignored, or whatever the misperception is. Before, my attitude was: "Let's sit down. Let's talk about it. Let's see if we can understand all sides of this thing."

But now I find I do not have time for this. Or maybe it's the patience for it. Perhaps the best way to say it is that a year and a day ago I was using a different model of how things "worked." I was using a different model with a different set of understandings and assumptions of what was important in life and at work and what the priorities were as I managed the affairs of a team trying to get tasks done. And in my old way of looking at the world, I can see that I spent a lot more time and energy on things that, now, quite frankly, seem trivial, inconsequential.

So here I am now, a year and a day later, and what I understood as important isn't the same anymore. Petty grievances between the kids or with a colleague at work or between two colleagues seem nearly irrelevant to me. In the past I would have taken the time to fully understand them and come to some resolution. But while I see that my old way of understanding the world isn't valid anymore, I don't have a solid, *new* understanding yet. I think we tend to walk around life with a whole set of understandings about the nature of reality and how our worldviews are based on culture and our parents and our religions and so on. And they're important because they create an anchor for us so we don't just float away. That set of assumptions about the nature of reality is really important. And now, for me, that old set of assumptions no longer fits my new reality, and I haven't quite worked out a new set of assumptions. So I still feel adrift. As if my anchor has come loose in a storm.

We don't necessarily ask ourselves the big questions—Why are we here? What's my purpose? Where am I going?—every day when we get up. Ugh, it's Tuesday morning. The alarm just went off. "Why am I here? What's my purpose? What's the meaning of life?" But these are the questions that lie underneath, perhaps, just waiting for some existential jolt, like Amy's death, to pop to the surface and stay there for a while.

When we're little kids we start to grapple with those questions, as they start to emerge in our consciousness, and we do our best to answer them for ourselves. First our parents or teachers help us answer those questions. The way other people view things—our friends, for example—can help us, of course, but at the end of the day we're left to figure it out ourselves. And when we hit those teen years the questions come up again and maybe we come up with different answers. But maybe the answers start feeling less certain. There are times in life when I think we return to the day-to-day probing that many of us go through in adolescence, and through the difficulties of being teenagers, heading out of our homes, discovering who we are in the world. Different life milestones can bring the questions back up again. Certainly, Amy's death forced a reevaluation for me.

So that is going on now, very much so, to the point where I'm about ready to declare that I know the answers don't exist. It sounds like hubris to basically state with certainty that thousands of years of religion, philosophy, and science are all for naught, but that's where I am. So my beliefs are simple now: This is life; it's what we have, just this one. I was talking to my shrink about this yesterday, and I started wondering, "How much time have I spent on Amy's death?"

It's a ridiculous, horrible question to ask, isn't it? Hundreds of hours of work get thrown off by someone's death. Not just the paperwork, but all the emotional work, those hours and hours of misery and pain and anguish, or numbness. Hours of therapy. Not to mention the cost of all the Scotch. And my capacity to do other things has been completely wiped out by the emotional pain and weight of this event. Add to that, then, the struggle to find and make an entirely *new* way of living, of being alone, of trying to help my boys come to terms with this event and live through it. Put on top of all that the pondering of the existence of who and what and where she is now. When Amy was alive I didn't spend much time at all thinking about death and what comes next. But now I do, with some frequency—when I'm driving to work, or in a meeting, or even trying to listen to a colleague's complaint. Something triggers a thought, and then I'm off wondering, is Amy aware right now of what we are going through? Is there an immortal soul, or not? I'm listening to a colleague, or pretending to listen, nodding my head, saying "uh-huh" at the right times, but I'm not really listening. I'm thinking about Amy and if she has a soul and if she can hear this crazy conversation I'm in.

So that's what I mean when I talk about "spending time" on Amy's death. How do you add all that up? How do you quantify that? I do not know if I could ever calculate how much time I've spent on her death. And for all the time I have been spending asking questions, I am beginning to see that many of the questions are unanswerable.

So why am I wasting my time trying to come up with the answers? Why am I reading these books on life and death, and the philosophy of death? Why am I pondering going back to the Bible and reading it? Because, in the end, so what? I'm not going to find an answer in any of those places, really. I'll find some suggestions. I'll find what other people thought. And to me, it's not that one's right and one's wrong. Or even if one is, how could we possibly know? And yet it feels we are cursed, in a way, to *want* to know. We *want* to know something that, in the end, is unknowable. We crave the answers. We fight over the answers. But there really is no answer. So why debate it?

I've been thinking about that. How it is that we so badly want to debate a right and a wrong out of everything—politics, science, religion. It's like the goddamn tree of the knowledge of good and evil. Not that I believe in a true Adam or a true Eve in the literal sense, but this notion of how we are cursed is coming alive for me now. We are cursed with this ability for rational thought, the ability to probe and to inquire and to wonder, and in so doing we're completely cast out and ripped apart from the rest of nature. We are put in conflict with the natural balance, the natural balancing forces. Our rational brains imagine wonderful things. Art, science, music, architecture. And we also imagine our own death. Unlike the other creatures in Eden who continue in blissful ignorance of their mortality, we are cursed with the awareness of ours. So we *actively* resist our mortality. We're in *active* conflict, against our own demise, against our own suffering. Symbolically, we're cursed: women with the pains of childbirth and men to toil forever. But that just scratches the surface of our suffering.

I've wondered about this before, and it might be in alignment with how the Buddhists would view life on earth and the endless cycle of suffering of birth, death, and rebirth, the recurrent lives, samsara. If you were going to design hell, would not a pernicious hell be one where you held in front of people beauty and love, let them smell it, let them taste it, taste all that is wonderful, only to snatch it away from them from time to time?

That would be a really diabolical hell, wouldn't it?

Here we are. We fall in love with someone, and they're taken away. We see beauty, and it is destroyed.

And I can't help but wonder if we humans weren't tricked from the outset. What if maybe we were tricked into believing that we are trying to avoid hell, when, in fact, that's exactly where we are.

What's my point? We don't have to look too far back in history to find all sorts of crimes humans have committed against one another in the name of, let's say, God. But even more than that, the social and cultural order of various periods have allowed for human sacrifice, or slavery, or oppression. Time passed, and we discarded those old cultural models for a better one. We stopped sacrificing humans and sacrificed only animals. And then we stopped sacrificing animals. But regardless of whether we still believe the old cultural model or a new one, there is still a fundamental assumption we typically make. That is, there is something behind all of this. A purpose. A plan. That's what we tell ourselves. But is that really true?

One day you're out doing your own thing. Whatever it is. You're going to school. Your kids are at school. You make love to your wife, then go to work. You just so happen to live on the coast of Japan—then boom, gone, in an instant, wiped out, destroyed by a tsunami. Or a tornado rips through your house but not your neighbor's house. Or you live in the Ninth Ward in New Orleans. Or in my case, some guy wasn't paying close enough attention while he was driving his truck and he drove over my wife. It's inexplicable. There is an endless list of "natural" disasters, and human failings. There's no explaining them. Acts of God. Forces of nature. Distracted drivers. Life is that way. Nature is that way. *We* are that way. Nature's not evil. Nature's just nature. Nature claims what nature claims. And we are part of nature. So we shouldn't take it personally.

So, why do we have—why were we given, why did we evolve—this need to understand what's around us as part of some purpose? What is it about human nature, or human beings collectively, and our desire for purpose? Is it just that we have this large frontal lobe that's trying to figure out something that can never be figured out? What is that?

Think of all we've created in that name, in the name of any religion, any philosophy, trying to understand life and death. If you took away our innate desire and need to figure that out, if you could take that out of humanity, what would remain? Could we still sit on the porch with our loved ones and enjoy our glasses of wine? Could love continue to exist if all the suffering went away? Could love continue if we removed our ability and desire to question what our purpose is?

But I still don't understand the suffering part. Why is it intrinsic to the human condition? Could you not conjure a physical universe where we're still as intelligent and probing, but without the suffering? If God created this, and God is all-powerful, then couldn't God declare there be abundant love and no suffering?

So now I'm wondering, why even ask the question? Why ask whether or not there's something "out there" to make my life have meaning, or purpose? Why even ask the question?

I'm asking: Could you create an existence, a human cultural existence, without those questions being even *part* of our existence? Could you remove the question, "Why am I here?" Could you remove the question, "How did we get here?" Could you remove the question, "Where are we going?" Could you remove the question, "Is there a God, or not, and what's beyond?" Could we remove those questions and simply accept that the sun comes up every day, birds chirp, and the leaves come out in spring?

I wonder what that existence would look like. It seems as though it would remove a lot of the suffering that comes from not being able to answer those questions. Maybe that's what Adam and Eve experienced before they ate of the tree of knowledge of good and evil: the bliss of ignorance. But then they ate of that tree. Maybe that is the fundamental human curse. What was it like for Adam and Eve before that? Do you see? When I read Genesis I am struck by that moment when their humanity is revealed to them. And then I have to ask, why would God even create the opportunity for them to do that? Do you see? I'll put it this way—if you believe in the God of the Bible, you either believe in the Adam and Eve story, literal or figurative, or you believe God set us in motion to evolve to have this intelligence, which, at least right now, is the source of our wisdom and suffering. To me, now, that seems like an amazingly creative hell.

So now, when someone dies young or tragically, the attempt to understand the purpose of that life when the death seems perfectly purposeless, becomes itself a purposeless exercise. If I have a model of how the world works that makes no consideration of purpose, then the tragedy of this life struck down too early can be taken strictly at face value. Amy and I can't be together anymore, and that is painful and sad. We no longer get the benefit of her presence, her many possible accomplishments. It's all very, very sad, of course. But there is no questioning, "Why did this happen?" "Why me?" "Why are my boys the ones selected to have no mother?" Why ask those existential questions, which have no answers? They only contribute to our torment as humans. If we can make those questions go away, with them will go the suffering that comes with that pondering.

Or we can more simply say that the natural world creates enough pain and suffering without us adding to it with our constant desire to answer questions with no answers.

So, I think year two for me will be about how to recast the model, some-how, to find a new home for these questions, which have been detached from the old model, and are swirling around out there, looking for a new landing. My old model of how it all worked included a large space for the inquiry into those matters. Call it philosophy, call it religion; it doesn't matter. But right now, for me, those questions don't have a clear landing area.

I will say this, though. Even though I *don't* have a clear model for myself, a *fuck it* part is emerging. You know, just: *fuck it*. Maybe this is what the Buddha experienced. Maybe instead of coming to some new clarity, his nirvana, he just said, "Fuck it. It is what it is. It's unanswerable." And so he was enlightened.

And I can see advantages to living that way, to abandoning the natural impulses to assert our will to control the forces that will ultimately take us. Letting go of all that. But that seems, somehow, not right to me, either.

I still want to believe that it's all about love. Somehow the creation of love is part of the story. That sounds clichéd, I admit. It sounds like the end of the Beatles song—it *is* the end of a Beatles song! But I still want that to be true. I'd be okay if that were true. But with that understanding must come the opportunity for greater pain when the person you love is destroyed. Think about two bodies, stars or planets, in gravitational connection. At least, in a Newtonian sense, if one of the bodies is removed, say the star explodes, or just disappears, that gravitational pull between those two stars is now zero. There is no gravity. But when two people love each other, and one of them is taken away, the other person left behind still feels that force. That force of love. You have two humans in a love force connection, and even if you take one away, the feeling remains.

So if I believe that, at her death, the Amy I knew was annihilated, completely gone, and that she did not continue on in some way, in some spirit world, as a soul, some transformed essence ... If I *truly* believe in annihilation and yet I still love her, what is the object of my love? I am in love with the memory of her, which is why it aches so badly. But—and this is the important part—I still feel *her* love for me. It's just part of the pain.

So what is the source of *that*? Where does the feeling I have that she still loves me come from? She isn't here anymore. Am I creating it in my own mind? Did her love continue on in some new form? Was her love instead cast out from her like an exploding star, and is it gradually diffusing out through the universe? Is that what happens? Because I still feel it. I don't feel it constantly; I'm not constantly aware of it. It's like gravity in that regard, too, I suppose. I don't really think about gravity that much, right? Who does? Until I drop something on my foot. Or maybe it's like the stars. I'm not aware of the stars right now because it's the middle of the day, and their presence is washed out by our own star, the Sun. At night, though, they "reemerge." But they're always here.

So, let's just say I'm more *aware* of Amy's love at certain times than at other times. When I hear a story that reminds me of her, or when her mom visits, or when I hear a Madonna song, I can still feel it. Is it coming from her, my memory of her, or is it something that I created in myself? She may have also created in herself an understanding of the love I had for her. So, was she *really* feeling my love for her? Or was she feeling in herself only what she had created as my love for her? Is it a true force that gets sent from one person to another, or do I create through words and actions an ability for her mind to generate my love for her internally?

I don't know the answer to that.

I can see an appeal on either side of this. She was completely annihilated, and I still feel love for her, and love from her. If that's really just a creation of my own imagination, I'm actually okay with that, because I can control that now. I can continue to feel her love, as long as I'm able to conjure it in my own brain.

And if she was *not* completely annihilated, and her essence *is* somewhere, in some way, then it still generates love for me. And I'm okay with that, too.

The point is that it doesn't really matter. So why should I muse about it? For me, the question is satisfied either way.

And even though I've just told you I want to let go of these unanswerable questions, I still can't. I have a better appreciation that no answers are coming for "Why this?" "Why us?" "Why now?" But the questions remain. And then new love is entering my life. New love that, I know, is attached to the suffering of losing the object of my love.

I can't help myself. I still want love to win.

—

I waited a moment for John, for me, to say more, and then I realized neither one of us needed to say anything. It was done. I turned off the recorder.

John and I sat there and looked at each other. I wasn't sure if I was going to laugh or cry. I reached for the cigars as John started pouring the Scotch. I sat back and in that moment felt a love for him that I've too rarely felt in my life. It was a deep, abiding sense of love. He had taken what life had given him—the death of his wife, and a cruel death at that—and was finding a way.

I thought back to one of our conversations last year, when he had described that first week, how members of his church had sat silent in mourning with him in his living room, and that one particular moment when they quietly reached out to lay hands on him, calming him, assuring him of his place in the world, helping him through their touch.

Their human touch.

I thought, human "touch" can also happen through words. It's why we started this project. It's why people read books. To touch another life. So I felt, I thought, healing can take place there, too. Through our conversations I had felt a healing, not a laying on of hands but a laying on of words. At this end of it, I could say to myself that our conversations were medicine.

We raised our glasses in toast, and I think we both understood, without saying it, that in sorrow there can be cause for celebration. For us, it was the end of the year, the end of our project. We had done what we set out to do. We spoke briefly about next steps, and then we stopped. I think we both wanted to go back to enjoying that moment by being present in the moment. We sat and smoked and smiled, and we were quiet together.

I watched John and thought of his year after Amy's death and what he had to face. You will face yourself, I thought, whoever that person is, and deal with it. I smiled and felt love for this man, for our shared experience. Our friendship.

I looked out to the backyard, searching to find Gina. I thanked God silently for her presence in my life.

I saw John's boys running around the backyard, laughing and playing with friends, in their childhood joy. And I thought about how they would grow up knowing their mother through some childhood memories, yes, but, hopefully, what John and I had set down.

And I thought of Amy, and her death, and what it meant to me now. Through John I learned what a remarkable woman she was and what impact she had on him, her boys, her community. I regretted never meeting her, but I felt that I had gotten to know her through talking with John. And then it occurred to me that only through Amy's death was I brought this close to this man. Friendship we shared, yes, but now something beyond my normal experience and what our culture typically regards as "male friendship." It was much more than that. What John and I shared was closer to kinship, or brotherhood. And as I was thinking on that I remembered something John had said. That, somehow, we could appreciate this fleeting life we are given because we are now confronted with the truth of death. I felt grateful to Amy for giving me that.

I watched Lori, and I was happy for her, and John, for them both, together.

We tell stories because we are storytellers, and we tell the stories of our lives and our love for one other. Those stories will be what endure, and it is up to us to tell them and share them as we weave our collective human history of life and love. Life wins out, I thought. Life has a way of finding new life. And why shouldn't it? That is its purpose. We fear death, I thought, but we need not. We fear death because we think it is the end, but it is not. Our lives are brief, true, and we perish, true, but who we are, what we do, and the stories we tell, endure.

Afterword

Two nights ago we celebrated New Year's Eve, for the second time, without Amy. And this holiday season, compared to last, fared better. So much of last year was looking back and saying to myself, "Dear God, *that* was our last Christmas together. If we'd only known, would we have done anything differently?" Now I compare this Christmas without Amy against last year without Amy and I see a noticeable difference.

But the question of whether or not we would have done anything differently is still there, and the answer is, without a doubt, "Yes." Emphatically so.

When I was younger, in college, I'd be out and about with my friends and we'd proclaim "Carpe Diem!" as we raised a pitcher of beer or a shot of tequila. As I understood "seizing the day" then, it was more about justifying any one of several deviant behaviors. After all, if this was really the last day, we might as well enjoy it.

Then it *was* the last day. And now I wonder about how well we really lived in the moment. Did we seize the day?

Yesterday I told my psychiatrist that the yin-yang symbol, the *taijitu*, of Daoism, has been floating about in my mind's eye. At first I see the two halves, the dark and the light, actually as the same shade of gray. It then gradually recomposes as I mentally dial up the contrast toward the brightest white and the darkest black. And I see now how the bright white can only exist with the dark black. I can't just dial up the white and leave the black as gray. Some years ago, after drifting through my first marriage, I called out to whomever would hear me (and if there is a God, then I guess to God) that I wanted to live life to the fullest. That I wanted to be a player in the game and not just the spectator I felt I had been, too scared to step up to the plate. Well, that is what I am getting with the full contrast of that black and white—death and life.

Not that long ago I worked hard. Very hard. I put in lots of hours for my job, and I missed things because of long hours and occasional travel. The first four months of my first son's life I was working crazy hours on two proposals and a killer, death march, IT project. In each case we accomplished good things. Important things, even. I was able to work with people at the CDC on IT systems supporting HIV and AIDS prevention. I got to travel to Ethiopia and help set up a resource center for HIV and AIDS awareness. I led a team developing the software and databases the FDA and CDC used for vaccine safety research. But there were times when I wasn't really around my family that much. I missed Adam's first Halloween because I was in Moscow on a project with USAID. Halloween was Amy's favorite holiday. I was at a hotel in Chiang-Mai, Thailand, when Amy sent me an email with an attachment, a jpeg, of her first ultrasound when she was pregnant with Bryan. Amy wasn't mad at me; she supported my work because she also saw it as serving a greater good. But that time is gone forever. And sometimes, even when I was physically at home, I now see that mentally and often emotionally I wasn't present. We'd be eating dinner and my mind would be running through the list of tasks left undone from work. I'd put my son to bed, then dash off to the computer for a couple more hours of email, to prepare a presentation for a client the next day, or to review budgets or staffing or schedules. I'd be at the playground with my toddler son and would push him on the swing and my mind would be working on how to solve some client complaint. I was there with my family, but not there. I think about colleagues of mine from those days. Long hours, proposals, contracts, demanding clients. Sacrificing family and time for a snatch of personal glory and maybe a nice bonus or stock option.

I remember a February day a couple years ago when it snowed several good inches—enough to shut down the schools and invoke liberal leave policies for many. As a billable contractor, I either needed to take vacation time, or work. I had a number of pressing deliverables, so I worked. And from home I dialed into conference calls, spit out emails, and did some other tasks. That morning, friends with kids called to invite us to go sledding on the big hill at the middle school. Amy told me she could "do me a favor" and get the kids out of the house so I could concentrate on work.

That sounds good, I told her, and said I would meet up with them around lunchtime for afternoon sledding. But morning turned into noon, then afternoon. Unexpected things popped up, and it was four o'clock by the time I got to the hill. I looked around and I couldn't find them anywhere. I finally called Amy, and she told me they had just left, and were heading to our friend's house nearby, for hot chocolate.

I stood there on the top of that snowy sledding hill with a hundred other kids and dads and moms in the fading winter sun, and it hit me. I felt alone. And resentful. Then jealous. And then I cried. For a moment I wanted to just drive home so I could continue to feel sorry for myself, but I didn't. Instead, I drove to our friends' house, and everyone was happy to see me, and I guess I was happy to be there, too, but I could hardly share in their tired giddiness, that special feeling that comes after a snow-day of sledding. Instead, I was most aware that I had just missed one of those family days that I'd never have again. That was the first moment I realized I was slipping into an unsustainable version of myself. It was later that month when I confessed this to Amy and told her I needed to quit my job for something saner, even if the money was less, much less.

She never hesitated.

And I found that better, saner job, but I was still in the same mode as before. With the mental lists, and my mind wandering from the playground to the office. And then Amy died. And I was forced, really, for the first time ever, to be present, always, and aware, as a parent—as a human being. It didn't happen right away. It took over a year. And it's still unfolding. I avoided the reality, at first, through alcohol—Scotch, mostly— but eventually I had no choice but to be present for my children.

And so it is that I conjure the image of the yin-yang symbol. I now have a growing relationship with two sons that would not have been possible, at least in the same way, were it not for Amy's tragic death. Lori has entered our lives and altered us, for the better. And with her came a dog and two cats whose healing powers, especially for my two boys, cannot be overstated.

The other morning as we were finishing breakfast and going through the routine to catch the school bus, my oldest son asked me, "Dad, if Mom hadn't died, would we have met Lori and Dolly (the dog) and Grits and Little Kitty (the cats)?"

I took a deep breath. This is, on the surface, a simple question. But scratch it ever so slightly and just below it gets mighty complex.

"No, Adam, probably not. Your mom was allergic to cats and we never really discussed a dog." And then I added, "It's a very difficult thing to think about, isn't it?"

He didn't say anything. What do you say? And we just went on, in silence, with getting ready for the day.

I also can't help but think about this. This book. This set of conversations with Robert. I was fortunate to already have the friendship I had with him. And then Amy died, and something called him to reach out, and we sat down together and opened our hearts to each other in ways most men don't. I consider it a gift. A tragic gift.

The truth is, with our immense loss, we have also gained. We have gained new understandings, new love, new appreciations. Another aspect of this grace has been with my mother-in-law, Amy's mom. We were always fond of each other, I think, but mostly in the best way a mother-in-law and a son-in-law can be. But as we close in on two years after Amy's death, we have discovered each other as our mutual, closest connection to Amy. And I now feel a special love for her that is singular in my experience. I love her, in some ways, as my own mother, but I also see Amy in her in a way I never noticed before. Before, others would often remark how much Amy and her mother were alike, both in their physical and intellectual beauty. I couldn't see it, as I was too close to Amy. Now I see it. And as unexpected as it is, I truly appreciate it and look forward to when Amy's mom visits us. How many sons-in-law can confess to that?

And while these new experiences unfold, I'm still not sure what exactly "carpe diem" means to me. But Amy's death reminds me of the brevity of life.

Last month, I was sitting at the computer catching up with work when Bryan asked me to play a game with him. As he asked the question I could feel the subtle resentment rising in me at being called on to do something by a demanding six-year-old. The words "not right now" were forming in my mind when something else came up and pushed that down, and I heard myself say, "Sure, I'm coming right now." It was as if some other force lifted me out of my chair and to the floor where my son had a card game started. And that's when I had my most recent awakening. That, when asked, I would find a way to say "yes" to my children rather than "not now" or "later." I'm noticing a shift. We talk more, and I actually have more fun with him. Both of them. It's something remarkable, really, in its utter simplicity. And just like the question about having cats and a dog, I wonder what else would have *not* happened had Mommy still been alive. I imagine some conversation it the future with my adult son when he asks, "Dad, if Mom hadn't died, would you and I have gotten to know each other as well?"

And this is the paradox I find myself in as I continue the lingering mourning of Amy's death—the paradox of losing the woman with whom I first really began to learn what it meant to love, and to be loved.

I've prided myself on thinking—or at least I had talked myself into *believing*—that I had no regrets. That I lived life in a particular way where I could accept my actions, own them, and know they served a purpose. To learn about myself. But I have to pause and wonder how engaged I really have been in life. In living life in the moment and truly seizing the day. I think of the times I set aside time from Amy in the interest of work, however noble, with the belief that "later" we'd spend time together, hold each other, continue to get to know each other. But it was all a dream. We ran out of "later."

And in this new dimension of time and space where the reality no longer holds a living Amy, but only our memory of her, I see there really is no such thing as "later." There is really only "now." And all the clichés—about living in the moment, the "now-ness" of the present, that "there is no tomorrow" and that "tomorrow never comes"—however trite, contain mystical truths. And I regret that it took the death of my most beloved to begin to comprehend this.

—

I had lunch recently with a colleague from work, someone I had come to know after Amy died. When we first met at work for a new project, we talked about work and what we had to do. As we came to know each other, we shared the normal office chitchat—the weather, sports, that sort of thing. There had never really been an opportunity for me to share that I was a widower, that my late wife had been run over by a truck. It just doesn't come up in small talk. Nor was there any real opportunity for him to share that he had lost a child. That his eighteen-year-old daughter, a college student, had been run over by a car. It came to light only after a third person, a mutual work friend who knew us both, mentioned my situation to him in passing. He reached out to me, and we met for lunch. And such is the world of personal tragedy and grief. You realize that you are not alone. And try as you may not to compare, there is always someone else with a story more gut-wrenching than your own. The spectrum of human tragedy seems catastrophically unbounded, though there must be that one most pitiful, lonesome soul, the outlier at the far end of the curve, who has suffered the most.

We talked about our tragedies over lunch. The complete ripping away of a loved one, and the shredding of a life's fabric. The ripple effects to those left to live. The depression and withdrawal and the coping mechanisms of alcohol or drugs. Other family relations pulled hard to the point where the connective fibers begin to snap. The erratic attempts to reconstruct a life. The thoughts of suicide. The "what if" scenarios. I shared with him my own personal "thank-God-for-my-two-boys" feeling. I told him that I like to think I would have chosen life and chosen some path to honor Amy after her death, had we not had children, but that I can also imagine in that case the complete sense of loss and the lack of any substantial motive to go on. I shared my fantasy of joining her in whatever other place she was in, if any. And I told him that now I could see with a new clarity one reason why suicide is prevalent among the elderly. You grow old with someone, your love, and they die. The kids are all grown by then. Were it me I can see asking myself, "Well, why go on?" I've lived my life, my children are on their own, and my life partner is gone.

Some years ago, before I met Amy, I went to a weekend-long Buddhist meditation and seminar. I remember one of the teachers, a Buddhist monk, describing what "mindfulness" meant. I don't remember his exact words, but what he said in essence was:

When I cook my rice, I cook my rice.
When I eat my rice, I eat my rice.
When I wash my bowl, I wash my bowl.

Aha, I thought, and filed it away, but didn't really act on it. But that really is all there is to it. Being present with the present. And now when I am with my boys, I am with my boys. And when I push them on the swing, I push them on the swing. And when I'm with my lover, I'm not thinking of the lingering tasks at work. It is mindfulness, and it is being present in the moment. It's also how to love. And I wish I could say with certainty it's how I now live my life but of course I don't. I fall short. So when I am not present I am denying my loved ones my love. Holding back from them. And at the end of the day, that is all that truly sets us apart from the rest of the animals. The profound and unrelenting gift, and curse, to love and be loved. And the greater the love, the greater the loss. Yin and yang.

But there isn't only love, for us. We are also driven by our dreams and desires to do good, to make our marks, create wealth, leave legacies. At least, most do, I imagine. So what happens when our naïve notion of seizing the day actually turns into forgetting the present? What happens when that drive, that very human drive to succeed, gets in the way of the love of now? When we say to ourselves, "Well, I'll just work one extra hour today and make it up to my loved ones next weekend"? Or, "If I just make that last sale I can get that bigger bonus, and then I can afford that retirement house." What happens then?

The line "carpe diem" comes from a Latin poem by Horace. The whole verse is:

You should not ask, it is unholy to know, for me or for you
what end the gods will have given, O Leuconoe, nor Babylonian
calculations attempt. Much better it is whatever will be to endure,
whether more winters Jupiter has allotted or the last,
which now weakens against opposing rocks the sea
Tyrrhenian: be wise, strain your wines, and because of brief life
cut short long-term hopes. While we are speaking, envious will have fled
a lifetime: seize the day, as little as possible trusting the future.

Seizing the day. We in America have this sense of entitlement that I believe is wrapped around a naïve notion of "carpe diem." And that justifies our drive toward wealth at all costs and unbridled consumerism—a drive that has led our country into unmanageable debt. We dream of the big car and the big house with the big yard. But why don't we dream, in America, of spending that time with those we love now? What is driving us to work so hard that we miss so much? What is it—this dream about money and possessions?

But all of this, all of this speculation on love, and yin-yang, and what it means to live in the present moment, to be mindful, our distractions with work and success and consumption—all of this—these are all wrapped within timeless questions that sages and philosophers, religions and cultures, have struggled with from the time we became aware of time. There is nothing new here under the sun. And yet we continuously fall short. Putting imagined worries of the future ahead of what is right in front of us. Setting aside the "now" for the "later." Maybe this is the curse of original sin. Maybe it's not so much that we are cursed to toil every day the rest of our lives, or to suffer the pangs of childbirth. Maybe it is that in our toil and pain we allow ourselves to be distracted from the real and present beauty with which toil and pain coexist. Maybe it is that we preoccupy ourselves with the looming dangers around the curve, preparing for the worst, rather than noticing each step we take on the path. And when we are cooking our rice we are thinking of cleaning our rice bowls, and when we are cleaning our rice bowls we are worried about having rice tomorrow.

My grief has ebbed over the past year and a half, but it lingers, and I imagine it always will. As the convulsive, physical symptoms of that earlier grief pain subside, a new, subtler sadness rises. It's an awareness that I actually do have regret. I didn't live in the present moment with Amy. Sometimes, but not enough. I let myself be distracted by work and future worries rather than being present with what stood in front of me. And I don't get that time back with her, nor those first precious years of my sons' lives. They're gone. But unlike Amy, I have been given a second chance through the—and this is so difficult to say—horrific grace and blessing that shines from her death. I imagine the ever-expanding glowing and fading gas from a star's explosive death, the afterglow that lights up the path of my life right in front of me. Each step simultaneously perilous and fragile, and sublimely beautiful.

And what else could it be?

—John Robinette
Takoma Park, Maryland

Acknowledgements

The authors thank Robyn Russell and Jason Buchholz
for their guidance and support.

CPSIA information can be obtained
at www.ICGtesting.com
Printed in the USA
BVHW031153111119
563462BV00001B/15/P